W9-DES-504

A Commentary on the Poems
of
THOMAS HARDY

A Commentary on the Poems
of
THOMAS HARDY

F. B. Pinion

BARNES & NOBLE

BOOKS

10 East 53d St., New York 10022
(a division of Harper & Row Publishers, Inc.)

2675950   3/22/79 кк

© F. B. Pinion 1976

First published 1976 by
THE MACMILLAN PRESS LTD
London and Basingstoke

Published in the U.S.A. 1977 by
HARPER & ROW PUBLISHERS, INC.
BARNES & NOBLE IMPORT DIVISION

ISBN 0-06-495572-9
LCN 76-15684

Printed in Great Britain

*Quid quod idem in poesi quoque eo evasit
ut hoc solo scribendi genere . . .
immortalem famam assequi possit?*

From A. D. Godley's public oration at Oxford in 1920 when the degree of Doctor of Letters was conferred on Thomas Hardy: 'Why now, is not the excellence of his poems such that, by this type of writing alone, he can achieve immortal fame . . .? (*The Life of Thomas Hardy*, 397–8)

'The Temporary the All'

(Hardy's design for the sundial at Max Gate)

Contents

List of Drawings and Maps

(Hardy's sketches were prepared for *Wessex Poems*, 1898, and are reproduced by courtesy of the City of Birmingham Museums and Art Gallery)

List of Plates

(*between pp. 46 and 47*)

Plates 2 and 5b are reproduced by permission of the City of Birmingham Museums and Art Gallery, 6 by permission of the Henry W. and Albert A. Berg Collection, the New York Public Library, Astor, Lenox and Tilden Foundations, 8a by permission of the Dorset County Museum; 4a and b and 7a and b were taken by the author, and the copyright in them is his.

Preface

(Superior numbers refer to Supplementary Notes, pp. 268–70)

THERE are 918 poems in the eight volumes of Hardy's published poetry, and notes of varying length are provided for all but a small number on which it seems superfluous to comment. Notes are also included on twenty-three which have remained uncollected until recently, and, more briefly, on units which may be regarded as poems in *The Dynasts* and *The Queen of Cornwall*. The book which is required most of all for references is F. E. Hardy's *The Life of Thomas Hardy* (see p. xiv).

About forty of Hardy's surviving poems were written by 1870,* before he settled down to novel-writing; and considerably more than half belong to the period after the completion of the novels and *The Dynasts*, most of them being written when he was over seventy. Some of the most interesting belong to the years 1865–7; the most moving relate to his wife Emma. In the first three volumes published after her death in 1912, nearly one third of the poems were written about her, or with her in mind.

When Hardy asserted that, in general, there was more autobiography in a hundred lines of his poetry than in all his novels, his hyperbole sprang from exasperation (*Life*, 392). Yet, the more one discovers about the poems, the more true this statement appears. Perhaps, if and when his life is ever seen in its true proportions, it will be found that nothing of great significance has been omitted from his personal revelations. The 'biography' which he and Florence Hardy prepared in his later years should be regarded as complementary to the poems. After the earlier portion (which only he could write), much of it suggests that the main task facing them was the selection of entries and

---

* How many of the poems written in London from about 1865 to 1867 were destroyed (*Life*, 47, 48, 54) is unknown, and his statements on 25 July 1926, as recorded by Virginia Woolf (*A Writer's Diary*, London, 1953, p. 92) are very imprecise. He said he had lost many copies, but had found the notes, and re-written poems from these. 'I am always finding them. I found one the other day; but I don't think I shall find any more.'

passages from notebooks and letters, and that Hardy's further interest extended little beyond checking the typed copy which his wife had prepared. He was much happier writing poetry.*

Although opportunities have been taken occasionally to comment on Hardy's style and craftsmanship, the principal aim throughout this commentary has been to provide as far as possible information and background which will assist in the interpretation of the poems.

However accurate one's interpretation, literary appreciation is ultimately dependent on individual experience and judgement. One reason why Hardy made a practice of publishing nearly everything he completed in verse was the discovery that poems he did not care for were sometimes highly regarded by readers (Collins, 67).[1] Literary judgement depends too on contemporary thought and taste. There must be many who find 'Neutral Tones' a remarkable poem, yet this was the comment it received in 1940:

> So Hardy wrote in 1867. So any young man who had read Browning and Swinburne might have written. It is a copy of verses, nothing more. His work was in the other harmony of prose.†

Perhaps the most significant truth for the reader of Hardy's poetry is to be found in Philip Larkin's declaration

> that he delights in Hardy's poems because one can read them for years up and down in the *Collected Poems*, and still be surprised by something newly discovered or previously overlooked.‡

Much of the groundwork for this volume was done in the preparation of *A Hardy Companion* (1968). Since then I have read the greater part of Hardy's correspondence, and there, and elsewhere, come across details that have thrown light on many poems. Uncertainties remain, and much no doubt has been overlooked, but I have done my best not to add to the biographical confusion which has spread in recent years. My principal indebtedness is to R. L. Purdy's notes; and it is to spare the reader some wearisome iteration that I have omitted references for many borrowings from his well-known bibliographical study. My

---

* Compare Florence Hardy's remark: 'He is now . . . writing a poem with great spirit. . . . Needless to say it is an intensely dismal poem' (26 December 1920; in Viola Meynell (ed.), *Friends of a Lifetime*, London, 1940).

† G. M. Young, in his introduction to *Select Poems of Thomas Hardy*, London, 1940.

‡ Donald Davie, *Thomas Hardy and British Poetry*, London, 1973, p. 27.

obligations to J. O. Bailey, with whom I discussed several of the poems some years ago, are expressed in the text. A number of Hardy manuscript details have been taken from James Gibson's notes for the new edition of Hardy's poems,* and I am very grateful to him for enabling me to see them.

Others have helped me in various ways, and to them I wish to express my deep appreciation: John Antell, Evelyn Hardy, A. C. Harrison, and Brigadier J. B. Willis; Miss Margaret Holmes, County Archivist, Dorset; E. J. Huddy, the British Library (Map Room); P. R. G. Marriott, Reference Librarian, Dorset County Library; R. N. R. Peers, Curator of the Dorset County Museum; Mrs L. L. Szladits, Curator of the Berg Collection, New York; Robert Gittings for the suggested link between Horace Moule and 'The Place on the Map'; Miss Mary Henderson for valuable information relative to the question of 'the Runic Stone'; Michael Millgate for a long note on Rosamund Tomson; Kenneth Phelps for news from Lyonnesse and kindly guidance along some of its roads and 'crooked ways'; and Mr and Mrs J. P. Skilling for topographical hints and confirmations. I am grateful to T. M. Farmiloe and H. W. Bawden for their co-operation on behalf of the publishers; and, above all, to my wife, whose assistance in checking both the text and the proofs has been quite invaluable.

* *The Complete Poems of Thomas Hardy*, London, 1976.

Reference Abbreviations

Hardy's Prose Fiction

CM	*A Changed Man*	PBE	*A Pair of Blue Eyes*
DR	*Desperate Remedies*	RN	*The Return of the Native*
FMC	*Far from the Madding Crowd*	TD	*Tess of the d'Urbervilles*
GND	*A Group of Noble Dames*	TM	*The Trumpet-Major*
HE	*The Hand of Ethelberta*	TT	*Two on a Tower*
JO	*Jude the Obscure*	UGT	*Under the Greenwood Tree*
L	*A Laodicean*	W	*The Woodlanders*
LLI	*Life's Little Ironies*	WB	*The Well-Beloved*
MC	*The Mayor of Casterbridge*	WT	*Wessex Tales*

The Dynasts

References take the form of D2.III.iv, where 2 indicates the second Part, III the Act, and iv the Scene.

Books relating to Hardy and Wessex

AHC   F. B. Pinion, *A Hardy Companion*, London and New York' 1968

HLMSq   Carl J. Weber, *Hardy and the Lady from Madison Square*, Waterville, Me., 1952

Life   F. E. Hardy, *The Life of Thomas Hardy*, London and New York, 1962

MGC   Carl and Clara Weber, *Thomas Hardy's Correspondence at Max Gate*, Waterville, Me., 1968

ORFW   Evelyn Hardy and F. B. Pinion (eds.), *One Rare Fair Woman, Thomas Hardy's Letters to Florence Henniker, 1893–1922*, London and Coral Gables, Fla., 1972

SR   Evelyn Hardy and Robert Gittings (eds.), *Some Recollections by Emma Hardy*, London, 1961

THN   Evelyn Hardy (ed.), *Thomas Hardy's Notebooks*, London, 1955

Authors

Archer   W. Archer, *Real Conversations*, London, 1904

Bailey   J. O. Bailey, *The Poetry of Thomas Hardy*, Chapel Hill, N.C., 1970

Collins   V. H. Collins, *Talks with Thomas Hardy at Max Gate, 1920–22*, London, 1928

Gittings   R. Gittings, *Young Thomas Hardy*, London, 1975

Hutchins   John Hutchins, *The History and Antiquities of the County of Dorset*, 3rd ed. in 4 vols. (as used by Hardy), London, 1861–1873

Lea   Hermann Lea, *Thomas Hardy's Wessex*, London, 1913

Orel   H. Orel, *Thomas Hardy's Personal Writings*, Lawrence, Kans., 1966 and London, 1967

Purdy   R. L. Purdy, *Thomas Hardy, A Bibliographical Study*, Oxford, 1954

Chronology

1840   (2 June) Thomas Hardy born in the house built for his grandfather on the edge of the heath at Higher Bockhampton.

1849–56   At school in Dorchester.

1856–61   Articled to the architect John Hicks of Dorchester, where he works in an office next door to the school kept by the Dorset poet William Barnes. Early during this period Hardy's interest in painting leads to a closer acquaintanceship with the Moule family at Fordington.

1857   Death of his paternal grandmother (widowed in 1837), who had remained with her son (married 1839) and his family in the home where she had lived since 1801. Hardy begins his almost lifelong habit of reading *The Saturday Review*.

1860   His sister and close friend Mary begins her teacher-training at Salisbury, which he visits for the first time.

1862–7   In London, employed by the eminent young architect Arthur Blomfield. Sketching and painting continue, especially when Hardy is on holiday or visiting places outside London. Sketches, for example, at Denchworth, where Mary Hardy is teaching, in April 1863; at Fawley, the 'Marygreen' of *Jude the Obscure*, where his paternal grandmother was born, in the autumn of 1864; and at Denchworth again at Christmas, 1865. Interest in music and opera; visits to art galleries and the theatre; dancing; strenuous reading. Most of his early poetry belongs to the 1865–7 period.

1867   Returns home for health reasons. Resumes architectural work with Hicks, and begins his first novel, *The Poor Man and the Lady* (never published).

1868–9   At Weymouth, working for Hicks's successor, Mr Crickmay.

Writes a number of poems, and begins *Desperate Remedies*.

1870 (March) Sent to St Juliot, Cornwall, to plan church-restoration. Falls in love with Emma Lavinia Gifford.

1871–4 *Desperate Remedies, Under the Greenwood Tree, A Pair of Blue Eyes*, and *Far from the Madding Crowd* published.

1874 (September) Hardy and Emma Gifford are married in London. They return from their honeymoon in Rouen and Paris to live at Surbiton.

1875 Hardy's lifelong friendship with Edmund Gosse begins about this time. Removal to Bayswater for scenes in *The Hand of Ethelberta*, which is completed at Swanage.

1876–8 After a short period at Yeovil, the Hardys' two-year 'idyll' runs its course at Sturminster Newton, where *The Return of the Native* is written.

1881 After another period in London, and the writing of *The Trumpet-Major* and *A Laodicean* (much of the latter during a severe illness), they move to Wimborne. *Two on a Tower* begun.

1883–5 In Dorchester. *The Mayor of Casterbridge* completed.

1885 They move to Max Gate, the house Hardy had designed for himself on the outskirts of Dorchester.

1886–91 *The Woodlanders, Tess of the d'Urbervilles*, and many short stories are written.

1891–2 The growing estrangement between Emma Hardy and Thomas, and between her and his family, leads to the 'division' which lasted for the remainder of her life.

1892 Death of Hardy's father. *The Well-Beloved* serialized.

1893 Hardy's friendship with Mrs Henniker, sister of Lord Houghton (later Lord Crewe) begins. It continued until her death in 1923.

1895 (November) *Jude the Obscure* (largely the imaginative outcome of strained relations at home) is published.

1896 In consequence of his domestic unsettlement, exacerbated by strong censure of *Jude* in the press, Hardy abandons the writing of novels, and decides to turn to poetry, which he can write to please himself.

1898 *Wessex Poems* published.

1901 *Poems of the Past and the Present* published.

1902 Hardy, having completed plans which had evolved over many years, begins *The Dynasts*, a major work based on the history of the Napoleonic War. It was published in three parts (1904, 1906, 1908).

1904 Death of his mother.

1907 Growing friendship with Miss Florence Dugdale. She had done research for Hardy at the British Museum. At various times in subsequent years she helps at Max Gate, giving secretarial assistance to both Emma and Thomas.

1909 *Time's Laughingstocks* published.

1912 (September) His brother and sisters move from Higher Bockhampton to Talbothays, West Stafford. (November) Death of Emma Hardy. Florence Dugdale takes charge of Max Gate at Hardy's urgent request.

1913 (March) Hardy revisits Cornwall with his brother.

1914 (February) He marries Florence Dugdale. Outbreak of the First World War. *Satires of Circumstance* published.

1915 Death of Mary Hardy.

1917 *Moments of Vision* published.

1922 *Late Lyrics and Earlier* published.

1923 *The Famous Tragedy of the Queen of Cornwall* published.

1925 *Human Shows* published.

1928 (10 January) Death of Hardy. (October) *Winter Words* published.

Comments and Notes

I

Wessex Poems

FIRST published in December 1898, this is much the shortest of Hardy's eight volumes of poetry. With the last five poems, which were a late addition, it comprises only 51 poems. It is a miscellaneous collection, presenting, among others, sample poems of two apprenticeship periods which are separated by thirty years. Several of the longer ones are distinguished by strong Wessex associations, and a few are related to Wessex novels. Altogether, only four had been published previously, two in Hardy's prose fiction. The narrative element is prominent, as could be expected of a writer who had devoted himself to fiction for over a quarter of a century. Poems relating to the Napoleonic War reflect an absorbing interest, which developed from Hardy's boyhood until it reached its full expression in *The Dynasts*.

Perhaps the most notable features are to be found in the early poems (far more of which are included here than in any subsequent volume), a large proportion in the sonnet form. Their hard, wiry style makes a break with tradition almost as startling as the radical modernity of their scientific outlook. A humorous narrative of this period is remarkable for its use of dialect, and for being the first of Hardy's poems to be published – nine years after it was written, and in a bowdlerized form. The style ranges from the plainness of speech to varieties of the lyrical; it is often laboured, with awkward inversions, quaint archaisms, and neologistic devices, the most peculiar arising from the use of the negative particle (as in 'unknows' for 'does not know'). Hardy's integrity is to be seen as much in his style as in his thought and vision of life. Euphony is the aim, but he is unwilling to sacrifice sense, vigour, and economy for the sake of achieving it. It is often difficult to draw the line between poems which are personal and those which are wholly 'dramatic or [im]personative'. A few of the former type have a lyrical quality which hints at Hardy's highest poetic achievements in the future. The most remarkable imaginative poem is 'Neutral Tones'; it is in a class apart, and was written as early as 1867.

Few of Hardy's illustrations for the volume are impressive. They fall into four main groups: local outdoor scenes, and those which are primarily symbolic, architectural, or Napoleonic in interest. Most are wholly linear or rather flat compositions; some are pen and black ink, grey wash, heightened with white body colour.[2]

The Temporary the All

outshow, 'show out', display.

The poem may suggest Hardy's tendency to romanticize the past, but all is sobered by the main, rather existentialist theme. The title has challenging overtones, even wider than the poem and probably owing much to the 'Conclusion' of Pater's Renaissance studies (*op. cit.*, p. 235). Hardy had lost his belief in Providence by the middle of the 1860s. Scientific philosophy – Darwinism, the essentials of Comte's Positivism, the views of J. S. Mill and Herbert Spencer – confirmed the tragic theme of 'change and chancefulness' in life, of which he had heard many harsh illustrations in his early years. It had been reinforced by the poetry of Shelley and Swinburne. In *Prometheus Unbound* (II. iv, 119–20) all earthly things are declared subject to 'Fate, Time, Occasion, Chance, and Change'. More recently, in a selection of Browning's poems presented to him by Mrs Henniker in 1894, when he was writing *Jude the Obscure*, Hardy had noted 'Chance, change, all that purpose warps' in 'St. Martin's Summer', a poem which must have had a complex personal significance for him. The theme gives sombre tones to much in his fiction, e.g. *A Pair of Blue Eyes* and *Two on a Tower*. It is found in the next two poems (cf. the ending of the preface to *Poems of the Past and the Present*).

'The Temporary the All', which seems to have been composed as an introduction to *Wessex Poems* (though the thought occurs in *PBE*.xiii: 'Circumstance, as usual, did it all . . . makeshift') conveys much of Hardy's disappointment in life. Perhaps he was induced to make this verse experiment by Swinburne's 'Sapphics' in *Poems and Ballads*, 1866. Unconventional diction (compounds, archaism, coinages) shows Hardy's partiality for Anglo-Saxon forms, and sometimes his refusal to waste words.

How specific the allusions are is conjectural. The friend is probably

Horace Moule; the 'Tenements uncouth' could be lodgings at Swanage and Yeovil, and the house in Dorchester where the Hardys lived before moving to Max Gate (*Life*, 107, 111, 163). Hints of the 'Maiden meet' will be found in many of Hardy's poems.

Amabel (1865)*

dorp, 'thorp', hamlet, village. *fell*, cruel.

The hour-glass in Hardy's illustration with two butterflies outside represents the flight of time and the imminent departure of the soul, which had known companionship on earth. The rhyme-scheme and close regular stresses reinforce the sense of fate. The repetition of 'Amabel' (perhaps remembered from W. H. Ainsworth's *Old St. Paul's*, one of Hardy's favourite novels in his youth, and perhaps signifying 'à ma belle') seems like a bell insistently tolling. For the probable origin of the poem, see *Life*, 18–20, 41, 102 (references to Julia Augusta Martin, the lady of Kingston Maurward House from 1845 to 1853); compare too the endings of *Two on a Tower* and *The Well-Beloved*.

Hap (1866)

unblooms, does not bloom.

This reflects the indifference of the universe to human fate; 'the Cause of Things . . . is neither moral nor immoral, but *un*moral: "loveless and hateless" I have called it, "which neither good nor evil knows"' (*Life*, 409). The poem provides a comment on misinterpretations of 'the President of the Immortals' passage at the end of *Tess*, which is figurative, reflecting how 'the Cause of Things' can appear. Chance or Casualty is also an appearance; given full knowledge of the complex 'web' of life and circumstances, one could explain all events in terms of cause-effect. It seems hardly possible that a year or less before 'Hap' was written Hardy had thought that a curacy in a country village would afford him a better chance of success as a poet than architecture appeared to have done (*Life*, 50). In this comforting aspiration he thought of William Barnes and perhaps John Keble.

unblooms . . . sown . . . sun and rain are part of one image. *for gladness*, instead of gladness. *Doomsters*, agents of fate, good or bad.

* The date after a title is the date of composition as given by Hardy.

'In Vision I Roamed' (1866)

Like 'At a Lunar Eclipse', this shows that Hardy's interest in astronomical space had developed long before he made a special study of it
for *Two on a Tower*. The theme anticipates that of the novel a little;
see Hardy's preface to the latter.

Dome, sky; cf. Shelley's 'Ode to the West Wind' and 'The Cloud'. *un-
caring*, indifferent to.

At a Bridal (1866)

For the treatment of the subject, compare 'To a Motherless Child'.

corporate . . . be, will never have a physical existence. *Mode's decree*,
convention. Cf. 'Amabel', line 2, and *JO.* iv.iii, v.iii. *found.* (Past
tense) 'found . . . a stolid line'. *miscompose*, form unsuitable unions.
the great Dame, Nature. Hardy had read Shelley's *Queen Mab* (vi. 197–
219). *care . . . types*. See Tennyson, *In Memoriam*, lv and lvi:

> She cries, 'A thousand types are gone:
> I care for nothing, all shall go.'

Postponement (1866)

lewth, shelter.

Autobiographically, this could be related to the previous poem;
possibly Hardy had in mind the H. A. referred to in his letters of 1863
and 1865 (*Life*, 39, 52). The thought is conveyed in imagery: 'leafless'
implies lack of money and security; 'evergreen', always wealthy.

A Confession to a Friend in Trouble (1866)

The friend was Horace Moule, son of the vicar of Fordington (on the
south-eastern side of Dorchester). He was a classical scholar, reviewer,
and leader-writer, who lent Hardy books and discussed them with him.
See *Life*, 32–4, 48. For Moule's 'trouble', see 'The Place on the Map'
(p. 98).

outer precincts. Cf. *DR*.xvi (end) and *MC*.xlvii: 'There is an outer
chamber of the brain in which thoughts unowned, unsolicited, and of

noxious kind, are sometimes allowed to wander for a moment prior
to being sent off whence they came.' *lawless*, 'of noxious kind'; cf.
'banned'.

Neutral Tones (1867)

starving, frozen.

The poem was written in London (*Life*, 54) before Hardy returned to
Higher Bockhampton. However much, or little, actual experience lay
behind it (by Rushy Pond or elsewhere),[3] the poem is experimental, an
imaginative feat of exceptional character. With it may be associated
Hardy's phrase 'a negative beauty of tragic tone' (*TD*.xlv), where we
are confronted with 'the most forlorn' of spots on a 'bleached and
desolate upland'. As will be seen, it is 'the Frost's decree' which 'unblooms the best hope ever sown'; and *Desperate Remedies* (xiii.1,4)
provides a more elaborate, narrative example of the use to which Hardy
puts such Shelleyan imagery in 1871 (if it were not copied or recast
from a scene in *The Poor Man and the Lady*, written in the autumn of
1867). With this poem in mind, Edmund Gosse wrote: 'The habit of
taking poetical negatives of small scenes . . . which had not existed in
English verse since the days of Crabbe, reappears' (*Some Diversions of a
Man of Letters*, London, 1919, p. 236). Apart from white and grey,
there is no colour in the scene. It is as if the poet were trying to present
a non-subjective impression. With the smile 'the deadest thing/Alive
enough to have strength to die' and the grin of bitterness sweeping
past like an ominous bird (cf. the 'murky bird' image in the previous
poem), the effect is far different. Feelings and setting are fused; all
warmth has left the sun, which seems 'God-curst' in its whiteness.
Nature appears dead, and love has reached its dying-point. A similar
parallelism is presented in imagery when Marty South's hopes have
died: 'The bleared white visage of a sunless winter day emerged like a
dead-born child' (*W*.iv).

as eyes . . . long ago, as if she were contemplating a tragic dilemma that
could be traced through the ages. *On which lost*, on the question of
which of us lost. . . . *wrings with wrong*. The alliteration intensifies the
reader's imaginative emotional response.

She at His Funeral (187–)

'At His Funeral' is the sub-title in the first edition. Hardy's illustration shows Stinsford Church and a woman gazing into the churchyard. Though brief, the poem is very expressive, especially in the contrast and climax of the concluding lines. The ironical contrast is further accentuated in the 'gown of garish dye'.

Her Initials (1869)

Readers partial to biographical interpretations should note the first two lines, '. . . I wrote/Of old. . .' . The letters of the illustration are Y (most probably) and Z. The poetry (Shelley's or Swinburne's?) remains unchanged, but all the radiance associated with 'her' has vanished. Compare 'At Waking' (p. 71), another poem of 1869.

Her Dilemma (1866)

The illustration presents the vertical section of a Gothic church. Immediately below ground-level, skulls and bones lie scattered in the earth; beneath are vaults with coffins and skeletons. The lovers stand within one of the pillared arches in the nave. The 'mildewed walls', 'wasted carvings', and the 'wormy poppy-head' (the carved finial at the end of a pew) are contrapuntal to the man's decline and imminent death.

Revulsion (1866)

table, tablet (as in *Hamlet*, I.v.98). *junctive law*, marriage bonds.

The alliterations (e.g. 'cuts like contumely', 'cede . . . superfluously') suggest the versifying of a transient thought, a mood, or a pose, rather than deep feeling. The indication that the writer's love sprang more from his thought and imagination than from experience –

> Though I waste watches framing words to fetter
> Some unknown spirit. . . .
> Let me then never feel the fateful thrilling –

could be significant for a number of Hardy's early poems. Compare his note: 'My 25th birthday. . . . Walked about by moonlight in the evening. Wondered what woman, if any, I should be thinking about in five years' time' (*Life*, 50).

She, to Him (1866)

These four sonnets were 'part of a much larger number which perished' (*Life*, 54); perhaps they were suggested by 'James Lee's Wife' in Browning's *Dramatis Personae*, 1864, though their dramatic style undoubtedly owes something to Shakespeare's sonnets. In their 'Amabel' theme and 'My eyes no longer stars as in their prime', the opening lines anticipate *Two on a Tower*.

I

excellencies, excellences. *Sportsman Time*. Cf. 'The Puzzled Game-Birds'.

II

Then may you pause. Cf. DR.xiii.4 (and Hardy's 1912 prefatory note to the novel): 'And they will pause just for an instant, and give a sigh to me, and think, "Poor girl!" believing they do great justice to my memory by this. But they will never, never realize that it was my single opportunity of existence . . .; they will not feel that what to them is but a thought, easily held in those two words of pity, "Poor girl!" was a whole life to me . . .: that it was my world, what is to them their world, and they in that life of mine, however much I cared for them, only as the thought I seem to them to be.'

III

Numb as a vane . . . canker came. Remarkable for its aptness, and also because extended imagery is rare in Hardy's poetry. Possibly developed from Swinburne's 'joy as a vane that veers' in 'Rondel', *Poems and Ballads*, 1866.

IV

unrecked, uncared for.

Ditty (1870)

knap, hillock.

The poem was written in May 1870 (*Life*, 76) after Hardy's first visit to Cornwall the previous March. The thought that, had he not met Emma Lavinia Gifford at this time, he might have fallen as deeply in love with

another has interesting implications: Hardy had never been deeply in
love before. It recalls Browning's 'By the Fire-side', where the element
of chance is stressed (ll. 191-215). The lyrical tone contrasts with the
more forced dramatic style of 'She, to Him'; at times it resembles
Browning's 'A Woman's Last Word'.

bond-servants of Chance. Cf. 'Hap', 'The Bedridden Peasant', and the
note to 'The Temporary the All'. *That where she ... Spread ... change,*
that a strange and withering change spread where she I know by
rote is. The syntax is awkward. The change would be unnoticed because
it is subjective; the "Here is she!" seems written everywhere upon 'that
fabric fair' only to the author in love.

The Sergeant's Song (1878)

The first two verses are included in *TM*.v, but the time-scheme for
the novel suggests 1804 as the period of the expected Napoleonic invasion near Weymouth ('Budmouth').

Valenciennes (1878-97)

snocks, crashes. *slats,* batterings. *slent,* shattered. *en,* it, him. *Nick,* the
Devil.

This is the first of five poems showing Hardy's interest in the war
between England and France from 1793 to 1815. Valenciennes is near
the French frontier with Belgium. The story is told by Corporal
Tullidge (see *TM*.iv), and the first edition suggests that Hardy had the
novel setting in mind for its narration:

> – God knows what year will end the roar
> Begun at Valencieën!

S. C. was probably one of the Chelsea pensioners to whom Hardy
talked on their campaign against the French (*Life*, 78, 106, 111, 123-4).
He could not have been Samuel Clark (*D3*.vii.v), who died in 1857.

Some of these war poems may have been designed as part of one of
the plans which culminated in *The Dynasts*. After his second visit to
Chelsea Hospital, in June 1875, Hardy wrote: 'Mem: A Ballad of the
Hundred Days. Then another of Moscow. Others of the earlier
campaigns – forming altogether an Iliad of Europe from 1789 to 1815.'

San Sebastian

gayed, made merry. *blink . . . bays*, ignore . . . successes. *vamped*, tramped. *ken*, sight.

Almost at the end of his successful campaign against the French in the Spanish peninsula, Wellington's troops were held up by garrisons at Pamplona and San Sebastian near the French frontier. Hardy found the hint for the crime against a girl of seventeen in Napier's *History of the War in the Peninsula*. The belief that 'we shape our offspring's guise/ From fancy' is found in 'An Imaginative Woman' (*LLI*).

Ivel Way. For Wessex names, see the glossary, p. 274. *fauss'bray . . . curtain-face . . . hornwork*. The fauss-bray was a mound thrown up outside the main rampart; the curtain-face was the section of wall between two bastions; the hornwork was an outer defence, consisting of a curtain between two demi-bastions, which was linked to the main work or defence by two parallel wings.

The Stranger's Song

This appeared first in 'The Three Strangers' (*WT*), perhaps the most popular of Hardy's short stories. His dramatized version, 'The Three Wayfarers', was produced by Charles Charrington, who took the part of the stranger or hangman, at Terry's Theatre, London, in June 1893 (*ORFW*. 1–2).

The Burghers

unshent, unharmed. *haw*, enclosure or field adjoining a house.

Hardy's illustration shows High West Street, Dorchester, with a flaring sunset behind the 'nearing friend'. Grey's is the bridge of that name to the east of the town; Dammer's Crest, the highest point on the road to Damer's Barn on the west. Pummery-Tout is Poundbury Camp, a prehistoric earthwork to the north-west; the Gibbet, Gallows Hill in the south-east (where supporters of the rebel Duke of Monmouth were hanged by order of Judge Jeffreys). The house is Colliton House, south of Colliton Park; the 'pleasaunce', the adjacent garden; the 'haw', probably a field which became part of the Park. The door in the wall of the courtyard is that described in *MC*.xxi. See the map, p. 272.

the Furnace held unshent. See Daniel, iii. 19–25. *Says Charity, 'Do . . . by.'* The quotation is attributed to Lord Chesterfield (1694–1773).

Leipzig

prow, valiant.

Hardy's illustration shows a fiddler outside the Old Ship Inn, Dorchester. The battle is presented in *D*3.III.i–v, where six stanzas of the poem are included. The 'One' is Napoleon, his power shrunken after the retreat from Moscow and Spain; the 'Three' are the allies, Russia, Prussia, and Austria.

swords . . . promised prime. Isaiah, ii. 3–4.

The Peasant's Confession

easted, travelled east. *capple,* with a red-and-white face.

In preparation for *The Dynasts,* Hardy bought Adolphe Thiers' *Histoire du Consulat et de l'Empire;* he also had an English translation, and appears to have been very familiar with the work. For details of the Waterloo campaign, see the last two acts of *The Dynasts.* The story of the poem seems to be Hardy's invention.

The Alarm

In the first edition the date is given as 1803, and the reader is referred to *The Trumpet-Major.* Yet in that novel (as in *D*1.II.v) the French invasion alarm occurred, for artistic reasons, in 1805, reaching its climactic resolution with news of the battle of Trafalgar. The actual date seems to be 1 May 1804 (*The Dorset Year Book,* 1971–2, p. 140). In his notes for *The Trumpet-Major,* Hardy states that the alarm period belongs equally to 1803 and 1804, 'so that the beacon-firing may be in either year'. He gave 1803 for the poem, since it was in the summer of that year that Molly (Mary Hardy, his paternal grandmother) was expecting her first-born. From her (see 'One We Knew') Hardy learnt much of this historic period, when his grandfather was a volunteer (*Life,* 12).

In the MS the year is 1804 (as in *RN*.II.vi), and Molly is urged to send the 'char-wench' via 'Yalbury' wood (to 'Weatherbury' no doubt) in an emergency. It was to 'Weatherbury' she was to drive if she heard that the French had cast anchor ('Kingsbere' was substituted probably to conform with 'The Alarm' measures in *TM*.xxvi). The first beacon was lit on the downs above Weymouth; another (the one described in the poem, and seen in Hardy's illustration), on Rainbarrow, little more than half a mile across the heath from the Hardy's home at Higher Bockhampton. Of the two illustrations by Hardy, the second, reproduced overleaf, shows the Volunteer at the top of Ridgeway, with Weymouth on the far side of the bay, and Portland beyond, connected to the mainland by a strip of Chesil Beach.

royal George's town, Weymouth, where George III had made a habit of spending his summer holidays with his family. *the Road*, outside the harbour at Weymouth. *He'th Hills*, on Puddletown Heath, behind the Hardy cottage (the 'Egdon Heath' of *The Return of the Native*). *Durnover Great Field and Fort*. As Fordington Field extended to the south-west of Dorchester, the Fort must be Maiden Castle. *Fencibles*, the 'Home Guard'. *vernal*, antithetical to 'sere', and used for the sake of rhyme. *Cunningham*, an officer for the Puddletown district; cf. *TM*.xxvii.

Her Death and After

Like other poems, this suggests that Hardy had a number of stories in mind when he abandoned prose for poetry. He said it would have made a prose tale (*HLMSq.* 137).

he Western Wall, the avenued walk where the Roman wall once ran on the western side of Dorchester. *the City*, business in London. *swinging trees/Rang*. Compare line 7 for harmony of scene and mood. *Field of Tombs . . . earthworks*. Hardy's illustration shows the cemetery on the Weymouth road and the Roman amphitheatre ('the cirque of Gladiators' or Maumbury Rings; see *MC*.xi); beyond is Dorchester. *ball or blade*. Cf. 'Her Immortality'. *Yet though, God wot*. This shows the influence of Browning; cf. the ending of 'The Burghers'; *wot*, knows.

The Dance at the Phoenix

leazes, meadowland. *durn* doorpost.

Dorchester was a barracks town, and the poem, according to Hardy, was based on fact. For the places, see the map, p. 272.

Parrett, Yeo, or Tone, rivers in Somerset. *bride-ale*, wedding-feast. Originally Hardy wrote 'bridal'. *The Wain by Bullstake Square,*

'The Alarm'

Charles's Wain (the constellation) over North Square. *moorland . . . elm-rows.* Just east of Dorchester the road was lined with elms; on either side stretched moorland by the River Frome. *Standfast Bridge, Prince's Bridge.* The three points chosen by Hardy form an imaginary triangle which includes the whole of the town. *steel and stone.* To light a candle or fire, tinder was ignited by sparks struck from a flint with a piece of steel. *Mellstock Ridge,* Stinsford Hill, one mile east of Dorchester.

The Casterbridge Captains

The names (J. B. Lock, T. G. Besant, and J. Logan) were carved on the upper part of a panel in All Saints' Church, Dorchester. Lock and Logan lost their lives in the battle for the Khyber Pass, 1842. Hardy's emphasis on chance is significant.

A Sign-Seeker

subtrude, steal in, thrust under. *moils,* toil and turmoil. *solve me,* bring about my dissolution.

weigh the sun. From Tennyson's 'Locksley Hall' (line 186). *signs the general word . . . suspense.* The signs which are found in the Old Testament are denied the poet. The first edition ran:

> Those signs the general word so well,
> Vouchsafed to their unheed, denied my watchings tense.

The 'general word' is God (see John, i.1). *Recorder . . . as in Writ.* In the Scriptures, prophets and visionaries are presented as recording God's word; see, for example, Habakkuk, ii. 2 and Revelation, i. 11. *Nescience.* Cf. '*February* 7. Carlyle died last Sunday. Both he and George Eliot have vanished into nescience' (*Life,* 148). The finality of the poem recalls Hardy's note of 29 January 1890 (*Life,* 224): 'I have been looking for God 50 years, and I think that if he existed I should have discovered him.' It will be seen that on the question of life-after-death he was not as positive in his later years.

My Cicely

lynchet, strip of land left uncultivated because it is too steep or rocky. *garth, church-hay,* churchyard.

This strange story seems to have arisen from the death of Hardy's cousin Tryphena (née Sparks). He had known her best from the summer of 1867 to the end of 1869, when she was a pupil-teacher. Hardy was eleven years her senior, and, according to her brother, more interested in her elder sister Martha. Much speculation has arisen on whether the ring which it is reported Hardy had in readiness for his engagement was ever intended for Tryphena. In January 1871, after two successful years at Stockwell Training College, Clapham, she began her career as headmistress in Plymouth. In 1877 she married Charles Gale, owner of the South-Western Hotel, Topsham, south of Exeter, where she often served at the bar. She died in March 1890 (see Hardy's note, *Life*, 224). According to her daughter, Hardy and his brother cycled to Topsham to visit her grave. The poem may convey some of his disillusionment at finding that his 'prize' in retrospect (see 'Thoughts of Phena') had acted as a bar-tender; in general, however, it communicates the heightened feelings of an excitable, rather neurotic, narrator. Distancing in time is a further disguise.

In a private letter, Hardy rightly called attention to 'the galloping movement of the verses'. With this as his paramount technical aim, he subordinated rhyme, reducing it to one, at the end of each verse, and boldly keeping it unchanged to the end of the poem.

The sketch at the head of the poem shows the rider on the open road immediately west of Dorchester. In the distance stands the gibbet which was transferred from Maumbury Rings in 1767; to the left, the end of 'triple-ramparted' Maiden Castle can be seen. The concluding sketch shows the towers of Exeter Cathedral.

Baals illusive and specious. This recalls Clym Yeobright (in some ways like Hardy; see *RN*.III.ii). *House of Long Sieging*, Basing House near Basingstoke, which was besieged by Parliamentary forces during the Civil War. *Stour-bordered Forum*, Blandford Forum on the River Stour. *fair fane of Poore's . . . see*, Salisbury Cathedral. Richard Poore was its first bishop. *the Icen*, the Icen Way, a Roman road from Norfolk to the south-west of England. *Weatherbury Castle*, a prehistoric earthwork on a hill east-north-east of Puddletown; it was used for the main setting in *Two on a Tower*. *Nine-Pillared Cromlech*. It stands by the roadside west of Winterborne Abbas. *Bride-streams*. In the valley on the south side of the road to Bridport. *Axe . . . Otter . . . Exe*, rivers in Devon. *Lions-Three* (beside the great Highway). This is fictitious. Originally, it was 'The Old Holly Tree', then 'The famed Fleur-de-Lis'. *seeming derision.* The first edition reads 'hocus satiric'.

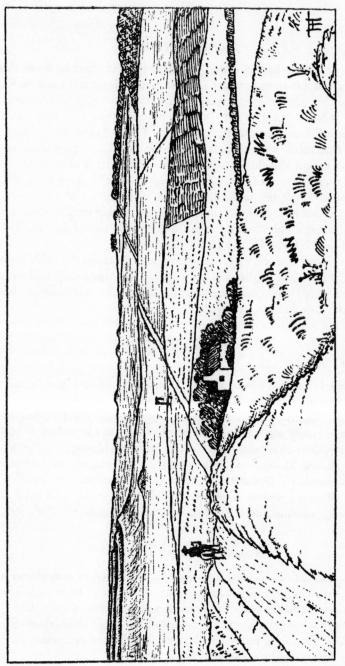

'My Cecily'

Her Immortality

Hardy probably had his cousin Tryphena in mind when he wrote this poem, but it is an imaginative exercise, not an elegy. It is based on the 'subjective' idea of immortality which Hardy referred to as early as 1874 (*FMC*.l) but does not appear to have accepted until he found it confirmed fourteen years later in Walter Pater's *Marius the Epicurean*. This rationalistic view offers little hope for the majority; not many can expect to join 'the choir invisible' of 'the immortal dead' who live in others' memories, as George Eliot hoped to do. The poem is fanciful. Hardy accepted the rational, Positivist view; he could never have believed that he would join the dead by committing suicide. There is a pseudo-heroic flourish in the poem which has its absurd side; the 'ball and blade' is found in 'Her Death and After'.

The illustration shows Hardy's familiar walk across the fields from Stinsford toward Higher Bockhampton. Seven years may well have passed after Tryphena's death when this poem was written, but Charles Gale had not remarried.

The Ivy-Wife

coll, embrace.

For the Darwinian outer meaning, compare *W*.vii and 'In a Wood'. The matrimonial implications recall Blake's 'The Clod and the Pebble' and Sue Bridehead's fear of the marriage bond in *Jude the Obscure*. Hardy was influenced by Shelley's note to *Queen Mab*, v. 189, 'Love withers under constraint: its very essence is liberty. . .' . The 'ha-ha!', like the 'Ho-ho!' of the next poem, is the utterance of the Spirit Ironic (from *The Dynasts*). Cf. 'All tragedy is grotesque – if you allow yourself to see it as such. A risky indulgence for any who have an aspiration towards a little goodness and greatness of heart!' (*Life*, 296).

A Meeting with Despair

'Egdon Heath' was deleted from the MS. In *The Return of the Native* it is presented as most itself when gloomy, though it varies according to the seasons, and the moods and fortunes of the principal characters. It is more in harmony with 'the moods of the more thinking among mankind' than fairer prospects; like man, it is 'slighted and enduring . . . suggesting tragical possibilities'.

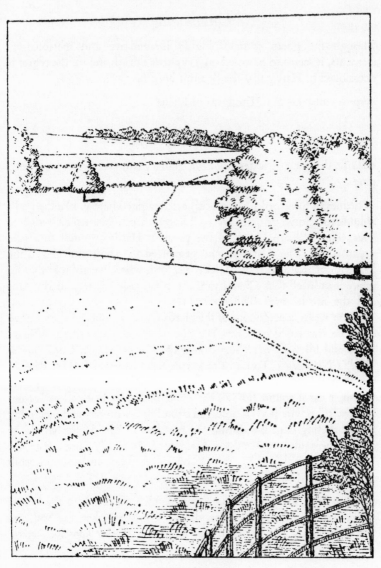

'Her Immortality'

Unknowing

Though the poem contains highly imaginative and 'personative' elements, it seems to be based on Tryphena's death and on the regret it occasioned in Hardy that she had not been his wife.

misprise, mistake. See 'Thoughts of Phena'.

Friends Beyond

stillicide, dripping of water. *grinterns*, granary compartments. *ho*, grieve, pine.

Worthies of Stinsford ('Mellstock') are imagined happy, like the gods, after death. Some of them are well known from *Under the Greenwood Tree*. The William Dewy of the poem is Hardy's grandfather (the volunteer of 'The Alarm'), who organized the choir and played the bass-viol or 'cello (*Life*, 9, 11); see *TD*.xvii, where we are told that his grave is in 'Mellstock Churchyard', 'just between the second yew-tree and the north aisle'. The tranter Reuben Dewy was drawn from William Keats, a neighbour of the Hardys; as a member of the stringed choir he was based on James Dart (see *Life*, 92, and 11,97). William Keats and his wife were buried near the Hardys (E. A. Last, *Thomas Hardy's Neighbours*, Toucan Press, 1969). So too was Robert Reason, the 'Robert Penny' of the novel and probably the 'Robert' of the poem. On their carol round (*UGT*) the choir makes its first call at Farmer Ledlow's; his wife (I.vi) is observed counting her money and reckoning her marketing expenses during the first lesson. The Squire would be one of the squires of Kingston Maurward. For Lady Susan, see 'The Noble Lady's Tale', p. 87; she was buried with her husband in a vault of the church (*Life*, 9).

the City stage. Lady Susan married an actor. *the weirs*, in the Frome valley near Stinsford. *the Trine*, the Trinity (the Father, the Son, and the Holy Ghost) of the Christian Church. *all that haps . . . moon*, sublunary or earthly affairs.

To Outer Nature

Hardy's illustration shows a vase with wilted flowers hanging round the rim. The subject is Nature and youthful illusion. He had thought that Nature was an expression of God's love; in the Darwinian era he sees it differently. 'Iris-hued embowment' alludes to the rainbow as a sign of 'the everlasting covenant between God and every living creature of all flesh that is upon earth' (Genesis, ix. 8–17). The last verse utters one of Hardy's wishes that time could stand still when all is well; cf. the fatuously tautological note of 14 July 1887:

It is the on-going – i.e. the becoming – of the world that produces its sadness. If the world stood still at a felicitous moment there would be no sadness in it (Life, 202).

Hardy probably thought there was sufficient warranty in Browning for the forced rhymes of the last verse. The iris-bow image recurs in his poetry in association with love and beauty. He first used it in The Woodlanders (xvi), where Fitzpiers says on the subjectivity of human love: 'it is joy accompanied by an idea that we project against any suitable object in the line of our vision, just as the rainbow iris is projected against an oak, ash, or elm tree indifferently'. Hence the 're-adorning' of the poem. It suggests the deceptiveness of the imagination.

Thoughts of Phena (March 1890)

See the note for 'My Cecily'. The opening of the poem was prompted by 'sympathetic telepathy'; the remainder was written when Hardy heard of his cousin's death (Life, 224). It is the only poem where we can be certain that he utters his actual thoughts and feelings about Tryphena. The three negatives which make the poem a cyclic whole are related to her 'late time'; he regrets he has nothing to indicate how she has fared. This seems to imply that he has received nothing from her. His ignorance or 'unsight' is total. All he has is a memory of her in the distant past.

Hardy's illustration showed the shrouded body of a woman laid out on a sofa, the original of which was given Hardy by his mother and kept at Max Gate (Basil Willey, Cambridge and Other Memories, London, 1968, p. 54).

In conjunction with the poem, the preface to Jude indicates that some of the 'circumstances' of the novel were suggested by Tryphena's death. These relate to her pupil-teaching rather than to training-college life, of which he learned most from his sisters. The heroine, however, owes more to Hardy's image of Mrs Henniker (ORFW, xxxvi–vii).

dame in her dwelling, as Mrs Gale at Topsham. *my lost prize*. Hardy's loves seemed to thrive imaginatively in retrospect. See 'The Opportunity', p. 178. *fined . . . the more/That*, refined, rarefied . . . all the more because . . .

Middle-Age Enthusiasms

The poem, dedicated to his sister Mary, suggests that in temperament and outlook she had much in common with Hardy. See *Life*, 371.

Passed the mortal door, the mortal door having been passed. For this awkward inversion, compare the end of 'To Outer Nature'.

In a Wood (1887, 1896)

The note should read *'See "The Woodlanders"'* (*'Vide'* in the first edition). No particular reference is intended; the novel shows many glimpses of the Darwinian conflict in Nature and its parallel in human affairs. In both the Unfulfilled Intention (*W*.vii; see the note on 'The Mother Mourns', pp. 38–9) is seen. The poem, the first draft of which was probably written after the completion of the novel, is more explicit, making clear that human nature offers room for hope.

Dreaming that sylvan peace. In the novel (xix) this is Fitzpiers' dream. *Combatants all*. Cf. *RN*.iii.vi and *W*.iii. *Ivy-spun halters*. See 'The Ivy-Wife'. *Since, then . . .* Compare the endings of 'A Plaint to Man' and *The Dynasts*. Some of the final poems in *Winter Words* indicate that Hardy in his last years lost confidence in man.

To a Lady

The lady who had admired Hardy's works was almost certainly Rebekah Owen, an American who came over to see Hardy, and eventually settled in England. She thought Zola's *La Faute de l'Abbé Mouret* healthier than *Jude*, in which she found 'nothing but the futility of all impulse, lofty or base' (*HLMSq*. 111–16).

dreams of me and mine, false impressions of Hardy and his works.

To a Motherless Child

The poem was rightly described as 'A Whimsey' in the first edition, since the 'dream' runs counter to natural law. It was indulged in by

Jude (III. viii), who pathetically hoped that his well-beloved would appear if he followed traditional rites according to Old Midsummer Eve superstition. She had just married, and he pictured her with children

> more or less in her own likeness around her. But the consolation of regarding them as a continuation of her identity was denied to him, as to all such dreamers, by the wilfulness of Nature in not allowing issue from one parent alone.

These thoughts and those of the poem may have arisen from seeing Tryphena's children at Topsham after her death. The change of title from 'To an Orphan Child' suggests Hardy's awareness of the contrast between his poem and 'The Motherless Child' of William Barnes:

> O little chile so near to me,
> An' like thy mother gone; why need I zay,
> Sweet moon, the messenger vrom my lost day,
> Thy looks be always dear to me.

mindsight memory-laden. Cf. 'Thoughts of Phena'. *mechanic artistry.* Nature works according to scientific laws. *dreams are all unknown.* See the end of 'At a Bridal'.

Nature's Questioning

The broken key in Hardy's illustration denotes not only the insoluble question but also misfortune, the 'glooms and pains' of the ages (as indicated, for example, by Egdon Heath; see the note to 'A Meeting with Despair'). For the superstition of the broken key, cf. *FMC.* xxxiii.

Like chastened children. Hardy probably recalled the school at Dorchester where Isaac Last was a martinet.[4] *Vast Imbecility . . . jest.* Not Hardy's view; see 'Hap', p. 5. *over which Achievement strides.* Not through mankind, as in 'A Plaint to Man' and, by implication, at the end of *The Dynasts.* This fourth theory regards man as 'the Forlorn Hope'. Of the four alternatives, the second is nearest Hardy's view, as may be seen at the opening of *The Dynasts*:

Shade of the Earth

What of the Immanent Will and Its designs?

Spirit of the Years
It works unconsciously as heretofore,
Eternal artistries in Circumstance,
Whose patterns, wrought by rapt aesthetic rote,
Seem in themselves Its single listless aim,
And not their consequence.

The Impercipient

The illustration shows a service in Salisbury Cathedral, and the poem (which in the MS is entitled 'The Agnostic') may have resulted from Hardy's visit with his wife in August 1897, when he underlined Jeremiah, vi. 20: 'To what purpose cometh there to me incense from Sheba, and the sweet cane from a far country? your burnt offerings are not acceptable, nor your sacrifices sweet unto me.'

Shining Land, the abode of the Shining Ones (*The Pilgrim's Progress*), the heavenly Jerusalem, a city that had no need of sun or moon, 'for the glory of God did lighten it, and the Lamb is the light thereof' (Revelation, xxi. 23). *All's Well*. This alludes to the restoration of Tennyson's faith (*In Memoriam*, cxxvi, cxxvii):

And all is well, tho' faith and form
Be sunder'd in the night of fear.

upfingered, pointing up to Heaven. *the glorious distant sea*. Cf. Wordsworth's 'Intimations of Immortality':

Though inland far we be,
Our souls have sight of that immortal sea
Which brought us hither . . .

I'd liefer not have be. Originally 'I'd rather to unbe'. There were some who believed that Hardy preferred to be pessimistic, to believe that God's *not* in his heaven: all's *wrong* with the world (*TD*.xxxvii).

At an Inn

Hermann Lea says that the poem was written at the George Inn, Winchester; perhaps Hardy told him that this was the inn of the poem. If so, it could refer to his visit with his new friend Mrs Henniker in August 1893, when she wished to see places associated with Tess (*ORFW*. 20 n). Cf. 'A Thunderstorm in Town' and 'Wessex Heights':

Yet my love for her in its fulness she herself even did not know.

O severing sea and land. Cf. Matthew Arnold's 'Isolation':

> Yes: in the sea of life enisl'd . . .
> We mortal millions live alone.

O laws of men. A subject Hardy took up in *The Woodlanders* and more strenuously (not without thoughts of Mrs Henniker; see *ORFW.* xxxvi–viii) in *Jude*.

The Slow Nature (1894)

A type of poem, turning on the ironies of fate, to which Hardy became over-partial.

In a Eweleaze near Weatherbury (1890)

eweleaze, sheep pasturage. *grizzel*, grey.

The date of the composition and the place (near Puddletown) suggest some association with Tryphena Sparks. The scene of the illustration, across which a pair of spectacles is extended (to suggest an aged person looking back over the years) could be to the south or south-west of Puddletown. Perhaps some of the details of the occasion ('a village picnic – a gipsying') are recalled in *RN.*IV.iii.

despite . . . teacher . . . men. Despite all that he has learned from experience in the intervening years, he is still the same at heart, still subject to 'fantasies' such as the 'iris-hued embowment' of love; compare the last verse of *Wessex Poems*. *chisel . . . Time.* Cf. 'The Revisitation' and *WB.*II.iii, where it is associated with Avice Caro, who like Tryphena had been another man's wife and was now dead.[5] *Thine for ever!* These are the words of transient Beauty (cf. *WB.*III.viii), from the hymn 'Thine for ever, God of love'. Hardy's memories were not deceptive. For the cleavage between his emotional life and his early intellectual convictions, see some of the poems he wrote in London before the dancing here recalled took place.

The Bride-Night Fire (1866)

goodman, husband. *wight*, person. *nightrail*, nightdress.

Written, like the poetry of William Barnes, in the Dorset dialect, this was the first of Hardy's poems to be published (November 1875). The novelist R. D. Blackmore wrote immediately on reading it to thank him for his 'jovial little ballad' (which appeared in a bowdlerized form). For Hardy's comments on over-serious criticism of the poem, see *Life*, 302. Perhaps the story had some influence on that of *Desperate Remedies*.

skimmity-ride. The traditional way in which the lower classes took delight in exposing marriage scandals among their social superiors; cf. *MC*.xxxix.

Heiress and Architect (1867)

engrailed, ornamented.

The poem is so well designed and finished that one wonders how much of it was composed at 8 Adelphi Terrace, where Arthur Blomfield, the London architect for whom Hardy worked, had his offices. It was probably presented when Hardy left in July 1867, and it would be interesting to know what Blomfield, son of 'the recently deceased' Bishop of London, thought of it.

The poet's vision of life gives him the cold, clear view of an arch-designer who cuts down demands and disposes of them one by one. The arch-designer is fate or 'the Cause of Things' responsible for the Unfulfilled Intention, and the poem contrasts reductively and ironically one's illusory hopes and the discoveries brought by time and experience. They are regarded as inevitable, 'the Frost's decree' ('For winters freeze'). 'For you will fade' recalls 'Amabel'. The general theme has links with 'The Temporary the All' and the opening of 'Let Me Enjoy'. The phrase 'the man of measuring eye' may derive from James Thomson (1700–48), 'To the Memory of Sir Isaac Newton' (l.95).

The Two Men (1866)

The MS has the title 'The World's Verdict. A morality-rime'. The conclusion of the theme recalls Ecclesiastes (which Hardy once proposed versifying, *Life*, 47): 'Vanity of vanities, saith the preacher; all is vanity.' In *not* providing the obvious contrast between the worldly failure of a sincere idealist (like Clym Yeobright) and the worldly success of an idle and hypocritical materialist, the poem presents from

an unusual angle the familiar Browning view that the world is a poor
judge of integrity and noble effort. Compare *TD*.xlix:

> [Angel Clare] now began to discredit the old appraisements of
> morality. He thought they wanted readjusting. Who was the moral
> man? Still more pertinently, who was the moral woman? The
> beauty or ugliness of a character lay not only in its achievements,
> but in its aims and impulses; its true history lay, not among things
> done, but among things willed.

The higher aim, 'to mend the mortal lot/And sweeten sorrow', links
this poem with the next.

Lines (July 1890)

This appeal was written at the Savile Club, to which Hardy was
elected in June 1878. Lady Jeune was a distant relative of Mrs Hardy.
Ada Rehan was an American actress who was brought to London in
one of his companies by Augustus Daly. She excelled in *The Taming of
the Shrew*; on the occasion when these lines were recited, she played the
part of Rosalind in *As You Like It* (*Life*, 211, 228).

The syntax of the last four lines is clear, but the second line is rather
clumsy. 'Might supernal' could be 'Power on high', but with 'do' it
suggests a collective plural and can mean only 'people in high positions',
people with the power to help the needy. Whether they belong to the
Government or not, they adopt a policy of laissez-faire, because
adequate action is against their interests.

Nature's quandary. Hardy means the defects of Nature which perplex
man; cf. 'Discouragement'. *vitalized without option*, conceived without
choice and subject to the chance of Nature (as well as of environment).

'I Look Into My Glass'

Much personal experience, which will be revealed in later poems (e.g.
'In Tenebris', 'Wessex Heights'), lies behind this brief lyric. The poet's
feelings are just as strong as ever though he appears to be ageing.
Hardy had in mind the criticisms and disapproval evoked by *Jude the
Obscure*, matrimonial tensions at home, the love he had felt for Mrs
Henniker. . . . All this is subsumed in the Time theme with which
Wessex Poems opened. Perhaps the poem was written when Hardy

revised the serial form of *The Well-Beloved* for book publication in March 1897. The hero reflects (ii.xii): 'When was it to end – this curse of his heart not ageing while his frame moved naturally onward?' Again (iii.iv), 'never had he seemed so aged . . . as he was represented in the glass in that cold grey morning light. While his soul was what it was, why should he have been encumbered with that withering carcase . . .?'

2

Poems of the Past and the Present

OF the 99 poems in this volume, which first appeared in November 1901, only thirteen had been published earlier, and only three from the pre-novel period were included. The majority cannot be dated, but most of them almost certainly belong to the years 1898–1901. The last ends on a hopeful note rather like that which concludes *The Dynasts*, and the volume is remarkable for the sustained onslaught* with which Hardy attempted to clear the way for John Stuart Mill's 'religion of the Future'.† Hardy wrote poems to please himself, not the public;‡ and, fortified by Arnold's declaration of the function of poetry,

> If what distinguishes the greatest poets is their powerful and profound application of ideas to life, which surely no good critic will deny,§

he meant to press on from where he left off with *Jude the Obscure*, as his note of 17 October 1896 shows (*Life*, 284–5):

* Cf. J. C. Powys, *The Pleasures of Literature*, London, 1938, p. 608: 'the main driving-force of his genius is a philosophical arraignment of the ways of God to Man'.

† From 'Theism', *Three Essays on Religion*, 1874. Cf. 'The Graveyard of Dead Creeds' (p. 208).

‡ Siegfried Sassoon, *Siegfried's Journey, 1916–1920*, 1945, p. 91.

§ From the essay on Wordsworth in *Essays in Criticism*, Second Series, 1888. In his Apology to *Late Lyrics and Earlier* Hardy states that 'the real function of poetry' is 'the application of ideas to life (in Matthew Arnold's familiar phrase)'. There is a gulf between the implication of his statement that 'a poet should express the emotion of all the ages and the thought of his own' (*Life*, 386) and the eighteenth-century view that the writer's principal aim could be summed up in 'What oft was thought, but ne'er so well expressed'. The scientific revolution in philosophy meant, Hardy believed, that 'If you mean to make the world listen to you, you must say now what they will all be thinking and saying five and twenty years hence' (*ORFW*, 26).

Poetry. Perhaps I can express more fully in verse ideas and emotions which run counter to the inert crystallized opinion – hard as a rock – which the vast body of men have vested interests in supporting. To cry out in a passionate poem that (for instance) the Supreme Mover or Movers, the Prime Force or Forces, must be either limited in power, unknowing, or cruel – which is obvious enough, and has been for centuries – will cause them merely a shake of the head; but to put it in argumentative prose will make them sneer, or foam, and set all the literary contortionists jumping upon me, a harmless agnostic, as if I were a clamorous atheist, which in their crass illiteracy they seem to think is the same thing. . . . If Galileo had said in verse that the world moved, the Inquisition might have let him alone.

Nevertheless, soon after sending his second volume of poems to the publishers, he seems to have been frightened by his temerity: 'I feel gloomy in the extreme when I think of it, and hope they will let me down easily', he wrote to Gosse on 17 September 1901.

Next to the philosophical poems, those relating to the Boer War and to travel abroad form the most important groups in this volume. The most poignant notes are to be found in a few poems of deep autobiographical significance among the miscellany which comprises the remainder of the collection.

V. R. 1819–1901 (27 January 1901)

This commemorative poem was written on 27 January 1901, five days after Queen Victoria's death; she had reigned more than sixty-three years. It ends with the familiar thought that only in time will her value be seen in its true proportions. The view that her life was designed by the Absolute shows the inconsistency of Hardy's 'seemings', for numerous presentations of 'the Cause of Things' in this volume show 'the All-One' proceeding by rote, unaware of, or indifferent to, humanity. It was with this in mind that Hardy gave the poem its subtitle 'A Reverie'.

WAR POEMS

These were written during the Boer War (1899–1902) between the British and the Dutch settlers in South Africa. 'I am happy to say that not a single one is Jingo or Imperial', Hardy wrote (*ORFW*. 99)

Embarcation

This French form of the word was quite common in English when Hardy wrote the poem. Its main stress is on the unchanging nature of mankind. In 'Yellow as autumn leaves' (though 'alive as spring') he hints at 'the tragical To-be'. He was horrified at the senseless slaughter of war, yet excited by its drama and pageantry. Hence his cycling to Southampton to see the troops depart; altogether he saw five thousand off (*ORFW*. 86).

Vespasian, subsequently Roman emperor, landed about 43 A.D. *Cerdic* landed (495 A.D.) in Southampton Water and founded the kingdom of Wessex. *Henry V* sailed from Southampton against the French in 1415.

Departure

bottoms, ships (Shakespeare, *Henry V*, III, Prologue).

The thought of the poem was repeated by Hardy in 1917: 'nothing effectual will be accomplished in the cause of *Peace* till the sentiment of *Patriotism* be freed from the narrow meaning attaching to it . . . and be extended to the whole globe' (*Life*, 375).

smalling. For this arbitrary use of 'small' as a verb, compare 'The Dead Quire', verse xxi. *puppets in a playing hand*. Hardy was planning *The Dynasts* when this was written.

The Colonel's Soliloquy

Hardy creates a lively, dramatic scene and poignant interest in the speaker. The colonel keeps a stiff upper lip, and hopes, rather excitedly, that the ardours of youthful enterprise will be revived. However, the emphasis is on 'the years', and pathos (relieved by humour) marks the conclusion of the poem.

The Going of the Battery

First printed in *The Graphic* with the following note: 'Late at night, in rain and darkness, the 73rd Battery [Royal Field Artillery] left Dorchester Barracks for the War in South Africa, marching on foot to the railway station, where their guns were already entrained.' Hardy told

Mrs Henniker that 'as they left at 10 at night, and some at 4 in the morning, amid rain and wind, the scene was a pathetic one'. The poem, he added, was 'almost an exact report of the scene and expressions I overheard' (*ORFW.* 87, 88). The poem has a pronounced stress-rhythm, to accord with the marching and band music.

At the War Office, London

The title suggests the occasion which was imagined for the poem.

Death waited Nature's wont. Death waited for people to die naturally. *unshent*, uninjured.

A Christmas Ghost-Story (December 1899)

Compare Hardy's poem 'Christmas: 1924'. His reply to the editor of *The Daily Chronicle*, who complained that a soldier (albeit a phantom) should protest against war, is a remarkable composition; it was written on Christmas Day, the day the editorial appeared (Orel, 201–3). The last four lines of the poem were added subsequently. Hardy gave the date as 'Christmas-eve', yet the poem appeared in *The Westminster Gazette* on 23 December.

Law of Peace . . . Crucified. See Luke, ii. 13–14 with reference to the birth of Christ. *what . . . 'Anno Domini' . . . years.* What sense does it make to refer to the years as A.D. ('in the year of our Lord')? *liveried thus*, in this uniform (all the same).

Drummer Hodge

Hardy's interest was quickened when he heard that one of the drummers killed in the war was 'a native of a village near Casterbridge'. War, however, is a subsidiary theme in this imaginative poem. It creates an initial sense of revulsion, but predominantly a sense of wonder. The main thought is an irony, that Hodge is transplanted (as it were) for ever to a foreign country and sky, so new and unexpected that it puzzled him. Each verse ends with an image of the strange constellations in the southern sky, suggesting the 'poetry of motion' which Hardy expressed in *FMC*.ii. The South African terms accentuate the strangeness of the landscape: *kopje*, small hill; *veldt*, open pasture land; *Karoo*, barren tract with extensive plateaus; *Bush*, uncleared or untilled land. 'Hodge' is a generic term for a country labourer, and Hardy had occasion to write in his defence; see 'The Dorsetshire Labourer' (Orel, 168–91) and *TD*.xviii.

A Wife in London

Flashed news, a telegram.

The Souls of the Slain (December 1899)

bent-bearded, covered with tufts of reedy grass. *mighty-vanned*, large-winged.

In this impressively imaginative poem a realistic perspective is given to war by setting the glory traditionally associated with the slain against the feelings and attitudes of those who held them dear at home. The note which accompanied the poem on its first appearance illustrates the precision which Hardy had acquired, largely from his architectural training. He pointed out that the Bill was the appropriate place for a bird (or the souls of the slain) to alight, as it was on the great circle from South Africa to the middle of the United Kingdom.

Bill . . . Race. The Bill is the southern tip of Portland or 'the Isle' (the Isle of Slingers in Hardy's Wessex). To the south-east is an 'area of troubled waters known as the Race, where two seas met to effect the destruction of such vessels as could not be mastered by one' (*TM*.xxxiv). *record was lovely and true*. There can be no doubt where Hardy's priorities lay:

> Finally, brethren, whatsoever things are true, whatsoever things are honest, whatsoever things are just, whatsoever things are pure, whatsoever things are lovely, whatsoever things are of good report; if there be any virtue, and if there be any praise, think on these things (Philippians, iv. 8).

like the Pentecost wind, which brought the Holy Spirit or Comforter (Acts, ii. 1–4, 17). These spirits were alive; the memories of these men were an inspiration to those who had known them. (There is a link here with the 'world's amendment' of 'A Commonplace Day' and therefore with the last, hopeful lines of *The Dynasts*.) The contrast in sound and sense between the last two stanzas, the movement (in context) of 'towering' and 'plunged', the stress (followed by a pause) on 'legions', the finality of 'surceased', and the continuity of 'Sea-mutter-ings' illustrate Hardy's artistry with words and a judicious use of alliteration.

Song of the Soldiers' Wives and Sweethearts

Occasioned by the return of the Household Cavalry near the end of 1900.

The Sick Battle-God

nimb, nimbus, halo. *outbrings*, brings out.

After more personal and imaginative poems, this is rather a metrical exercise, with obvious 'poetic diction': 'fulgid beam', 'blue demesne'. The alliteration is more regular and mechanical: 'peoples pledged', 'heart and hand', 'murk and murderous', 'rape and raid', 'rune and rhyme'. . . . On the subject of war Hardy is more optimistic here than he was in his later years. The First World War made him admit that his optimism was unjustified; see *Life*, 365–6 and 368, where he says that this conflict destroyed the belief in 'the gradual ennoblement of man' which he had held for many years, as 'The Sick Battle-God' shows, and that he would 'probably not have ended *The Dynasts* as he did end it if he could have foreseen what was going to happen within a few years'.

POEMS OF PILGRIMAGE

As this group includes a poem on an invitation to the United States, which Hardy did not visit, 'pilgrimage' (as in one of his favourite poems, Byron's *Childe Harold's Pilgrimage*) implies travel as well as visits to places held in honour. His Italian journey is described in *Life*, 187–96; the visit to Switzerland ten years later, *Life*, 292–5.

Genoa and the Mediterranean

The poem was written 'a long time after' the visit in 1887 (*Life*, 187). It is a study in anticlimax, but the concluding lines suggest unintentional bathos in a poem which is serious in tone.

Central Sea refers to the derivation of the name 'Mediterranean'; it is 'epic-famed' in Homer's *Odyssey* and more directly in Virgil's *Aeneid*.

Torino, Turin. *Superba*. Described as 'La Superba' in Hardy's Baedeker. *Palazza Doria*. The city 'nobly redeemed its character when they visited its palaces' (*Life*, 187). Cf. *JO.III.ix*.

Shelley's Skylark

Shelley was Hardy's favourite poet. His 'To a Skylark' was written at Leghorn. Perhaps the association of the bird and the memory of Shelley in Browning's poem 'Memorabilia' gave Hardy the thought for a poem which never quite rises to its subject.

In the Old Theatre, Fiesole

dim Etruria. Little is known of this ancient state (modern Tuscany), which was overcome by the Romans. Fiesole is near Florence, and Tuscany extends to the south on the west side of the Tiber. *my distant plot*. Roman remains had been found at Max Gate (Orel, 191–5), and it was this memory which made Hardy realize in a flash 'the reach of perished Rome'.

Rome: On the Palatine

Hardy would remember the Strauss; perhaps he needed to refer to Baedeker to recall the classical details, for he admits that his notes on Rome were 'of a very jumbled and confusing kind' (*Life*, 189). The Palatine is the largest of the seven hills of ancient Rome, and here had stood the palace of the Roman emperors (Caesars).

where Victor Jove was shrined, the temple of Jupiter Victor. *Livia's red mural show*. Livia Drusilla was the wife of the emperor Tiberius Claudius Nero. The reference is to the red walls of the dining-apartment. *Criptoportico*. A passage once 'covered by the buildings of Tiberius' (Livia's son). *Caligula*, a Roman emperor of the first century, A.D. *peristyle*, surrounding columns.

Rome: Building a New Street in the Ancient Quarter

Once again Hardy is struck by the contiguity of the ancient and crumbling with the new. The 'caustic monitory gnome' is conveyed in a letter he wrote to Edmund Gosse: 'how any community can go on building in the face of the "vanitas vanitatum" reiterated by the ruins is quite marvellous'; see also *Life*, 189.

outskeleton, present the skeleton features. *metope*, a square space of stone between the triglyphs of a Doric frieze. Hardy's familiarity with architectural terms (cf. 'entablature') is rarely as obtrusive as in this poem. *cove and quoin*, architectural terms which refer to the joining of ceiling and wall, and of walls at corners.

Rome. The Vatican: Sala delle Muse

Hardy (*Life*, 189) states that the suggestion for the poem came from 'his nearly falling asleep in the Sala delle Muse . . . the weariness being the effect of the deadly fatiguing size of St. Peter's'.

the Muses' Hall, the 'Sala delle Muse', the hall of the nine classical muses. *Dance, and Hymn*. Hardy's works, as later poems will illustrate, show very amply his love of these; cf. *AHC*. 187ff. *river-weed as the ripples run*. It is swayed by chance. Compare Hardy's description of history as a stream, not a tree (from Matthew Arnold's 'The Literary Influence of Academies'): 'now a straw turns it this way, now a tiny barrier of sand that' (*Life*, 172).

Rome: At the Pyramid of Cestius near the Graves of Shelley and Keats

After reading Shelley's *Adonais*, Hardy could not fail to make his pilgrimage to the Protestant Cemetery in Rome, where two of his favourite poets were buried near the pyramidal tomb of Cestius. The irony is that Cestius, of whom little is known, has a tomb which catches immediate attention and guides the visitor to the humble graves of the two 'matchless singers'. But for this he would probably be forgotten.

thick, crowding (with an unfortunate ambiguity). *of mine*. This expresses Hardy's pride in his compatriot poets. *Slew . . . threatening*. From a description of the fierce intentions of Saul (later St Paul) against the early Christians (Acts, ix. 1).

Lausanne. In Gibbon's Old Garden: 11–12 p.m.

See *Life*, 293-4, where Hardy quotes the passage from Milton's *The Doctrine and Discipline of Divorce* from which the last two lines of the poem derive. He was thinking of the furore raised by *Jude*; cf. the ending of 'To a Lady'.

Zermatt: To the Matterhorn

From Lausanne the Hardys proceeded to Zermatt, where at night he gazed at the darkness created by the Matterhorn among the stars.

He meant to make a poem of the strange feeling implanted by this black silhouette of the mountain on the pattern of the constellation; but never did so far as is known. However, the mountain inspired him to begin one sonnet, finished some time after – that entitled 'To the Matterhorn' – the terrible accident on whose summit, thirty-two years before this date, had so impressed him at the time of its occurrence (*Life*, 294).

He was then living in London, and remembered 'people standing at the doors discussing something with a serious look' as he walked from Westbourne Park Villas to Harrow, where two of the victims had lived. In 1894, when staying with his friend Edward Clodd at Aldeburgh, he met the mountaineer Edward Whymper, the only survivor of the four Englishmen who had been climbing when the accident occurred. According to Clodd's *Memories* (1916) it was at Aldeburgh that Whymper marked 'on a sketch of the Matterhorn a red line showing the track of the adventurers to the top and the spot of the accident' (*Life*, 264). Hardy kept the sketch, which is now preserved in the Dorset County Museum.

It is strange that Hardy, who had adopted a scientific outlook, chooses supernatural events as the most memorable changes witnessed in the sky. They are connected with Joshua, Julius Caesar, and Jesus (at the Crucifixion): Joshua, x; *Julius Caesar*, II. ii. 19–21; and Mark, xv. 33 or Luke, xxiii. 44.

The Bridge of Lodi

thrid them, thread their way. *palinody*, recantation.

In his *Life* (195–6) Hardy recounts how he and a young Scottish officer who had never heard of Napoleon's victory at Lodi in May 1796 went there from Milan, and fought the battle over 'the quiet flowing of the Adda'. He describes the poem as a 'pleasant jingle'. For the French dance tune 'The Bridge of Lodi' which Hardy, when he was very young, heard his father play at home (*Life*, 15), see 'The Dance at the Phoenix'. He inquired about the tune in Milan, but without success. The collocation of the battle and the making of cheese in Baedeker suggested verse ix (Bailey, 138).

Milan's Marvel, the cathedral, which Hardy had just visited. *all Lodi, low and head ones*, all the people of Lodi, unimportant or great.

On an Invitation to the United States

emprize, enterprise. *wonning* dwelling.

Details of this invitation are unknown. Though he had had a number of invitations – two, for example, in July 1906 and January 1909 (*Life*, 331, 343) – Hardy never visited the States. The poem owes something to a passage in Henry James's *Hawthorne* (1879), from which Hardy copied extracts. The first contains most of the following:

> History, as yet, has left in the United States but so thin and impalpable a deposit that we can very soon touch the hard substratum of nature ... the light of the sun seems fresh and innocent, as if it knew as yet but few of the secrets of the world and none of the weariness of shining. .... A large juvenility is stamped upon the face of things, and in the vividness of the present, the past which died so young and had time to produce so little, attracts but little attention.

Hardy described England as a 'palimpsest' on which many a historical record had been written only to be erased for another.

MISCELLANEOUS POEMS

The Mother Mourns

soughed, sighed deeply. *outshape*, develop. *soul-shell*, body. *rank*, rebellious.

The 'Mother' is Nature. She is distressed that her imperfections have been discovered by scientists. Hardy touches on his theory of the Unfulfilled Intention, that the First Cause has (*Life*, 149)

created so far beyond all apparent first intention (on the emotional side), without mending matters by a second intent and execution, to eliminate the evils of the blunder of overdoing. The emotions have no place in a world of defect, and it is a cruel injustice that they should have developed in it.

If Law [i.e. natural law, Nature or the 'Mother'] had consciousness, how the aspect of its creatures would terrify it, fill it with remorse!

For further comment on this, see *Life*, 163, 218 and *JO*.VI.iii. The poem illustrates the influence on Hardy of astronomy and Darwin's *The Origin of Species* (1859).

needle-thicks, tufts of needles on the pine trees. *mechanize*, work or create in an unconscious, mechanical way; cf. the quotation from *The Dynasts*, p. 24. *aped my own slaughters*. The Darwinian struggle for existence is aggravated by the slaughter for which man is responsible. *laud of my cunning*, praise of my skill. The wonder of creation, God's handiwork, was the theme of writers from the setting up of the Royal Society (for science) in 1660 throughout the greater part of the eighteenth century; cf. Pope's *Essay on Man*:

> All nature is but art unknown to thee;
> All chance, direction, which thou canst not see;
> . . .
> And, spite of pride, in erring reason's spite,
> One truth is clear, *Whatever is, is right*.

'I Said to Love'

The thought runs: man has seen that love is nature's lure to continue the race; he realizes that it is deceptive and leads to distress. If this realization extends till it leads gradually to the extinction of the race, let it be so.

the Boy, the Bright . . . sun, Cupid, whose influence was thought by the ancient to extend throughout the universe. *thine agonies*. The 'pain outweighing the pleasure in all love' is stressed in Eduard von Hartmann's *The Philosophy of the Unconscious* (W. R. Rutland, *Thomas Hardy, A Study of his Writings and their Background*, Oxford, 1938, p. 255). *darts . . . cherub air . . . swan . . . dove*. All are associated with Cupid and his mother Venus.

A Commonplace Day

The best of the poem is in those glimpses of the scene which express the poet's mood. On such a dull uninspiring day, when he has done or thought 'nothing of tiniest worth', he hopes that any 'enkindling ardency' awakened elsewhere has not been snuffed out before it can become part of 'the general Will' and contribute to the 'world's amendment'. See 'He Wonders About Himself', p. 148.

scuttles . . . fits and furtively. The various changes in the light around the room as the day wanes are vivified by this personification. *pale corpse-like birth.* Compare the dawn of a similar day at the opening of *W*.iv, the poem 'At Waking', and the note on 'Neutral Tones', p. 7. *wakens my regret.* An echo of Tennyson's *In Memoriam*, cxv. *I wot of, was toward . . . prime*, I am aware of, prospered . . . at his dawn (the first hour of the day). *impulse . . . ardency.* The poem may have been inspired by the following lines from Browning's 'Cristina', which Hardy marked in the selection of Browning's poems given him by Mrs Henniker in 1894:

> Oh, we're sunk enough here, God knows!
>   But not quite so sunk that moments,
> Sure tho' seldom, are denied us,
>   When the spirit's true endowments
> Stand out plainly from its false ones,
>   And apprise it if pursuing
> Or the right way or the wrong way,
>   To its triumph or undoing.
>   . . .
> While just this or that poor impulse,
>   Which for once had play unstifled,
> Seems the sole work of a life-time
>   That away the rest have trifled.

from whose maturer glows/The world's amendment flows. See Shelley, *The Revolt of Islam*, IX. xxviii (a stanza which concludes a passage of great moment in Hardy's early imagery and more optimistic evolutionary thinking).

At a Lunar Eclipse (MS, 186–)

moil, turmoil.

Central Sea. See 'Genoa and the Mediterranean', p. 34. *the stellar gauge*, the proportion and significance of human affairs in the universe at large. Compare, however, 'In Vision I Roamed', the preface to *Two on a Tower*, and the final hope of *The Dynasts*.

The Lacking Sense

The questions on Nature, the Mother or the Lacking Sense, who is blind or unaware of all her defects and the internecine struggle of her creatures, are addressed to Time, the omniscient forerunner of the Spirit of the Years in *The Dynasts*. The sad-coloured landscape which shows the Mother's look is Waddon Vale between Upwey and Portisham, west of the road from Dorchester to Weymouth.

world-webs. This suggests the link-up of cause and effect throughout the universe; for a parallel, compare 'the great web of human doings' (*W.*iii). *Assist her ... clay.* Compare the general note to 'A Commonplace Day'. Since man is one of Nature's creatures, his evolution can contribute to the amelioration of life generally; cf. Hardy, 'The discovery of the law of evolution, which revealed that all organic creatures are of one family, shifted the centre of altruism from humanity to the whole conscious world collectively' (*Life,* 346).

To Life

The contrast between the rather cynical, forced gaiety of this poem and the sad, pleading, sympathetically hopeful tone of the previous is reflected in the verse.

mumm, mum, mime (not necessarily in dumb show; cf. the mummers' play, *RN.*ii.v).

Doom and She

Nature is compelled by law (cf. 'The Mother Mourns' above), and by her 'dead-reckoning' inflicts doom on her creatures (cf. 'The Lacking Sense'). Doom, therefore, is both Nature's 'lord' and 'her ever well-obeyed'. Though personified for this dramatic presentation of a point

of view, Doom is an abstraction. He therefore has no feeling. Nature
is alive, but a blind Mother, who sometimes senses, however, that the
creatures she has brought forth are doomed to suffer. Having no feeling
or moral sense, he is unable to confirm what she helplessly suspects.
Doom or Fate is 'the Cause of Things' working insentiently through
Nature; it is the First Cause or Immanent Will. Compare 'God-
Forgotten': 'Thou shouldst have learnt that *Not to Mend*/For Me could
mean but *Not to Know*.' Originally Nature's sighs were associated with
Wessex hills, first High Stoy and Pilsdon Peak, then Pilsdon Pen and
Lewsdon Peak. 'Alpine' and 'Polar' are more appropriate, suggesting
not only a greater cruelty in Nature (cf. *TD*.xliii) but also something
of more universal incidence.

The Problem

Probably inspired by Tennyson's *In Memoriam*, xxxiii:

> Leave thou thy sister when she prays
> Her early Heaven, her happy views;
> Nor thou with shadow'd hint confuse
> A life that leads melodious days.

When Hardy included this verse in *Tess* (xxvii), he appears to have
thought it 'less honest than musical'.

The Subalterns

wight, person, man or woman. *fell*, cruel.

freeze . . . North. Cf. 'The Caged Thrush Freed and Home Again', p. 51.
little ark, the body, sometimes referred to by Hardy as the 'fleshly
tabernacle' (from II Corinthians, v. 1–4). As the body is the 'soul-shell'
('The Mother Mourns') so the Ark contained the Covenant between
Jahweh and his chosen people, which was later kept in the holiest part
of the Tabernacle.

The Sleep-Worker

coils, troubles.

The 'Mother' is Nature, working by rote (according to fixed laws) and
unwittingly engendering pain and wrong; cf. 'The Lacking Sense' and
the note on 'Doom and She'.

The Bullfinches

The main interest of the poem is its relation to a scene in *Tess*, where Hardy on two occasions at least uses imagery in narrative to suggest overtones of meaning with reference to his own mythology. For example, the threshing-machine (xlvii) is the *primum mobile* maintaining a motion which distresses Tess; she is a slave to it ('Once victim, always victim – that's the law!). Since the *primum mobile* imparted motion to the concentric spheres containing the universe, from the stars on the outer sphere to the stationary earth at the centre, it became synonymous with God, the Prime Mover, in medieval philosophy (Arthur Koestler, *The Sleepwalkers*, London, 1959, p. 59), just as for a Positivist like Hardy's friend Frederic Harrison it became synonymous with the First Cause (*The Positive Evolution of Religion*, 1913, p. 213). Tess's life is conditioned by circumstances and events over which she has little control. Since Positivism stresses humanitarianism rather than belief in supernatural forces, it is not surprising that *Tess* seemed like 'a Positivist allegory or sermon' to Harrison.

Mrs d'Urberville, a blind mother, is unaware of what goes on in and around her house. Tess whistles to the caged bullfinches in her bedroom, and it is there that she becomes aware of her danger. Similarly the bullfinch realizes how unprotected Nature's creatures are left:

> Busy in her handsome house
> Known as Space, she falls a-drowse;
> Yet, in seeming, works on dreaming,
> While beneath her groping hands
> Fiends make havoc in her bands.

In the same chapter (*TD*.ix) the evil to which Tess falls a victim is associated with the Arch-Fiend; Alec d'Urberville leaps over the wall into the garden just as Satan did in *Paradise Lost* (IV. 172ff.). Quotation makes his Satanic role more obvious in the garden scene at Tess's home (l). In the poem Hardy is able to make his meaning less obscure.

The link with the *caged* bullfinches is clear from a note written by Hardy in 1885, after watching people in London and reflecting on the 'hum of the wheel': 'All are caged birds; the only difference lies in the size of the cage. This too is part of the tragedy' (*Life*, 171). He implied that people's lives are conditioned to an unrealized extent; there is little opportunity for the exercise of free choice, especially among the poor.

Blackmoor Vale. For Hardy this is the country in upper Dorset west of Shaftesbury and north of the chalky line of hills running west from Blandford. Its woods were associated with fairies (*TD*.l). *let us sing . . . of old.* Rather like 'what advantageth it me, if the dead rise not? let us eat and drink; for to-morrow we die' (I Corinthians, xv. 32). In its totality therefore the poem has much in common with the *Rubáiyát of Omar Khayyám*, from which Hardy asked that a verse should be read just before his death; it is quoted on p. 446 of his *Life*.

God-Forgotten

A direct attack on the idea of Providence. In this fantasy Hardy employs a theory which he did not believe in to explain the Creator's indifference to human woe; cf. the Spirit of the Years, *D*i. Fore Scene, 20–30:

> As one sad story runs, It lends Its heed
> To other worlds, being wearied out with this;
> Wherefore Its mindlessness of earthly woes.
> Some, too, have told at whiles that rightfully
> Its warefulness, Its care, this planet lost
> When in her early growth and crudity
> By bad mad acts of severance men contrived,
> Working such nescience by their own device. –
> Yea, so it stands in certain chronicles,
> Though not in mine.

their tainted ball. Cf. the precocious discussion between Abraham and Tess Durbeyfield (*TD*.iv). *Homing at dawn* suggests the return of a bird.

The Bedridden Peasant

Compare *RN*.vi. i:

> Human beings, in their generous endeavour to construct a hypo-thesis that shall not degrade a First Cause, have always hesitated to conceive a dominant power of lower moral quality than their own; and, even while they sit down and weep by the waters of Babylon, invent excuses for the oppression which prompts their tears.

bondage . . . To Time and Chance. Cf. Crass Casualty and dicing time in 'Hap', and 'What bond-servants of Chance/We are all' in 'Ditty'.

By the Earth's Corpse

The Lord informs Time that he regards the Earth as one of his failures, and wishes he had never created it. The nub of the poem is neither his repentance nor his awareness of wrong; it is the admission of 'the Unfulfilled Intention' (*Life*, 149):

> the wrongs endured
> By Earth's poor patient kind,
> Which my too oft unconscious hand
> Let enter undesigned.

Mute Opinion

outwrought, worked out, fully developed, revealed.

Hardy seems to agree with Thomas Hobbes, who wrote, 'heresy signifies no more than private opinion' (*Leviathan*). It is always so: 'It is the customary fate of new truths to begin as heresies and to end as superstitions', wrote T. H. Huxley. G. B. Shaw's *Saint Joan* embodies this theme. Compare 'Lausanne. In Gibbon's Old Garden'.

grown a Shade, become a spirit (after death).

To an Unborn Pauper Child

A note on the MS – ' "She must go to the Union-house to have her baby." Casterbridge Petty Sessions.' – recalls the Union which Fanny Robin reached to have her baby (*FMC*.xl–xlii); Hardy, however, struck out 'Casterbridge'. For the view that it is better not to be born, see 'Thoughts from Sophocles'. This was one Hardy mood; 'Great Things' expresses another. Far from being cynical, the last verse, though consistent with the remainder of the poem in its pessimism, shows heartfelt concern for the child's welfare. Compare Louis MacNeice's 'Prayer before Birth'.

Doomsters. Cf. 'Hap'. *take life so*, accept life on the terms outlined (ll.4–11). *some shut plot . . . wold*, shelter from unhappiness and misfortune; 'wold' suggests open, exposed country. Cf. 'Heiress and Architect'.

To Flowers from Italy in Winter

Hardy's 'altruism' (see 'The Lacking Sense', p. 41) made him grieve to think that trees and plants suffer.

mix with alien earth. Cf. 'Drummer Hodge'. *frigid Boreal flame,* cold light of the North.

On a Fine Morning (February 1899)

heyday, time of exalted feeling.

Just as sunshine creates a new impression, so the Dream makes the 'gray things' of life seem golden. For Hardy's 'gray' philosophy, cf. 'The Lacking Sense', with its sad-coloured landscape, and 'The Darkling Thrush'. The deceptiveness of the imagination, its 'iris-hued embowment', has been seen in 'To Outer Nature' (pp. 20–21). The same attitude to the solace of dreams occurs in a poem written in 1867; see 'A Young Man's Exhortation'.

To Lizbie Browne

The name was changed for lyrical reasons. Lizbie was Elizabeth Bishop (Gittings, 25–6), 'a gamekeeper's pretty daughter, who won Hardy's boyish admiration because of her beautiful bay-red hair. But she despised him, as being two or three years his junior, and married early' (*Life,* 25–6, 206). The date for the latter reference (1888) may offer a clue to the time when the poem was written (Purdy, 112). Like 'Thoughts of Phena' and other poems, 'To Lizbie Browne' illustrates Hardy's retrospective indulgence in the Dream, the 'iris-hued embowment' of girls he had known in his early years:

> The desire of the moth for the star,
> 　　Of the night for the morrow,
> The devotion to something afar
> 　　From the sphere of our sorrow.
> 　　　　　　　　　　(Shelley, 'To ————')

Song of Hope

doff, take off. *don,* put on. *shoon,* shoes. *null,* cancel. *gleaming . . . no gray.* Cf. 'On a Fine Morning'. The increasing strength of the stress with

Hardy's birthplace, drawn by him

Max Gate in 1893

T———a.

At news of her death.

~~Phantasmagoria~~

Not a line of her writing have I,
  Not a thread of her hair
No mark of her late time, her ~~~~ bower, her ~~lattice~~, whereby
  I may image her there;
And in vain do I urge my insight
  To conceive my lost prize
In her close, whom I knew when her dreams were upbrimming with *light*,
  And with laughter her eyes.

What scenes spread around her last days,
  Sad, sharp, or serene?
Did the Fates & Affections combine to embow her sweet ways
  With an irisèd sheen?
Or did lifelight decline from her years,
  And mischances control
Her full daystar; unease, or regret, or forebodings, or fears
  Disennoble her soul?

Thus I ~~have~~ *do* but the vision ~~to~~ *retain* ~~clasp~~
  Of the maiden of yore
As my relic, yet haply the best of her — fined in my ~~grasp~~ *brain*
  It may be the more
That no line of her writing have I,
  Nor a thread of her hair,
No mark of her late time, her ~~~~ bower, her ~~lattice~~, whereby
  I may image her there

                                        March, 1890

'Thoughts of Phena' (see p. 21)

[2]

Beeny Cliff (Aug. 22:70)

The Figure in the Scene.

.....": I stood back that I might pencil it
With her amid the scene ;
Till it gloomed & rained".

(Moments of Vision.)

Church Way, Stinsford (showing Stinsford House)

Kingston Maurward

High East Street, Dorchester, 1891

Outside the Old Ship Inn, High West Street, Dorchester: Hardy's drawing for 'Leipzig'

[5]

Hardy's sketch of the Celtic Cross at St Juliot

The footbridge, Sturminster Newton

The Frome valley below Lower Bockhampton

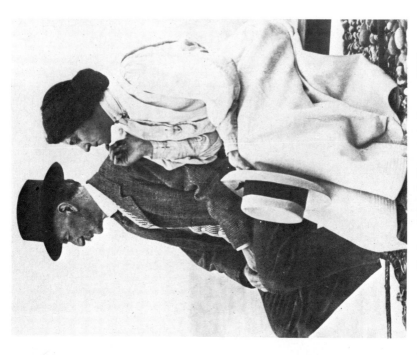

Hardy and his wife Florence by the sea, 1915

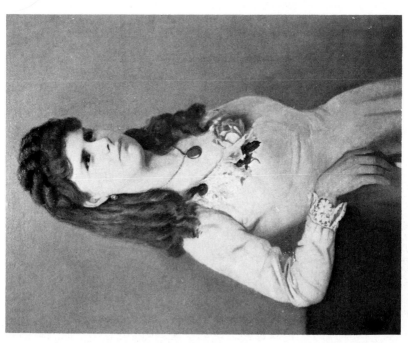

Emma Lavinia Gifford, 'The woman whom I loved so'

which the lines open towards the end suggests a special effort to make the most of the time. The broken viol-strings recall 'The Darkling Thrush'.

The Well-Beloved

The verse suggests the influence of Wordsworth's *Lyrical Ballads*. The theme of *The Well-Beloved* is presented here; it is nothing more than the deceptiveness of the Dream or the 'iris-hued embowment' which Hardy made explicit in *The Woodlanders* (see the note on 'To Outer Nature', pp. 20–21).

the Ikling way, the Roman road from Dorchester to Old Sarum (Salisbury). *Pagan temple*. Hardy had read in Hutchins that there was a Roman camp and temple on Woodbury Hill, east of Bere Regis; for the 1912 edition of *Wessex Poems* and *Poems of the Past and the Present* he changed the scene to the Roman site at Jordon Hill near Weymouth (and Portland, the main setting for *The Well-Beloved*). *I have ever stood* . . . This implies that the beauty the lover sees is a 're-adorning' of the actual. Hence for the hero of *The Well-Beloved* it is a 'Jill-o'-the-wisp' which makes him fall in love with one person after another. That this was a fascinating theory to Hardy and not a fixed belief may be seen in his note of 28 October 1891: 'It is the incompleteness that is loved, when love is sterling and true. This is what differentiates the real one from the imaginary, the practicable from the impossible, the Love who returns the kiss from the Vision that melts away' (*Life*, 239; cf. the endings of *FMC* and *WB*).

Her Reproach (1867)

This dramatic sonnet may have been intended as part of the 'She, to Him' sequence. Though not identical, the thought derives from Milton's 'Lycidas':

> Were it not better done, as others use,
> To sport with Amaryllis in the shade,
> Or with the tangles of Neaera's hair?

the dead page. The writer studies, neglecting the woman who thought he loved her and who bitterly compares the unreality of love he prefers to read about with the love he might, if he were more sensible, enjoy.

The Inconsistent

Possibly suggested by Hardy's visit to the grave where his cousin Tryphena was buried. See p. 16.

A Broken Appointment

Florence Hardy, who seems to have had no difficulty in obtaining biographical clues from her husband, must be the authority for associating this poem with Mrs Henniker and the British Museum (cf. Purdy, 113). With the line from 'Wessex Heights' –

Yet my love for her in its fulness she herself even did not know

– it throws important light on what her friendship meant to him, 'a time-torn man' (originally 'soul-sad'), especially from their meeting in May 1893 (*Life*, 254–6) to 1895–6. For 'time-torn', see 'The Ghost of the Past', ll.21–4 (and *TM*.xli).

'Between Us Now'

flushest, most colourful.

This lyric has a lighter, Browning touch, so much so that, though it could have originated from thoughts on Hardy's own domestic disharmony, it echoes no distress.

'How Great My Grief'

Though occasioned by thoughts of marital disillusionment, this is little more than a versifying exercise. The form (derived from the French and probably designed for music originally) suggests a simple theme rather than personal suffering. The 'triolet' (diminutive of 'trio') is regular: the main thought occurs three times, in the first, fourth, and seventh lines; the second line is repeated in the eighth (the concluding line). There are only two rhymes: *abaaabab*.

'I Need Not Go'

overgot, got over, overcome.

As Hardy did not always think it worth while to point out Lea's errors, one would like to know what truth there is for the statement (Lea, 270) that 'Stinsford Churchyard holds the tomb in which *She* lies'.

The Coquette, and After

fancy, love.

Hardy aimed at a striking ironical pattern in these two triolets. The idea that beneath apparent farce there may be tragedy is common in his works (cf. *TD.* xxi, xxix), and derives from Walpole's letters: 'I have often said, this world is a comedy to those that think, a tragedy to those that feel.'

A Spot

If this is autobiographical rather than imaginary, it recalls Hardy's early love of Emma Gifford. The glen would be the Valency valley.

sereward, towards old age, 'The sear, the yellow leaf' (*Macbeth*).

Long Plighted

The subject is anticipated in 'Postponement', a poem of 1866, and was suggested by Browning's 'The Statue and the Bust' (*Men and Women*). It is the theme of 'The Waiting Supper' (*CM*). Ultimately the wills of the lovers were 'somewhat enfeebled', 'their hearts sickened of tender enterprises by hope too long deferred'. . . . 'Is it worth while, after so many years?' she asked. This story provides the background to the poem. Its main setting is in the grounds of Stafford House near Stinsford ('Mellstock'). Meaning is stressed through structure, each verse opening with the same postponing question, each opening line ending with a hint of passing time ('now', 'when', 'since').

The Widow Betrothed

Written in the Wordsworth ballad metre, this is another poem on love and Time. When the lover hears that the woman he has loved and lost is widowed, his hope is renewed, only to find that she is 'betrothed' to her child. The lodge is on the right of the road from Dorchester to Stinsford Hill (see the map on p. 273); from it the avenue runs straight to Stinsford House (the first edition gives 'By Mellstock Lodge and

Avenue'). This poem and the previous are local and fictional; both lovers are baulked, the women deferring for different reasons. Hardy told Edmund Gosse that he thought of the poem about 1867; he added that it must have been written after he had read Wordsworth's preface to *Lyrical Ballads*, which 'influences the style of the poem, as you can see for yourself' (Purdy, 113). His notes on poetic diction and Wordsworth's volume (*Life*, 306) suggest that the poem could have been written about 1900.

At a Hasty Wedding

From the story 'A Changed Man' (*CM*), which Hardy wrote early in 1900. The third line ran, 'By lifelong ties that tether zest', echoing views expressed indirectly in *Jude the Obscure*. The poem contains a wry sort of contradiction; the lovers are blest only if hours extend to years, if the eastern stars never 'west' (for this verb, compare 'Drummer Hodge') or if fire is never succeeded by 'pallid ashes'. The wedding in the story is hasty; the poem is written by an invalid observer who felt subconsciously that 'though the couple might be happy . . . there was sufficient possibility of their being otherwise to colour the musings of an onlooker with a pleasing pathos of conjecture'.

The Dream-Follower

The dream is the illusion, as in 'On a Fine Morning'. It may have been occasioned by a recollection of Julia Augusta Martin, as the poet looked from Max Gate over the meadows toward Kingston Maurward (see p. 5). The poem is almost perfect in form and expression; its imagery epitomizes an important aspect of his outlook.

His Immortality (February 1899)

See the note to 'Her Immortality', p. 18. Few will remember him, and his memory will die with them.

The To-Be-Forgotten (MS, 9 February 1899)

foregone, gone before. *bourne*, limit.

Another poem on the 'second death' in posthumous memory. Only a few, to whom 'world-awakening scope' has been granted (the element of chance enters here) gain a lasting memory. The MS indicates that Hardy imagined the scene first in All Saints' churchyard, 'Casterbridge', then in 'Stourcastle' churchyard.

Things true . . . good report. See 'The Souls of the Slain', p. 33.

Wives in the Sere

A rounded, balanced poem in which a serious thought on love and the effect of Time on beauty is lightly conveyed, partly owing to the alternate feminine rhyming in a bold two-rhyme pattern.

The Superseded

The subduing effect of Time is seen, not from the outside as in the last poem, but by the ageing themselves.

An August Midnight (1899)

dumbledore, bumble-bee.

Hardy's altruism has been seen to include all conscious things. Here he recognises that Earth's humblest creatures may in some ways be superior to man. With the ending, compare 'The Darkling Thrush'. The inversion of the last line is perhaps an extreme example of the awkwardness and disregard for sound that Hardy sometimes accepted for the sake of verse pattern.[6]

The Caged Thrush Freed and Home Again

treen, trees (archaic plural).

The thought of the opening lines is similar to that at the end of the last poem. The caged thrush (see the note to 'The Bullfinches', p. 43) has been able to judge man's situation from being in a similar position: he is subject to suffering and mischance like every other creature. 'The Frost's decree' is the subject of six consecutive poems. As a symbol of the harshness of Nature and circumstance, it may be traced from Hardy's experience as a child, when he discovered its lethal possibilities *Life*, 23–4, 444). It was confirmed by Shelley's use of Winter imagery in *The Revolt of Islam* (IX. xx–xxx), 'The Sensitive Plant', 'Epipsychidion', 'Ode to the West Wind', etc. For its use in the novels, see *DR*.xiii. 1–4 and *TD*.xliii.

Hardy's interest in old French forms of verse such as the triolet and villanelle was stimulated by English examples in Gleeson White's anthology *Ballades and Rondeaus*, a copy of which Mrs Henniker sent him in July 1893 (*ORFW*, 15). The villanelle ('country-piece') normally consists of five tercets with a final quatrain and only two rhymes throughout.

Birds at Winter Nightfall

The rhyming is not of the best, especially with 'crumb-outcaster'; 'cotonea-aster' is more recognisable as 'cotoneaster'.

The Puzzled Game-Birds

In the 1912 edition this appeared as 'The Battue'. Hardy remembered the battue near Wimborne in 1882. Seven hundred pheasants were shot in a day. They were driven into a corner of a plantation, where they flew up and were shot wholesale. Next morning one hundred and fifty were found to have fallen from the trees. He pictured the night scene, the moon, and the birds fluttering and gasping as the hours passed; cf. *TD*.xli. He told Clive Holland that his books were 'one continued plea against man's inhumanity to man – to woman – and the lower animals'.

feed us. The birds were reared for the shooting-season; cf. 'Sportsman Time but rears his brood to kill' ('She, to Him').

Winter in Durnover Field

The scene is Fordington Field, an area stretching south of Dorchester and to the south-west between Maiden Castle and the Bridport road. The main theme (triply expressed) is reinforced by the 'cruel' frost alliteration in the second and eighth lines. For another field with the same metaphorical significance, see *TD*.xliii.

The Last Chrysanthemum

retrocede, move back, return. *witlessness*, ignorance.

Here we are presented with a particular example of 'The Lacking Sense', behind which must be a First Cause or Prime Mover (the 'Great Face' which is masked in Nature).

The Darkling Thrush

outleant, stretched out.

'Darkling' (in the dark) has a literal meaning with reference to the thrush, but its overtones express Hardy's mood and outlook. It does not echo Keats's 'Ode to a Nightingale' so much as Arnold and John Keble, the latter particularly. The subject of Arnold's 'Dover Beach' is the loss of faith and the intellectual uncertainty and groping which followed Evolutionary discoveries:

> for the world, which seems
> To lie before us like a land of dreams,
> So various, so beautiful, so new,
> Hath really neither joy, nor love, nor light,
> Nor certitude, nor peace, nor help for pain;
> And we are here as on a darkling plain
> Swept with confused alarms of struggle and flight,
> Where ignorant armies clash by night.

Arnold was probably influenced by John Keble's *The Christian Year*. Hardy's copy shows that he was thoroughly familiar with many of its hymns. Though the poet of 'The Twenty-first Sunday after Trinity' retained his Christian faith, the same theme appears in much of his poem as in 'The Darkling Thrush'. The setting is grey and autumnal, but in the 'dreary blast' a redbreast warbles a 'cheerful tender strain'. 'That', concludes Keble,

> is the heart for thoughtful seer,
> Watching, in trance nor dark nor clear,
> The appalling Future as it nearer draws:
> . . .
> Contented in his darkling round,
> If only he be faithful found,
> When from the east the eternal morning moves.

Hardy's change to mid-winter (the first edition title is 'The Century's End, 1900') has its obvious poetic cogency, and it explains why he chose the thrush, probably after reading (as Carl Weber pointed out in *Hardy of Wessex*, 1965, p. 234) the following passage from the thirteenth chapter of W. H. Hudson's *Nature in Downland* (1900):

> There is one thing to make a lover of bird-music happy in the darkest weather in January in this maritime district. Mid-winter is the season of the missel-thrush . . . when there is no gleam of light anywhere and no change in that darkness of immense ever-moving cloud above; and the south-west raves all day and all night, and day after day, then the storm-cock sings his loudest from a tree-top and has no rival. A glorious bird! . . . you must believe that this dark aspect of things delights him; that his pleasure in life, expressed with such sounds and in such circumstances, must greatly exceed in degree the contentment and bliss that is ours, even when we are most free from pain and care, and our whole beings most perfectly in tune with nature. . . . The sound is beautiful in quality, but the singer has no art, and flings out his notes anyhow; the song is an outburst, a cry of happiness. . . .

All the imagery in this passage is in accord with Hardy's mōod and thought, but attention must be called to 'flings' in Hudson's description of the bird's song; Hardy's thrush flings 'his soul/Upon the growing gloom'.

The end of a day in mid-winter at the end of the English year harmonizes with the utter fervourlessness of the poet. Within this general image, the mood is reinforced by the detail: the spectral Frost, Winter's dregs, the Century's corpse, and the tangled bine-stems like strings of broken lyres. The joyful song of a frail gaunt thrush 'in blast-beruffled plume' surprises Hardy, and makes him think that possibly the bird is instinctively more aware of the truth in Nature than he is. The poem shows less intransigence, a greater humility and wisdom, than 'The Impercipient', a readiness to agree that his intellectual pessimism may have misled him (cf. 'Night in the Old Home'). It creates a chiaroscuro effect, the 'joy illimited' of the song contrasting with the appearance of the bird and the scene and the poet's mood. The imagery of the poem is more traditional than is usual with Hardy, and rather Shelleyan.

Frost was spectre-gray. Cf. 'Neutral Tones'. *eye of day.* A Greek image which appears elsewhere in Hardy, e.g. *TT.*xviii, 'great eye of the sun'. Here it describes the weakening light at winter sunset. *tangled . . . broken lyres*. The image suggests not only lack of joy but also of faith; the bine-stems (bindweed which had grown up and over the neighbouring hedge) were dead and tangled like broken lyre-strings (with a hint of the music of old in 'scored'). *His crypt . . . death-lament*. Cf. Shelley's 'Ode to the West Wind':

> Thou dirge
> Of the dying year, to which this closing night
> Will be the dome of a vast sepulchre.

The Comet at Yell'ham

That this was Encke's Comet, October 1858, is confirmed by Hardy's letter to the Vice-Chancellor of the University of Oxford, on discovering that the latter had honoured him by quoting the poem in his address at the Sheldonian in 1908. The 'sweet form' may refer to Hardy's sister Mary. To Yellowham 'Height', via the heath and woodland tracks that existed then, was less than a mile from Higher Bockhampton.

Mad Judy

With ironical relish Hardy attributes some of his own views to the insane Judy.

A Wasted Illness

Although '(Overheard)' was added for the 1912 edition, the poem is probably based on Hardy's recollection of his long illness at Upper Tooting, 1880–1, when he was engaged to write *A Laodicean*. The mood seems to have been engendered by later experience; cf. 'In Tenebris'. The title and conclusion indicate why the poem follows 'Mad Judy', and make 'all was well' (cf. 'The Impercipient') most ambivalent.

A Man

clown, rustic. *untold*, unrecorded. *close with*, come to terms with. *rude*, unskilled.

It seems to be agreed that the house (to which Hardy referred when he was given the freedom of Dorchester in 1910; see *Life*, 352) was that of the Trenchards at the junction of Shirehall Lane and High West Street; it was demolished before 1849. H. of M. has not been identified.

Eliza, Elizabeth I, who reigned from 1558 to 1603. *cornice, quoin, and cove*. The cornice is an exterior horizontal moulding; for 'quoin' and 'cove' see the note to 'Rome: Building a New Street in an Ancient Quarter' (p. 36). Hardy regrets the loss of so much fine ornamental moulding both outside the building and around its rooms. *backed his tools*, put them on his back.

The Dame of Athelhall

The story depends on the ironical twist in the tail (the satire of circumstance, a favourite recipe with Hardy).

The Seasons of Her Year

The MS title 'The Pathetic Fallacy' may accord with Ruskin's definition (Bailey, 171). In this poem of contrasts the imaginative-emotional recolouring of the scene is comparable with that in 'The King's Experiment'; cf. 'The Waiting Supper' (*CM*), iv:

> The nook was most picturesque; but it looked horridly common and stupid now. Their sentiment had set a colour hardly less visible than a material one on surrounding objects, as sentiment must where life is but thought.

My song-birds moan. Compare Burns's lyric on a similar betrayal, 'Ye banks and braes o' bonnie Doon'.

The Milkmaid

ruminating, chewing the cud.

This provides a miniature analogue to *Far from the Madding Crowd*. All may appear delightfully pastoral to the traditionalist, but the milkmaid who appears idyllic is torn by sexual jealousy. The contrast between the outer scene and what passes through her mind forms the larger irony; incidental irony seems to puncture the description of both, in the 'rich red ruminating cow' and the 'poetries' of Phyllis's frustrated spirit.[7]

The Levelled Churchyard (1882)

passenger, passer-by.

Written at Wimborne with reference to the Minster and its restoration in 1855-7. Hardy treats the subject with pleasantry; at the end he imitates the Church Litany. The verse is hymnal. See his 'Memories of Church Restoration' (Orel, 207-8 in particular).

The Ruined Maid (1866)

barton, farmyard. *sock*, sigh deeply.

A distinctive poem without parallel in Hardy. In the dramatic dialogue, the metre suits the excitement of the country girl and her innocent wonder at the transformation of the friend she suddenly meets in town (London). The satire in the varying refrain is not too prolonged to lose its effect.

The Respectable Burgher

Hardy was amused to think that many a respectable citizen would find Voltaire's scepticism 'moderate' compared with 'The Higher Criticism', which began with German scholars whose policy was to examine the Scriptures from a historical and scientific angle. For Hardy the most important product of the movement in England was the publication of *Essays and Reviews* in 1860. Such was the outcry against it that its authors were dubbed 'The Seven against Christ' (cf. *Life*, 33). Hardy's scientific outlook made him welcome the rejection of the miraculous and supernatural in Biblical studies; some of his poems (e.g. 'Panthera') show his readiness to venture into 'the higher criticism' himself. Yet he was convinced that the progress of civilization depended on the maintenance of Christian values, especially the composite virtue of Charity.

banjo-player. In soothing Saul during his fits of depression (1 Samuel, xvi. 14-23). *Solomon sang the fleshly Fair.* In 'The Song of Solomon'. For its orthodox interpretation, see the headings of its chapters and JO.III.iv, where Jude complains that Sue is 'quite Voltairean' in criticizing them. *Esther . . . royal wear.* Esther, v. 1-3. *Mordecai . . . Jair.* Esther, ii, 5ff. *Balaam's ass.* Numbers, xxii. 21-35. *Nain widow.* Luke, vii. 11-17. *Lazarus.* John, xi. 1-46. *Piombo*, Sebastian del Piombo, Italian painter (1485-1547). His 'Raising of Lazarus' had been seen by Hardy in the National Gallery. *Malchus' ear.* John, xviii. 10. The crowning scepticism relates to the Resurrection: 'That [Jesus Christ] did not reappear!'

Architectural Masks

On the irony of appearances and common judgements.

The Tenant-for-Life

For an example of Hardy's imaginative contemplation of the various dwellers in a house, see the fourth paragraph of *W*.iv. Here he considers lifeholders from another aspect: they are soon dead and forgotten. The poem combines two points of view expressed in *Tess*: the literal one, when Tess's family is evicted (see the sixth paragraph of *TD*.liv), and the more general one on the insignificance of the individual in the course of time (*TD*.xix; see *AHC*. 170-2 for further reference to the theme).

The King's Experiment

coombs, valleys among hills. *een*, eyes.

Compare 'The Seasons of Her Year' (p. 56) and 'The Difference'. The poem suggests Hardy's familiarity with Crabbe's 'The Lover's Journey' (*Tales*, 1812).

Nature . . . King Doom. Cf. 'Doom and She' (pp. 41-2).

The Tree

A tale of passion and crime. The spirit of evil seems to have entered the tree with which it is associated, and even to persist in the roots that bristle 'like some mad Earth-god's spiny hair' after it has been felled by the midnight storm. For a possible connotation of the Sweetheart's madness, see 'On the Portrait of a Woman about to be Hanged'.

Fiord (Norway), *Strom*, *Fleuve* (stream in Germany and France).

Her Late Husband

Hardy's mother was born at 'King's Hintock, but it need not be assumed that the story or tradition of the 'strange interment' is connected with Hardy's ancestors. For his interest in their graves at Melbury Osmond, see *THN*. 68.

The Self-Unseeing

When this poem was written, the Hardys still lived at Higher Bock-hampton. Thomas Hardy's father had died in 1892. The poet recalls dancing to his father's fiddle when he was very young (*Life*, 15). At that time the front door gave direct access to the living-room. For the implications of the title, compare 'The Self-Unconscious'.

In Tenebris (I)

in unhope, with no hope.

The three poems were entitled 'De Profundis' in the first edition. The Latin quotations are all from St Jerome's version of the Psalms (which are numbered differently in the English Bible). The first is from cii.4: 'My heart is smitten, and withered like grass.' Even after rejecting Christian theology, Hardy accepted the ethical teaching of the Bible, and found more wisdom and spiritual sustenance there than from any other source. Perhaps Keble's practice in *The Christian Year* encouraged him to prefix some of his most serious poems with Biblical quotations. Hardy's bouts of depression in 1895-6 must be related to his matri-monial problems and *Jude the Obscure*; see 'Wessex Heights' (pp. 95-7.) The wintry imagery expresses unpropitious circumstances (see pp. 51-2). 'Bereavement-pain' and 'severing scene' both allude to the death of love. Some loss of friends may have occurred after the publication of *Jude*, though the poem expresses a mood rather than a situation.

In Tenebris (II) (1895-6)

'I looked on my right hand, and beheld, but there was no man that would know me . . .; no man cared for my soul' (Psalm cxlii. 4). Hardy's subject is the pessimism with which he had been charged. The period suggests that this arose from *Jude*.

All's well with us. See 'The Impercipient' (p. 24). *one born out of due time*. I Corinthians, xv. 8. *Best killed . . . First*. It may be that as an evolutionary meliorist Hardy assumed that the First was the Worst, that civilization had to progress slowly against the forces of evil and unenlightenment. See the note to 'The Church-Builder' (pp. 60-61) and the Apology to *Late Lyrics and Earlier*. *delight is a delicate thing*. This is the view of Blake, and the subject of dramatic scenes in *Jude* (V.v and VI.ii).

In each of the first three stanzas the subject of the last three lines is the public point of view, while that of the last is the poet's self-condemnation. Its continuation in the last stanza forms the climax of the poem.

In Tenebris (III) (1896)

quoin, corner. *listing*, desire. *unweeting*, ignorant.

'Woe is me . . . that I dwell in the tents of Kedar! My soul hath long dwelt with him that hateth peace' (Psalm cxx. 5–6). Against the lines which follow 'Ah, love, let us be true to one another' in 'Dover Beach' (they are quoted on p. 53) Hardy wrote, 'Sept. 1896 – T.H./E.L.H.' This may explain his depression; see 'The Dead Man Walking', which was also written in 1896. He recalls childhood experiences not recorded elsewhere, and thinks how much he would have been spared if he had died on one of these occasions.

in the midmost of Egdon. 'Egdon' is the Wessex name for the heath behind the Hardy's home at Higher Bockhampton. *baptism of pain*. Some early illness. It is easier to understand why Hardy chose this as a suitable time for his 'ending'. The first and second experiences suggest times of happy or confident illusion. *with no . . . longing to join*. Hardy's reluctance to grow up when he was young, to escape from the 'ongoing', may be seen in his *Life* (15–16) and more explicitly in *JO*.i.ii. *sweets . . . mouth . . . belly . . . bitter*. Revelation, x. 9–10.

The Church-Builder

dossal, ornamental cloth behind the altar. *chore*, choir, chancel.

The MS title is 'Nisi Dominus Frustra' from Psalm cxxvii, 'Except the Lord [build the house they labour] in vain [that build it].' The verse is braced in masterly style, as befits the building theme. After this the subject seem to express the mood, thoughts, and background of the 'In Tenebris' poems. The ghastly conclusion makes one feel that the 'crucifixion' scene in *Jude*, after Little Father Time has hanged Sue's two children and himself, also expresses Hardy's loathing of life. The lines –

> And powerful Wrong on feeble Right
> Tramples in olden style

– seem to paraphrase 'the low-voiced Best is killed by the clash of the First' in 'In Tenebris' (II).

The Lost Pyx

vill, village.

The pillar Cross-in-Hand stands on a ridge above Batcombe, between Bubb Down and High Stoy, overlooking the Vale of Blackmoor to the north. Two other traditions relating to its origin are given briefly in *TD*.xlv. The poem is placed here because the site marks the beginning of Tess's final tragedy.

Abbey north . . . Vale, Sherborne Abbey. Cernel's (line 5) was at Cerne Abbas.

Tess's Lament

durn, doorpost. *unbe*, not be, cease to be.

The sadness of this lyric is accentuated by artful repetition. Tess laments the ending of her happiness with Angel Clare at Talbothays dairy farm before their marriage and her desertion. One needs to know *Tess of the d'Urbervilles* well to appreciate the poem to the full, though the recollections of the third verse are based on scenes not included in the novel.

The Supplanter

The MS title is 'At the Cemetery Lodge'. There is no reason (especially as both poems include the phrase 'Field of Tombs') to assume that this is not the same cemetery as for 'Her Death and After' (p. 13). Perhaps the two poems were written at about the same time. It is a strange Gothic fancy, a ballad derivative in a modern setting.

IMITATIONS, ETC.

Sapphic Fragment

In 1897 Hardy informed Swinburne that, after examining several imitations of it, he attempted 'to strike out a better equivalent': 'I then stumbled upon your "Thee, too, the years shall cover", and all spirit for poetic pains died out of me. Those few words present, I think, the finest *drama* of Death and Oblivion, so to speak, in our tongue' (*Life*, 287). Sappho, a Greek poetess of the seventh century B.C., has often been thought unsurpassed for depth of feeling and grace.

Catullus: XXXI

Hardy's note does not indicate that this was written in April 1887, only that passing Sirmione at that time was one of the factors that led to the translation. In this poem the Latin poet celebrated his return from Bithynia in Asia Minor to the peninsula of Sirmione on Lake Garda. Hardy's translation does not suggest that Catullus was the 'tenderest of Roman poets' (see Tennyson's 'Frater Ave atque Vale').

pined for couch at last. In word and spirit this almost echoes the end of Arnold's 'Sohrab and Rustum'.

After Schiller

Hardy copied the first stanza of 'Ritter Toggenburg' in his notebook, and added a translation (slightly different from this) in 1889 (Purdy, 117).

Song from Heine

The song is 'Ich stand in dunkeln Träumen' from the *Reisebilder* (*Die Heimkehr*, no. 25). Hardy owned at least two selections of the poetry of Heinrich Heine (1797–1856) in translation.

From Victor Hugo

'A une Femme' (*Les Feuilles d'Automne*). See *Life*, 311 for Hardy's great tribute to Hugo's works.

Cardinal Bembo's Epitaph on Raphael

Hardy showed deep interest in the Italian painter Raffaello, and entered many quotations in his notebook from a biography of him. Cardinal Bembo's Latin epitaph was carved on Raphael's tomb.

RETROSPECT

'I Have Lived with Shades' (2 February 1899)

Hardy was a modest man. Lady St Helier (formerly Lady Jeune) met many distinguished people, but never one more modest (*Memories of Fifty Years*, London, 1909, p. 241). If this was his view of his posthumous significance, he miscalculated. The poem, like those on 'subjective immortality', illustrates his sense of the insignificance of the individual in the time-space continuum of the universe. His future poetry shows how he lived more and more with Shades (not spirits but memories of the departed) as he grew older.

Memory and I

outflickers, flickers out.

The poet's disillusionment could not be more unequivocally expressed; cf. the 'In Tenebris' poems. The climax comes with the death of his love (cf. 'The Dead Man Walking'); Emma's fondness belongs only to a phantom, one of the Shades of memory. (She was not blind to his meaning, and asked Rebekah Owen to read some of the poems in this volume as fiction – 'moans & fancies, etc. Written "to please" others or himself – but not me, far otherwise.')

Ἀγνώστωι Θεωι

The title, 'To the Unknown God' is from the Greek Scriptures (Acts, xvii. 23). The subject is an appropriate one to conclude a volume designed largely to eradicate 'weak fantasies' of the Will. Perhaps Hardy rationalized too much on the unknowable (cf. *Life*, 410). The end of the poem anticipates that of *The Dynasts*. As an 'evolutionary meliorist' he believed that the diffusion of 'Altruism, or the Golden Rule, or whatever "Love your Neighbour as Yourself" may be called' (*Life*, 224) would make the General Will more percipient and sensitive, since man's awareness is part of It (see 'He Wonders About Himself').

3

Time's Laughingstocks

IN the eight years between the publication of his last volume of poetry
and this, Hardy had been busy writing *The Dynasts*, which appeared in
three parts (1904, 1906, and 1908). *Time's Laughingstocks* was published
in December 1909, the title, initially used for the first poem, coming
from Tennyson's *The Princess* (IV. 496). Most of the 94 poems were
written during the period when Hardy's major preoccupation was *The
Dynasts*, but twelve are early, dating from 1866 to 1871. Twenty-nine
of the later poems had been previously published, from 1901 to 1909.
There is a noticeable increase in lyrical verse, but several of the more
outstanding poems are narrative. Hardy described this collection as 'a
miscellany'. It contains some light-hearted poems, but the general tone
is sombre. So unmistakable are the notes of personal unhappiness in
some of the poems, it seems strange that Edmund Gosse did not suspect
the reality behind them. Of the volume as a whole he wrote on 7
December 1909: 'how poignantly sad! What makes you take such a
hopelessly gloomy view of existence?'

TIME'S LAUGHINGSTOCKS

The Revisitation

This rather odd tale was first published under the title of 'Time's
Laughingstocks, A Summer Romance'. Cf. 'Long Plighted' (p. 49).

ancient country barrack. At Dorchester ('Casterbridge'). *ridge of Water-
stone.* North-east of Dorchester, and named after Waterston House,
the original of Bathsheba's in *Far from the Madding Crowd. lane of Slyre.*
Slyres Lane, which proceeds over the ridge to the Piddle valley ('the
vale'). *Sarsen stone,* a large stone from which the surrounding chalk has

been washed away (from 'Saracen' because such stones were sometimes associated with pagan rites). *Milton Wood to Dole-Hill.* From the hills above Milton Abbas to Dole's Hill Plantation north of Puddletown. *Time's transforming chisel.* See 'In a Eweleaze near Weatherbury' (p. 25).

A Trampwoman's Tragedy (April 1902)

tap, inn. *fancy-man*, sweetheart.

Hardy thought this 'upon the whole, his most successful poem' (*Life*, 311–12), a view which suggests that the author's love of an unusual story could tip the scales of his poetic judgement. In 1910 he told his publisher that such stories were popular, and added, 'I can do them with ease.' There is much to admire in the manipulation of the stanza, which is generally vigorous and well-knit, with effective repetition and rhyme.

Nearly all the place-names are actual. Hardy informed Edmund Gosse that the poem was written after a bicycle journey over Poldon Hill to Glastonbury, and that 'the woman's name was Mary Ann Taylor'. A note at the head of the poem on its first publication (in *The North American Review*) indicated that the events took place in 1827.[8]

the Great Forest, the New Forest. *Marshwood*, Marshwood Vale in west Dorset. *Lone inns.* King's Stag, south-west of Sturminster Newton; Windwhistle on the Exeter road west of Crewkerne; The Horse at Middlemarsh on the Dorchester-Sherborne road; The Hut on Long Bredy Hill, on the Dorchester-Bridport road; Wynyard's Gap on the road to Crewkerne, north of Beaminster. Some of them no longer exist. *My lady.* Hardy regretted that he could not use the word 'doxy' here; it 'has some sort of endearment', whereas the word 'lady' may be 'stern'. *Blue Jimmy.* When he was a boy, Hardy had heard that a horse belonging to the father of William Keats, the tranter who lived almost opposite the Hardys at Higher Bockhampton, had been stolen by this notorious thief. *his last fling.* He was hanged on 25 April 1827 (F. E. Dugdale, 'Blue Jimmy: The Horse-Stealer', *The Cornhill Magazine*, February 1911). *thinned.* The word seems suited to a ghostly illusion; cf. 'A Spellbound Palace' (p. 207) and 'smalled' in 'The Dead Quire'. *the Western Moor*, Sedgemoor, below the Poldon (Polden)Hills.

The Two Rosalinds

mammet, doll.

This seems an improbable piece of fiction. Hardy stated (*Life*, 228) that the poem might have occurred to him after he had seen Ada Rehan as Rosalind. This was in 1890; 'in eighteen sixty-three', 'some forty years ago', indicates a much later date.

'*Arden*' . . . *running brooks. As You Like It*, II. i.

A Sunday Morning Tragedy (January 1904)

traps, belongings. *poppling*, bubbling.

Perhaps the most notable thing about this tragic laughingstock of Time is that Hardy first intended it as a play; two sketches for this are preserved in the Dorset County Museum, 'Birthwort', the title of one, indicating the 'herb' used. The poem was rejected by *The Fortnightly Review* and *The Cornhill Magazine*. Ford Madox Hueffer (Ford) said that he founded *The English Review* to publish it (Purdy, 139). It is written in ballad form. Lea (303) claims that the banns were called in Piddlehinton Church 'in circumstances reputed to be veracious'.

loved too well. Othello, v. ii, 'Of one that lov'd not wisely but too well'.
picotee, an attractive kind of carnation, edged with a darker colour. The heroine's sister in *The Hand of Ethelberta* is named Picotee.

The House of Hospitalities

outset, set out.

This was identified by Hardy as the 'house by the well' (Purdy, 140), about half way along Higher Bockhampton lane. The well (cf. *Life*, 3) served the local inhabitants. Opposite it stood the house, once occupied by Mr C— (John Cox) and later divided into two cottages (*CM*. 'Enter a Dragoon'). The Christmas scenes in *Under the Greenwood Tree* seem to have been drawn in part from festive 'hospitalities' at the house before it was divided.

Bereft (1901)

Grey's Bridge is on the London road just outside Dorchester; 'Durnover Lea' is the meadowland by the Frome which the road traverses in this neighbourhood.

John and Jane

Such names suggest that this kind of tragedy is too common. The build-up, particularly in the last lines of the verses, leads to a sudden shattering of happiness and illusion. Once again, feelings affect impressions of the outside world; cf. 'The Seasons of Her Year'.

The Curate's Kindness

A tragi-comic satire of circumstance.

Pummery or Ten-Hatches Weir. Both are outside Dorchester. The Frome runs below Poundbury (Pummery; see 'The Dance at the Phoenix'), a prehistoric hill fort on the north-west side. The pool above Ten Hatches Weir (and Grey's Bridge), where Michael Henchard prepared to drown himself, is on the east side.

The Flirt's Tragedy

grizzle, turn grey. *coign-stone*, corner stone.

The 'drama' unfolds in the mind of an old man whose guilt makes him feel Cain-like as the shadows on the wainscot (created by the dying flames of the fire) remind him of the past. The opening of the poem, though the syntax is broken, suggests he is alone, yet the ending presupposes a listener. One rhyme only runs through the whole poem.

the manor she goddessed. Tintinhull Manor, north-west of Yeovil, Somerset, belonged to the Napier family in the eighteenth century. No record has been found authenticating Hardy's story, nor need it be assumed that it is wholly based on fact or tradition. *played . . . lines*. An angling metaphor. *calle*, a 'street' (off the Grand Canal, 'That still street of waters . . . two'). *Tophet*, used synonymously for Hell. *Time unveils*. Another twist of fortune proves that the lover is one of Time's laughingstocks.

The Rejected Member's Wife (January 1906)

Here is the atmosphere of real life, and the lyric conveys rather delicately the poet's pity. The elections at the beginning resulted in sweeping Liberal gains (*ORFW*. 126). The rejected candidate was Colonel W. E.

Brymer of Ilsington House, Puddletown, previously Conservative member (Parliamentary representative) for South Dorset. The results were declared at the County Hall, High West Street, Dorchester.

The Farm-Woman's Winter

limber, frail.

Autumn in King's Hintock Park (1901)

Hardy's interest in the Melbury district where his mother was born led to this poem. 'I happened to be walking, or cycling, through [the Ilchesters' park] years ago, when the incident occurred on which the verses are based', he wrote in December 1906 (*ORFW.* 131). The second of two contrasting poems, it conveys by its movement the vital, bustling character of the old woman. She had often sighed at the thought of life's passing (and the reader is frequently reminded of it by the recurrence of 'Raking up leaves'), but is comforted by the larger, more philosophical vision of the process of renewal in the seasons and generations; cf. 'Life and Death at Sunrise'.

Shut Out That Moon (1904)

At first the moon is associated with youthful happiness and 'sweet sentiments',

> When living seemed a laugh, and love
> All it was said to be.

The first verse closes with thoughts of the dead; the second, with beauty that has faded with age; the third, with the death of love; and the last, with general disillusionment. The theme of deprivation is hinted at in the 'stealing' moon which the poet does not wish to see; the romance and happiness of which it reminds him have proved to be nothing but illusory. Cf. 'The Absolute Explains', vii–viii.

Lady's Chair, Cassiopeia's Chair, a W-shaped constellation on the side of the Pole Star opposite the Great Bear. *mechanic speech*. Perfunctory, fervourless.

Reminiscences of a Dancing Man

jaunty jills, lively young women. *moue*, make grimaces at. *chaps*, cheeks.

One MS indicates that the poem was written in 1895, the year Hardy revisited Almack's (Willis's) Rooms with his wife (*Life*, 274). It reminded him of the dances he had enjoyed there (*Life*, 42–3) and at the Argyle Rooms and Cremorne (*Life*, 34, 43),[9] which he 'drew upon' largely 'in the destroyed novel *The Poor Man and the Lady*'. The collocation of this poem and the final lines of 'Shut Out That Moon' is one of Hardy's bitterest personal ironies. It is continued in the next poem. Hardy has succeeded, especially in the recollection of 'gay Cremorne', in making his measure evoke the rhythm of the music and dancers. For an excellent impression of a typical dancing scene in Cremorne Gardens (near the Thames, Chelsea), see the painting in the London Museum by Phoebus Levin (1864). Lady St Helier (*op. cit.*, p. 73) recalls being disappointed when she was taken there 'under promise of inviolable secrecy' in the 1860s: 'The gardens were pretty, but badly illuminated; the dancing was ungraceful, and the various grottos, or what we should now call side-shows, were tawdry and uninteresting.'

Jullien. Louis Antoine Jullien was a French conductor who did much to popularize music in London. Cf. *Life*, 123.

The Dead Man Walking (MS, 1906)

A most uncompromising revelation of relations between Hardy and his wife Emma.

died of late years. Cf. 'In Tenebris' (I). *ceased Time's enchantments . . . Life for lyre*. Cf. 'Shut Out That Moon'. *The goal of men . . . iced me*. Although Hardy found that 'he was "up against" the position of having to carry on his life . . . as a scientific game', and that he was committed to novel-writing as he had been to architecture 'as a regular trade' (*Life*, 104), yet he 'constitutionally shrank from the business of social advancement, caring for life as an emotion rather than for life as a science of climbing, in which respect he was quizzed by his acquaintance for his lack of ambition' (*Life*, 53; cf. 87). *my friend, my kinsfolk*. Horace Moule had committed suicide in 1873; see 'Before My Friend Arrived' (p. 231). Hardy's father died in 1892; his mother, in 1904. *my Love's heart kindled/In hate of me*. See 'The Voice of Things', p. 121.

MORE LOVE LYRICS

1967 (1867)

The ending is reminiscent of John Donne.

Her Definition (1866)

outfigure, delineate, present. *fitless*, unfitting.

Although eked out with an extended image, this early sonnet helps to clarify Hardy's reasons for eschewing a figurative and colourful style in poetry.

The Division (1893)

On 24 April 1899 Emma Hardy wrote to a friend, 'I have been a devoted wife for at least twenty years or more – but the last four or five alas!' Compare 'After a Journey':

> Summer gave us sweets, but autumn wrought division.

The poem may have been written in London, and almost certainly after Hardy's friendship with Mrs Henniker began. Although the distance by road from Dorchester to London is 120 miles (*CM*. 'A Changed Man'), it is approximately 100 'as the crow flies'.

On the Departure Platform

The poem is associated with Florence Dugdale, who was a welcome visitor to Max Gate by 1907, gave secretarial assistance to both Hardy and Emma, and married Hardy in 1914. She must be the authority for this identification (Purdy, 142). Since *Time's Laughingstocks* was published in Emma Hardy's lifetime, the fictitious conclusion to this dramatic lyric is not surprising.

In a Cathedral City

The footnote implies that the poem was *written* at Salisbury. On existing evidence, it seems rather futile to attempt any identification, though 'beauty's fame' suggests Mrs Henniker.

I Say, 'I'll Seek Her'

The poem is mainly fantasy, but it could have been written with 'Her Immortality' and Hardy's 'lost prize' Tryphena in mind, when his mood and situation were like those which engendered 'In Tenebris' (III). The 'cockcrows' suggest the departure of the spirit which has been calling him (cf. *Hamlet*, I. i. 147–65).

Her Father (MS, 1869)

Like the following Weymouth poems, this appears to be fictional. It is very ordinary compared with 'I Say ,"I'll Seek Her"'.

At Waking (1869)

The poem embodies the vanishing of a lover's enchantment. As truth strikes him in the cold light of dawn and reason, he realizes that the girl who had charmed him is commonplace. The last stanza particularly seems too light to convey deep feeling, and the poem generally suggests the inspiration of an idea which fascinated Hardy (cf. p. 47, on the difference between true love and 'the Vision that melts away').

dawn . . . Dead-white as a corpse. Cf. 'A Commonplace Day' and the note, p. 40. *the prize*. Hardy was engaged in writing *Desperate Remedies* when the poem was written. The same thought was in his mind when he wrote about the hero's poems (ii.3): 'He says that your true lover breathlessly finds himself engaged to a sweetheart, like a man who has caught something in the dark. He doesn't know whether it is a bat or a bird, and takes it to the light when he is cool to learn what it is . . . later he ponders whether she is the right kind of prize for him.'

Four Footprints

The scene may be at Weymouth.

In the Vaulted Way (MS, 1870)

Whether this is autobiographical or fictional is uncertain. Purdy (142) thinks the date of composition indicates 'an episode of Hardy's court-ship' in Cornwall. If so, it would be during his second visit in August

1870 (*Life*, 78–9). 'Dear' suggests an engagement; 'one long aim', a rather longer engagement than Hardy's had been. There is nothing in the poems or elsewhere which hints at any contretemps directly between Emma Gifford and Hardy; nor has anything approaching a long engagement been substantiated between Hardy and any other young woman at this time. No evidence has been found that the poem is not fictional. It is a well-contrived narrative lyric, ending in dramatized reflection, plainer, but after the manner of Meredith's *Modern Love*.

In the Mind's Eye

The title in the first edition is 'The Phantom'. In his copy Hardy underlined this, and wrote in the margin 'Ghost-face' (Bailey, 215). The heroine of this lyrical fantasy was dead.

The End of the Episode

dumbles, humble-bees.

Although it has been associated with Emma Hardy, the poem in its context and generality suggests no more than a dramatic lyric on a common situation, though the last lines seem to be weighted with bitter experience.

The Sigh

A light but more evenly successful lyric.

'In the Night She Came'

The dream is imaginary.

The Conformers

cohue, people of conventional outlook.

The poem strikes an attitude rather like that of Browning's more dramatic 'Respectability'. It recalls Bathsheba Everdene's father, who, in order to be romantic, was in the habit of taking off his wife's wedding-ring and pretending they were not married. 'And as soon as he could thoroughly fancy he was doing wrong and committing the seventh, 'a got to like her as well as ever' (*FMC*.viii).

The Dawn after the Dance (1869)

Another aspect of nonconformity. The 'formal/Matrimonial common-place' links this poem with the previous. As the winter of 1869 approached, Hardy joined a dancing-class at Weymouth, and found it 'a gay gathering for dances and love-making by adepts of both sexes' (*Life*, 64). From this it was but a short distance to most of Hardy's Weymouth poems.

no brighter. Hardy said he thought he could originally have written 'the brighter' (Collins, 23). The woman is expectant.

The Sun on the Letter

The MS title 'A Discord' was deleted. The last three verses show a continuity in syntax which is rare in Hardy's poetry, and should be read in one breath (as it were). The last verse runs, 'as if it had shown her true, [as if it] had teemed/With passionate thought . . . expressed with the ardency of the sun's rays'. A subordinate implication of the scene is the sun's indifference and its link with the Scriptures: 'for he maketh his sun to rise on the evil and the good, and sendeth rain on the just and on the unjust' (Matthew, v. 45).

The Night of the Dance

quiz, gaze at (as if questioning). *backbrand*, log placed at the back of the fire.

This recalls *Under the Greenwood Tree*. Whether 'Old Robert' is 'Robert Penny' (*Life*, 92) is doubtful; if the recollection is of Higher Bockhampton, it could be of either Hardy's home or 'The House of Hospitalities' (p. 66).

Misconception

Vanity of vanities, saith the preacher. Hardy had found himself so much in tune with the Book of Ecclesiastes that he began turning it into Spenserian stanzas, 'but finding the original unmatchable abandoned the task' (*Life*, 47).

moils, turmoils, the turn of the 'wheel' (*Life*, 171) or the 'diurnal spin/ Of vanities'.

The Voice of the Thorn

Although the down is likely to be elsewhere, the idea of the poem seems to be born from the kind of impression Hardy formed in October 1887, when looking at thorn bushes by Rushy Pond: 'In their wrath with the gales their forms resemble men's in like mood' (*Life*, 202). The first two stanzas present contrasts in mood and season; the third links the whole by telling what the voice says at all seasons when the unfaithful lover is near. The thorn reflects impressions made on viewers, human or animal; its voice is psychological.

From Her in the Country (1866)

For a variant of this, see 'The Musing Maiden'; for a contrast, 'Dream of the City Shopwoman'. All three were written in London in 1866.

Her Confession (1865–7)

Hardy sometimes uses the sustained comparison (characteristic of the early Shakespeare) to elaborate thought in his early poems.

To an Impersonator of Rosalind (21 April 1867)

Written at Arthur Blomfield's towards the end of Hardy's training as an architect in London. At this time the part of Rosalind in *As You Like It* (at the Haymarket) was taken by Mrs Mary Frances Scott-Siddons, great grand-daughter of the famous actress Mrs Siddons. The quotation comes from Act IV, Scene i of the play.

To an Actress (1867)

Rather hyperbolical and Elizabethan.

The Minute before Meeting (1871)

These lines (weakened by 'full-up') express a lover's thoughts. Hardy visited Emma Gifford at St Juliot in May 1871.

He Abjures Love (1883)

Placed here as a contrast to the last poem. Hardy regards himself as Time's laughingstock.

daysman, arbitrator (Job, ix. 33). *the gray hour golden*. Cf. 'On a Fine Morning'.

A SET OF COUNTRY SONGS

Let Me Enjoy

The opening reveals an attitude all too rare in Hardy. As it progresses, the poem seems less authentic and more 'impersonative'. The poems which follow express a variety of moods.

AT CASTERBRIDGE FAIR

I. The Ballad-Singer

The movement of the lines succeeds in conveying the effort of the 'speaker' to be hearty.

II. Former Beauties

Written in a more sober style, to accord with the subject.

III. After the Club-Dance

The heavy stress and sombre background imagery suggest the influence of A. E. Housman's *A Shropshire Lad* (1896).

have done the same. Reminiscent of Hardy's comment on Tess's downfall (*TD*.xiii).

IV. The Market-Girl

causey, paved road.

V. The Inquiry

sengreen, houseleek. *hurdled*, set up hurdles for sheep.

Hermitage is north of High Stoy and on the edge of Blackmoor Vale. The eager excited questioning of Patty Beech is subtly conveyed in the rhythm. Three of Hardy's common themes combine in the last four lines.

VI. A Wife Waits

The harsh truth between 'before' and 'after', between pledge and performance, is strongly pointed in the collocation of the last lines, which illustrate the general truth expressed at the end of the previous poem.

Club-room below. Although said to be in North Square (Lea, 305), the poem suggests it was lower down the High Street, below the Bow, a curved wall by the east end of St Peter's and on the northern side of the crossways of 'Casterbridge', the 'Cross' of the next poem and the *carrefour* of *MC*.xxiv.

VII. After the Fair (1902)

drong, lane.

The Cornmarket-place (Cornhill) above South Street is the main centre for the market; the 'stammering' chimes are St Peter's (cf. *MC*.iv); the Clock-corner refers to the Town Hall. People are seen wandering off down the High Street, past the White Hart at the end of the town, and over Grey's Bridge beyond, into the country towards Stinsford. The poet is left with ghosts (recollections) of citizens, stretching back to the Romans, whose remains were to be seen in the neighbouring Museum (cf. *GND*, at the conclusion of the first story).

The Dark-Eyed Gentleman

A song by a simple woman, rather like the more fortunate Mrs Green (*TT*.xvii).

Crimmercrock Lane. See the note to 'Toller downland' in 'The Home-coming' (p. 78).

To Carrey Clavel

coll, embrace.

The tones of speech are exquisitely conveyed in this dramatic poem.

like a tulip. Cf. 'peony lips' in 'Julie-Jane'.

The Orphaned Old Maid

This story of hypocrisy, selfishness, and self-sacrifice illustrates the traditional inequality of the sexes; 'the woman pays'.

The Spring Call

Compare Tess's dialect, 'the characteristic intonation . . . for this district being the voicing approximately rendered by the syllable UR, probably as rich an utterance as any to be found in human speech' (*TD*.ii).

Julie-Jane

The gusto of the first three stanzas communicates her character in a remarkable way. It does not change: 'She chose her bearers . . . From her fancy-men'. For the footnote, compare 'Retty's Phases' and 'The Hatband' (p. 263).

peony lips. As in *TD*.ii.

News for Her Mother

Another poem in which the metre conveys the almost breathless excitement of the central character. It is a dramatic lyric, in the Browning style, with an admirable close.

The Fiddler

This recalls 'Julie-Jane', and even more the 'witchery' of 'The Fiddler of the Reels' (*LLI*), one of Hardy's best short stories.

The Husband's View

A drama with an unusual happy ending. The wife confides in an old woman (a friend she can trust, no doubt) and is overheard by her husband.

Rose-Ann

The lyric presents a highly dramatic situation, and sufficient of the past to suggest a story. The metre suggests a man who is vexed but still in love with Rose-Ann.

The Homecoming (December 1901)

poppet, darling.

A change of situation and tone. The wife is very young and dependent; the husband is older, and seems to have learned wisdom from the elements. No greater change can be imagined than the girl's, for she has left a town home, where she was her father's darling, to live on the lonely and exposed Toller Down. The humour of the poem suggests that all will be well. The domestic situation is presented in lively dramatic style. None the less, the most important element is the wind, and the repetition at intervals of the couplet with which the scene opens and ends is most effective. This is the best example of rustic humour in Hardy's poetry, and it occurs too rarely.

Toller downland. From Maiden Newton, the Dorchester road to Crewkerne climbs up Whitesheet Hill and 'Crimmercrock's long lane' to the crossroads on Toller Down, where it is joined by Benvill Lane (the upper part of a road from Evershot) which continues on the southern side to Beaminster. Toller Down is about 825 feet high, near the setting for the opening scenes in *Far from the Madding Crowd.* *skimmer-cake.* So called because it is baked on a metal skimming-ladle.

PIECES OCCASIONAL AND VARIOUS

A Church Romance

This suggests that Hardy's mother met his father when she was a servant at Kingston Maurward House (the 'Knapwater House' of

Desperate Remedies). Both his father and grandfather played in the gallery string-choir at Stinsford Church (see *Life*, 9–11 and, with more particular reference to the poem, 13–14). It will be noticed that here, at a much later period in his life, Hardy has changed the date to 'circa 1836'. 'New Sabbath' and 'Mount Ephraim' are tunes for hymns (metrical psalms).

The Rash Bride

linhay, lean-to shed.

For *Under the Greenwood Tree* Hardy preferred the title 'The Mellstock Quire'. 'Quire' (choir) generally implies the instrumentalists, before organs were installed in churches. Whether the story is based on fact or tradition is not known, but 'Swetnam' was the surname of Hardy's maternal grandmother at Melbury Osmond (*Life*, 6–7); Woolcombe is about two miles to the south-east (cf. *Life*, 214–15). Both places are in *The Woodlanders* country, as the first edition shows.

Michael, Michael Mail (*UGT*); cf. the end of 'The Paphian Ball'. *Our old base player*, William Dewy (*UGT*); see 'Friends Beyond' (p. 20). *Ninetieth Psalm*. Its verses were appropriate for the occasion.

The Dead Quire (1897)

Hardy's Christmas stories and poems are often supernatural, e.g. 'A Christmas Ghost-Story' and 'The Paphian Ball' (another legend of the Mellstock Quire). Stanzas xx and xxiii (the latter a very apposite repetition of iii) were added for *Time's Laughingstocks*. The poem turns on the old belief that Christmas Day should be observed as sacred (cf. *UGT*. i.vii, where William Dewy allows no dancing to begin until Christmas Day is 'out'. 'Jigging parties be all very well on the Devil's holidays', said Mrs Penny). The scene of revelry is at Lower Bockhampton. The sound of the traditional hymn-carol seems to move along the path (beyond the bridge over a tributary of the Frome) towards Stinsford Church, where it gradually dies away.

Mead of Memories, the churchyard where the quire leaders and many others who were remembered (including Hardy's father and grandparents) lay buried. *Old Dewy*. Hardy's grandfather; cf. 'Friends Beyond' (p. 20). *For two-score years*. Hardy's grandfather took the choir in hand in 1801 and played in it until his death in 1837; his

father (and uncle) continued playing in it until its dissolution in 1841 or
1842. *his listener.* He is introduced too late to be significant. *Moaning
Hill* is in the field above the church, and named after the sound of the
wind in the trees thereon. (The clump has recently been cut down.)

The Christening (1904)

Intrinsic worth ('this paragon/Of mortals') is set against false, inhuman
assessments of Convention. The poem is artificial; the mother obviously
speaks for Hardy:

> This gem of the race
> The decent fain would smother.

The child is literally a love-child, and love is rated higher than con-
formity. See 'The Conformers' and the views expressed by Sue Bridehead (*JO*.v.i). They were summed up by Thomas Campbell in a poem
which was one of Hardy's favourites in *The Golden Treasury*. He knew
its bitter truth from his own faded romance:

> How delicious is the winning
> Of a kiss at love's beginning,
> When two mutual hearts are sighing
> For the knot there's no untying!
> . . .
> Can you keep the bee from ranging?
> Or the ringdove's neck from changing?
> No! nor fetter'd Love from dying
> In the knot there's no untying.

Criticism of the Church is clearly implied in Hardy's poem. Tess's child
was not a love-child, but the attitude of the Church towards her and
its christening evoked one of his greatest fictional scenes (*TD*.xiv).

A Dream Question

The poem has a link with the previous one. The question is whether the
old orthodox Church views of God are correct, or Hardy's. The
answer is that the Lord is indifferent to both (an indirect way of saying
that the First Cause is more or less as Hardy presented him at various
times).

as Moses wrote. Possibly Deuteronomy, i. 26–7 and 34–5. *he orders pain.*

So it may seem. This is a figurative statement, and only apparently inconsistent with Hardy's views on the Immanent Will, which works unconsciously according to natural laws. *fourth dimension*. At the time it was commonly postulated as the clue to much that was incalculable in the universe; see 'The Absolute Explains', (p. 214).

By the Barrows

The action of a woman in coming to the rescue of a defenceless child is more worthy than the heroism of prehistoric chieftains buried in the 'The He'th' barrows. As they are near 'Mellstock', they must be the three Rainbarrows, the highest of which is familiar to readers of *The Return of the Native*. See 'The Alarm', 'The Sheep-Boy', and *D*I.II.v. *bosoms . . . Multimammia*. Hardy used the image (from Diana Multi-mammia, goddess of the Ephesians) three times; see *MC*.xlv and *TD*.xlii.

A Wife and Another

This short story has something in common with 'The Christening'. It raises a moral question; but the ending, with its reference to God, seems rather weak and complacent compared with Browning's more dramatic way of raising such issues. As in 'Her Death and After', the protagonist in a moral crisis appears to be a person of conventional outlook. In 'A Dream Question' Hardy dismisses the idea that 'the Lord' is stirred to wrath by human actions. The cumulative import of *The Dynasts* and numerous declarations in *Poems of the Past and the Present* is that the failure of the Immanent Will to improve the lot of the living on earth signifies unawareness of it: 'Not to Mend' means 'Not to Know'.

The Roman Road

Associations which have a basis in reality and are linked to the affections are more memorable and significant than those which, however great historically, do not evoke living experience. Hardy had something similar in mind when he wrote on the methods of the painters Boldini and Hobbema, 'of infusing emotion into the baldest external objects either by the presence of a human figure among them, or by mark of some human connection with them' (*Life*, 120). The theme of the poem is not quite parallel to that of 'By the Barrows', but similar. The Roman road (now overgrown) passes south of Higher Bockhampton across 'The He'th'; another 'Egdon Heath' road is described like a 'parting-line in hair' in *RN*.i.ii.

The Vampirine Fair

Entitled 'The Fair Vampire' in the MS. The style echoes Wordsworth rather than the old ballads. Wingreen Hill is east-south-east of Shaftesbury. The Coomb (valley) runs down below Rushmore (site of the Manor Court) near Tollard Royal. For Hardy's visit in 1895, see *Life*, 269. There is no evidence to suggest that the story is historical.

The Reminder

An untimely Darwinian reminder during the festive Christmas season. For Hardy's bird and frost associations, see p. 51.

The Rambler

By juxtaposition this provides a comment on 'The Reminder'. In addition to religious writers, Hardy has Wordsworth's poetry in mind, especially the phrase 'Nature's holy plan' in 'Lines Written in Early Spring', where enjoyment is associated with flowers, birds, and trees. For a further comment on this, see *TD*.iii.

constellated daisies. Prompted by Wordsworth's 'To the Daisy' ('With little here to do or see') or Shelley's 'The Question':

> Daisies, those pearled Arcturi of the earth,
> The constellated flower that never sets.

Receives their. The sense is 'All receive their'. *keen appraisement.* The cutting irony here can be felt. *far back ones.* Hardy disagrees with the Providential view of Nature, but what he opposes to it is not explicit. If 'far back' is chronological, it seems to imply personal associations which emerge and grow with memory, but which were not appreciated until it was too late. The juxtaposition of the next two poems supports this view. For an illustration of it, see 'The Self-Unconscious'.

Night in the Old Home

my perished people. Hardy's grandparents and parents at Higher Bockhampton. *pale . . . thoughts.* Cf. *Hamlet*, III. i. 85, 'sicklied o'er with the pale cast of thought'. *Life in the sere*. After the death of his parents, Hardy had reached his middle-sixties; cf. *Macbeth*, v. iii. 22-3, 'My way of life/Is fall'n into the sear, the yellow leaf.'

After the Last Breath (1904)

list, listen. *outshapes*, appears.

Hardy's mother Jemima died on Easter Sunday, 1904 (see *Life*, 321). A photograph suggests that she looked younger and more serene after death.

Wrongers. Not so much 'Crass Casualty' as the infirmities and suffering of old age. *momentary*, i.e. in the course of time.

In Childbed

weetless, ignorant, unaware (of its future). *Such strange things did mother say to me*. Despite the context, the last line may be literally true. The poem reflects Hardy's philosophy; cf. *TD*.xix.

The Pine Planters

For the scene, see *W*.viii. The 'one fairer' is Grace Melbury. The significance of the second part is conveyed briefly but at least as adequately in the novel, where Marty South concludes, 'It seems to me as if they sigh because they are very sorry to begin life in earnest – just as we be.' This was true of Hardy (*Life*, 15-16). In the poem, he implies that it is better not to be born. See 'At Day-Close in November' (p. 101).[10]

The Dear (1901)

Though 'Fairmile' (in the sense of a 'good mile') was the local name for a long hill on the old Sherborne road from Dorchester (Lea, 312), the absence of quotation marks suggests that the name was well known. It is probably the hill on the road to Exeter from Honiton, a route with which Hardy was familiar. He told Sir Henry Newbolt that the poem was based on a real incident (Bailey, 245).

One We Knew (20 May 1902)

The subject of the poem is Hardy's paternal grandmother, Mary (Head) Hardy of 'The Alarm'. At the age of thirteen, she left Fawley, Berkshire (the 'Marygreen' of *Jude*). She lived in Hardy's birthplace from the time of her marriage in 1801, was widowed in 1837, and remained in her old home until her death in January 1857. The poem shows what interests she aroused in Hardy in his early years. She is probably the original of Mrs Martin (*TT*.ii). See *Life*, 215, 420.

dip, candle made by dipping a wick into melted tallow. *poussetting*, dancing round and round with hands joined. *spot . . . maypole . . . bandsmen*. This seems to be local; cf. *RN*.VI.i, where the scene is near the heath that neighbours the Hardy cottage. *King of France . . . Terror . . . Bonaparte*. Hardy's interest in the French Revolution and the Napoleonic Wars was extended in his boyhood when he discovered illustrated numbers of a periodical which his grandfather had bought. They comprised C. H. Gifford's *History of the Wars of the French Revolution* (1817), and their 'torn pages' with their 'melodramatic prints' were 'the first to set him on the train of ideas that led to *The Trumpet-Major* and *The Dynasts*' (*Life*, 16–17).[11] *warlike preparations*. Cf. 'The Alarm'. *the gibbet*. Possibly near Fawley, on the road to Wantage (cf. *JO*.I.xi). The sequence of events suggests, however, that 'the neighbouring town' is Dorchester; see 'My Cecily' (pp. 16–17).

She Hears the Storm

Thorncombe Wood is south of the Hardy cottage. The poet may have been thinking of his mother's loneliness after his father's death in 1892. The position of the poem suggests the possibility that he had his grandmother in mind, after the death of her husband in 1837.

A Wet Night

Hardy's route on his way home from Dorchester to Higher Bockhampton is carefully traced: along the London road across 'Durnover Moor' to Stinsford Hill, across the 'ewe-leaze' (as shown in the illustration to 'Her Immortality') into Cuckoo Lane. . . . The sonnet form and the subject suggest a relatively early poem, which was probably revised.

Before Life and After

The thought is regressive and related to the Unfulfilled Intention theory (*Life*, 149). Hardy's 'seemings' are inconsistent, as he was quick to point out when his 'philosophy' was attacked; they express moods. His faith depends on the growth of human sympathies, yet he can deplore the development of consciousness and wish for a return to 'nescience'; cf. 'The Mother Mourns' and *D*1.v.iv:

> The cognizance ye mourn, Life's doom to feel,
> . . . came unmeant . . .
> By listless sequence – luckless, tragic Chance.

A time there was. This alludes to the opening of Wordsworth's 'Intimations of Immortality'. The implication is that 'nescience' would create heaven. Hardy does not stop to consider whether creatures in this state would know they were alive or even be aware of physical enjoyment. *disease of feeling.* Compare Clym Yeobright: 'He already showed that thought is a disease of the flesh, and indirectly bore evidence that ideal physical beauty is incompatible with emotional development and a full recognition of the coil of things' (*RN*.II.vi).

New Year's Eve (1906)

unweeting, nescient. *in this tabernacle groan.* See 'The Subalterns' (p. 42). *use ethic tests I never knew.* Cf. *TD*.xiii (end).

God's Education

The subject of the last two poems is continued with reference to the ageing process; cf. the 'Wrongers' in 'After the Last Breath'.

To Sincerity (February 1899)

Compare Hardy's note of 7 October 1888: 'The besetting sin of modern literature is its insincerity. Half its utterances are qualified, even contradicted, by an aside, and this particularly in morals and religion' (*Life*, 215); also 'A Dream Question' (stanza ii) and 'By truth made free' in 'He Resolves to Say No More'.

would men look . . . disesteeming. Parallel to 'if way to the Better there be, it exacts a full look at the Worst' ('In Tenebris, II'). The meaning is, 'If men would face facts, life might be better than appears possible'; *count*, expect.

Panthera

fell, severe. *naysaying*, refusing.

The main story, as Panthera told it, is in blank verse. It is repeated by the speaker, whose framework of dramatic monologue is distinguished by its couplet rhymes. The story relating to Jesus, the nub of the poem, is therefore set at three removes from the reader. It is easy to see why Hardy placed 'To Sincerity' before this supremely crucial example of 'The Higher Criticism'. Among the sources he lists is Strauss, a reference to the translation of David Strauss's *Das Leben Jesu* by Mary Ann Evans (later 'George Eliot').

at a change in the air. Compare Corporal Tullidge in 'Valenciennes'. *Cappadocian*, from Cappadocia, part of Asia Minor. *Calabria*, that part of southern Italy from which the legion came. *Tabor*, a mountain south-west of the Sea of Galilee. *Pyrrhic*, a kind of armed dance which originated in Greece. *he would raze it*. A reference to John, ii. 18–21. *Fors Fortuna . . . hostages to hazardry*. Lucky Chance! 'He that hath wife and children hath given hostages to Fortune' (Bacon, 'Of Parents and Children'). *Mauretania and Numidia*, northern Morocco and Algeria. *Parthia*, north Iran. *Son of Saturn*, Jove (Jupiter). *the Three*, the Parcae or Fates of Greek mythology who presided over the birth and destiny of mankind.

The Unborn

The Will is 'all-immanent'; it resides in all created things. The poem does not say 'Better not to be born' so much as pity the illusions of the born. It was written at least as early as 1903; 1905 is probably the date of revision, when a final stanza was substituted. The earlier title ('Life's Opportunity') and conclusion strike a more positive note:

> A voice like Ocean's caught from afar
> Rolled forth on them and me:-
> 'For Lovingkindness Life supplies
> A scope superber than the skies.
> So ask no more. Life's gladdening star
> In Lovingkindness see.'

This thought kindled Hardy's hopes at the end of *The Dynasts*.

The Man He Killed

nipperkin, tot. *traps*, belongings.

First published in November 1902 with a note on the scene and characters: 'The settle of the Fox Inn, Stagfoot Lane. The speaker (a returned soldier) and his friends, natives of the hamlet.' (This is Hartfoot Lane, in the chalk hill country six miles north of Puddletown.) In a very simple and telling form, Hardy sums up his views of war, and the Boer War in particular.

Geographical Knowledge

Austral, in the southern hemisphere.

In memory of Mrs Christiana Coward, postmistress at Lower Bockhampton (Purdy, 147), the poem provides an unusual illustration of the way in which affection creates and sustains interest. She remembered the directions of places in many parts of the world which her son had seen and told her about, but she knew little of the tracks across the Frome meadows immediately below Lower Bockhampton or through Yellowham Wood near Higher Bockhampton; nor did she know the direction of towns 'ten miles off or so'.

One Ralph Blossom Soliloquizes

The rhymes which conclude each verse suggest a light-hearted rogue. 'What's done is done' recalls Mrs Durbeyfield when she hears of Tess's downfall, and of the breakdown of her marriage (*TD*.xii, xxxviii).

The Noble Lady's Tale

fay, faith. *quire*, chancel.

Hardy's interest in Lady Susan (1743–1827) began at home when his father recalled seeing her as an old widow walking in the garden at Stinsford House in a red cloak. He read about her in the *Letters* of Horace Walpole and *The Journal of Mary Frampton* (1885). She was the daughter of the first Earl of Ilchester, and eloped in 1764 with 'the handsome Irish comedian' William O'Brien, whom she met at Holland House in London. Hardy's grandfather had constructed a vault for both of them in Stinsford Church. See *Life*, 9, 163–4, 250. The story is imaginary.

grey hall, Stinsford House (by the church). *the sock*, comedy, from *soccus* (Latin), the low shoe worn by actors in Roman comedy.

Unrealized

poll, hair.

Wagtail and Baby

An unusual way of commenting on the artificialities of society. Cf. 'I Am the One' and *RN*.iv. ii, where Clym Yeobright, having turned his back on the pomps and vanities of Paris, is not shunned by the creatures of Egdon Heath. This scene, like the poem, embodies a Rousseauistic criticism of modern civilization.

Aberdeen

Hardy explained (Collins, 23) that the 'Queen' is Knowledge. The poem gives his impressions when he received an honorary degree in April 1905 (*Life*, 323).

George Meredith (May 1909)

Poet and novelist, he was the reader for Chapman and Hall who advised Hardy in 1869 to write a novel with a more complicated plot than that of his first (unpublished) story, *The Poor Man and the Lady*; the result was *Desperate Remedies* (*Life*, 60–62). Hardy visited him at his home near Box Hill in 1894. He saw the announcement of Meredith's death when he was on his way to the Academy, and went on to the Athenaeum (one of his two London clubs), where he wrote this poem, which was published a day or two later in *The Times* (*ORFW*. 138–9). Hardy attended the memorial service in Westminster Abbey (*Life*, 345–6).

He spoke ... Compare Lord Morley's description, 'His voice was strong, full, resonant, harmonious, his laugh quick and loud' (Siegfried Sassoon, *Meredith*, London, 1948, p. 91). *his green hill*, Box Hill near Dorking, Surrey. *vaporous vitiate*, obscure and tainted, making it difficult for truth to prevail (cf. ll.7–9).

Yell'ham-Wood's Story (1902)

The message sums up the theme of *The Woodlanders*, where the Un-fulfilled Intention is seen in the woods and serves as counterpoint to the story.

Coomb-Firtrees. By Beacon Corner north of Puddletown Heath, half a mile east of Yellowham Wood. *Clyffe-Hill Clump*, firs crowning a hill further east above Clyffe House near Tincleton; see 'The Paphian Ball'.

A Young Man's Epigram on Existence (1866)

In reply to Alfred Noyes's criticism, Hardy stated that he printed these lines 'merely as an amusing instance of early cynicism' (*Life*, 409). Their position at the end of his third published volume of poetry suggests he was not telling the whole truth. 'By experience we find out a short way by a long wandering', wrote Roger Ascham (*TD*.xv). It is a lesson Henchard learns, and which Hardy affirms in his reference to the irony of chance, 'the ingenious machinery contrived by the Gods for reducing human possibilities of amelioration to a minimum – which arranges that the wisdom to do shall come *pari passu* with the departure of zest for doing' (*MC*.xliv).

4

Satires of Circumstance

THE poems for this volume were collected and arranged in July 1914, just before the outbreak of the First World War. It was published the following November. One war poem, 'Men Who March Away', was included as a last-minute 'postscript' to the 106 poems which form the present collection; later it was transferred to 'Poems of War and Patriotism' in *Moments of Vision*. The group of fifteen minor poems which provided the title* appeared in the 'Lyrics and Reveries' section. Hardy knew that the issues they raised were light and trivial compared with the reality around him when they were published, but he seems to have realized too late how incongruous and superficial they would appear in the same volume as 'Poems of 1912–13'. The unforeseen death of his first wife in November 1912 had removed the hardened resentments which had divided them for years. He could overlook what he had endured, and recognize with regret the neglect and lack of tenderness from which Emma had suffered. He was moved by the record of her early life which ended with their Cornish romance,† and the pilgrimage which he made in expiation to Cornwall recalled the radiance of the past vividly and at times intolerably. His emotions and imagination were stirred as never before, and the result was 'Poems of 1912–13' (and many more subsequently), the 'only amends' he could make.‡ They comprise the most genuine love-elegy in the English language. In them and the story behind them lies a satire of circumstance more profound and far-reaching than in all the poems with which they are published. Not surprisingly, Hardy's second wife wondered whether readers of *Satires of Circumstance* would conclude that he had found his greatest happiness with his first, and now longed for refuge with her in the grave.§

* The choice was the publishers', not Hardy's (Purdy, 172).
† *Some Recollections* (see p. xiv). ‡ *ORFW*. 163.
§ Letter of 8 December 1917 in Viola Meynell (ed.), *Friends of a Lifetime* (letters to Sydney Cockerell), London, 1940.

LYRICS AND REVERIES

In Front of the Landscape

nimb, bright haze. *bypast*, in the past.

Like 'Wessex Heights' in subject, it has a rhythm more in harmony
with the poet's troubled spirit. It is a phantasmagorial poem; the inner
world of memories creates a screen between the poet and the landscape,
in which may be seen features towards Higher Bockhampton and
down in the meadows, from the vicinity of Stinsford churchyard where
Emma Hardy was buried. Within the generalizations of stanzas iv–viii,
she is the central figure. Only the short alternate lines rhyme, and the
rhymes alternate, each occurring three times once the poem is under-
way.

a headland, Beeny Cliff, Cornwall, at the time of Hardy's first visit to
St Juliot. See *Life*, 75, 'Ditty', 'Beeny Cliff'. *Clay cadavers*, his parents
and his wife. *one of the broad brow*, Emma; cf. 'A Dream or No' (line
8). *the clump*, probably the trees on Moaning Hill; see 'The Dead
Quire'. *Much had I slighted . . . body-borne eyes*. A continual cause for
self-criticism; cf. 'The Self-Unseeing', 'The Rambler'.

Channel Firing (April 1914)

When *Satires of Circumstance* appeared in November 1914, the First
World War had been raging three months. The poem is not without
humour, but it shows Hardy's fears –

> All nations striving strong to make
> Red war yet redder.

With the possibility of another war with Germany in mind, he described
the 'unreason' of nations as a 'demonic force' in 'We are Getting to the
End'. It had been the subject of *The Dynasts*. 'He said that he would
probably not have ended [it] as he did end it if he could have foreseen
what was going to happen within a few years' (*Life*, 368).

blow the trumpet. At the Day of Judgement (I Corinthians, xv. 52).
Parson Thirdly. Of 'Weatherbury' (*FMC*.xlii), so named probably
from his habit of dividing his sermon into three parts, with great

emphasis on 'Thirdly' when he reached his climax; possibly from the stress he placed on the 'Thirdly' section of the introduction to the marriage service.[12] *Stourton Tower*, King Alfred's Tower on Kingsettle Hill near Stourton, Wiltshire, which marks the site where a Saxon king erected his standard against the Danes. *Camelot*, the hill-fort known as Cadbury Castle, south of Castle Cary, Somerset, and traditionally associated with the legendary King Arthur. The question of the whereabouts of Camelot prompted Hardy's footnote remark in *D*3.VI.ii (à propos of the site of the room in Brussels where the famous ball took place on the eve of the battle of Waterloo) that 'the spot is almost as phantasmal in its elusive mystery as towered Camelot, the palace of Priam, or the hill of Calvary'.

The Convergence of the Twain

Written for the souvenir programme of the Dramatic and Operatic Matinée in aid of the bereaved at Covent Garden on 14 May 1912. The liner *Titanic* was sunk on her maiden voyage, after colliding at full speed with an iceberg on 15 April. The contrast between the pride and vaingloriousness of this ship and its fate at the bottom of the ocean, and the change of rhythm to communicate a sense of sudden impact at the end, are finely conceived and executed. The major theme is 'luckless, tragic Chance', 'listless' coincidence (see the note to 'Before Life and After', p. 85). The mating concept ('being anon twin halves of one August event'; cf. 'News for Her Mother') is reminiscent of the humour of the Spirit Sinister in *The Dynasts*.

The Ghost of the Past

Hardy is thinking predominantly of Emma, with happy memories before he became 'a time-torn man' (ll.21–4). The original 'westward' for 'wayward' is significant. The poem was probably written before her death. Otherwise, the main idea is fanciful, 'Poems of 1912–13' showing that the early years of their romance were never more vividly alive than during the period immediately preceding the preparation of this volume. The stanza opening is like that of 'A Trampwoman's Tragedy', and both poems employ effective repetition throughout.

After the Visit

drouthy, suffering drought.

See 'On the Departure Platform' (p. 70). Both poems suggest that Florence Dugdale's visits to Max Gate, like an appointment with Mrs Henniker, had soothed 'a time-torn man', and that he had often wished she could be his wife. When the poem was published (1910) there was, of course, no ascription.

the ancient floors. Introduced to conceal the truth from Emma Hardy. Max Gate was built in 1884–5.

To Meet, or Otherwise

Addressed to Miss Dugdale, and first printed in December 1913.[13]

How vast the difference . . . Nay. Cf. Browning, 'By the Fire-side'. *Cimmerian*, gloomy (classical); cf. 'Groan in their bondage', 'sick Life'. *undo the done.* Reminiscent of Browning's 'The petty Done, the Undone vast' ('The Last Ride Together').

The Difference

Another example of Ruskin's 'pathetic fallacy' or false impressions of the outward scene which are created by strong feelings; cf. 'The Seasons of Her Year' and other poems.

The Sun on the Bookcase

'Beyond the hills' and 1870 (the MS gives 1872) point to Emma Gifford. The apple-tree shadows suggest Higher Bockhampton for the scene.

'When I Set Out for Lyonnesse'

This well-known lyric recalls Hardy's fateful journey from Higher Bockhampton to St Juliot, Cornwall, where he fell in love with Emma Gifford. He rose at four, 'starting by starlight from his country retreat' (*Life*, 65) on Monday, 7 March 1870, reaching Launceston by rail at four in the afternoon. The remainder of the journey by road is recalled

in *PBE*.ii and 'A Man was Drawing Near to Me'. Lyonnesse, the
romance name for the Cornwall of Arthurian legend (Malory) was
familiar to Hardy through Tennyson ('Morte d'Arthur' and *Idylls of
the King*) and Swinburne's poetic drama *Tristram of Lyonesse*. The form
of the poem is simple: the departure, the stay, the return. Each verse
has the main feature of the rondeau or rondel, the last two lines
repeating the first two.

A Thunderstorm in Town

Florence Hardy must have been told that this poem related to Mrs
Henniker, the 'one rare fair woman' of 'Wessex Heights' (cf. Purdy,
161). One suspects a difference between the actuality and the poetic
re-creation. Between the impulse and the reality fell convention.

The Torn Letter

Hardy thought man enjoyed only a modicum of free will; when swayed
by a force beyond him, passion or (as here) impulse, he was subject to
the Immanent Will (Apology to *Late Lyrics and Earlier*). The story
does not carry conviction.

Beyond the Last Lamp (MS, September 1911)

A real scene is recalled from the period 1878–81, when the Hardys lived
at Upper Tooting. Such was the tragic expression on the faces of the
'linked loiterers', and so great the mystery of their pacing for hours one
dark wet evening, that Hardy never forgot them. He seems to have
adapted the scene to express the misery of Tess and Angel Clare when
their marriage founders (*TD*.xxxv): they are seen 'walking very slowly,
without converse, one behind the other, as in a funeral procession',
with 'anxious and sad' faces. The same person sees them later 'in the
same field, progressing just as slowly, and as regardless of the hour and
of the cheerless night as before'. The recurrence of 'slowly . . . sadly'
throughout the fourth lines contributes largely to the effect of the
poem, and the change of title from 'Night in a Suburb' enhances one's
impression of the scene.

The Face at the Casement

embowment, embrace. *garth*, churchyard.

Facts put forward in support of the view that Emma Gifford had a suitor at St Clether, a village about seven miles from St Juliot, are unconvincing. He married in 1864, and Emma did not live at St Juliot or near it until 1868.[14] Hardy's rather implausible story could be founded on the jealousy he experienced in August 1870 (see 'The Young Churchwarden'). Jealousy plays an important part in *A Pair of Blue Eyes*.

long-suffering, kind. I Corinthians, xiii. 4. *jealousy . . . grave.* Song of Solomon, viii. 6, 'jealousy is cruel as the grave' (epigraph to *PBE*. xxxviii).

Lost Love

Hardy can now imagine Emma's thoughts as she played 'some of her favourite tunes', and he proceeded upstairs to his study; cf. 'The Last Performance'.

'My Spirit Will Not Haunt the Mound'

Hardy wrote the poem shortly after his wife's burial at Stinsford. Speaking through her, he recalls their love in Cornwall before marriage. He was 'another' person then.

will not haunt. The 'will' is insistent, not just a reference to time. *my curious air.* As a phantom. The last lines stress the subjectivity of her existence. They suggest that Hardy was contemplating the visit to Cornwall which he made the following March.

Wessex Heights (MS, December 1896)

The poem expresses Hardy's depression, particularly when his division at home was aggravated by brooding over strong disapproval of *Jude the Obscure* from reviewers, friends,[15] his wife, and perhaps his mother. ' "Wessex Heights" will always wring my heart', wrote Florence Hardy, adding that it was written shortly after the publication of *Jude*, 'when he was so cruelly treated'. In another letter of 1914 she stated that 'the four people mentioned in the poem are actual women. One was dead and three living when it was written – now only one is living.' It is not clear whether more than four people are alluded to in the poem; if so, some may be fictional.

The four heights form the corners of a large area of 'Wessex': Wylls-Neck in the Quantocks, Somerset; Ingpen (Inkpen), the highest chalk hill in England, south of Hungerford and the 'Marygreen' country of *Jude* in Berkshire; nearer home, Bulbarrow overlooking Blackmoor Vale, and Pilsdon Pen near the Devon boundary of Dorset.

Each stanza marks a distinct progression in the theme, the last returning to the first.

was before my birth, and after death may be. These are strange words from the rationalist of the 'Immortality' poems and the Impercipient who could believe in neither spiritual pre-existence nor in life-after-death. The opening words of the line show that Hardy's thought is no more than one of his 'seemings'. On these heights, away from worldly cares and places with unpleasant associations, he experiences a sense of harmony and release from time. It is as if he had found his spiritual home. 'The Schreckhorn' and two later poems suggest, however, that there were times when Hardy's less rational self accepted the possibility of spiritual life after death; see, for example, 'He Prefers Her Earthly'. *Her who suffereth long . . . kind,* Charity; see 'The Face at the Casement'. *mind-chains,* thoughts from which he cannot free his mind, e.g. of 'Men with a wintry sneer, and women with tart disparagings'. *weird,* uncanny (almost supernatural). *crass cause.* Cf. 'Crass Casualty' ('Hap'). Hardy sees his youthful self watching him, wondering how he could have become what he is, at odds with the world, 'A thinker of crooked thoughts upon Life in the sere' ('Night in the Old Home'). *my chrysalis.* This metaphor implies that a startling change has taken place in the man emerging from youth; he is a 'strange continuator' of his former, simple self. *the great grey Plain.* Hardy did not change his Wessex topography, and there can be no doubt that this is Salisbury Plain; see *LLI.* 'On the Western Circuit' (i) and *TD.*lviii, where it is viewed from Stonehenge. In this verse Hardy could be thinking of both *Tess* and *Jude,* the two novels which did more to cast a blight on his popularity in high places than anything else. He often visited Stonehenge, and had no doubt that it was best seen by moonlight (Orel, 196, 200). Yet, if the figure he saw against the moon was Tess before her arrest (*TD.*lviii), it is strange that he writes 'Nobody sees it but I'. On the other hand he takes the same unduly despondent view with reference to the forms fixed in 'long vision' (retentive memory; cf. *Life*, 378) in 'the tall-spired town' (Salisbury, the 'Melchester' of *Jude*); they are 'now passed' (no longer in existence) for everybody else. He did not wish in any way to be reminded of the public disapprobation which he associated with these two novels.

The alternative is to assume that both places recalled encounters or incidents which he preferred to forget. For example, he visited Berkshire with his wife in April 1895, and they may have stopped for a view of Stonehenge en route. *a ghost*. As the 'one rare fair woman' of the next stanza is Mrs Henniker, who died in 1923, the three 'ghosts' are particular memories of the three 'actual' women who died before 1914. These seem to be Emma Hardy (d.1912), Hardy's mother (d.1904), and his cousin Tryphena (d.1890). The associations with Yellowham Bottom (the level stretch of London road opposite Higher Bockhampton and below Yellowham Hill) and the Frome meadows remain very conjectural. The first makes one wonder whether Hardy remembered sharp words from Tryphena as he accompanied her home to Puddletown (for her link with *Jude*, see 'Thoughts of Phena', p. 21). The 'thin-lipp'd' ghost in 'a shroud of white' (cf. 'a white sea' of summer fog, *TD*.xx and 'The Head above the Fog') may be a memory of Hardy's mother crossing the Frome meadows from the 'Church-way' at Stinsford to visit Max Gate before the ties between her and Emma Hardy were severed. The ghost in the railway carriage who says things Hardy does not wish to hear is a recollection of his wife. She had a habit of leaving home suddenly. The occasion may have been her departure for London, to see Dr Richard Garnett of the British Museum in the hope that he would persuade Hardy not to proceed with *Jude*.[16] *now I can let her go*. A transient thought from Hardy in a black mood. He and Mrs Henniker maintained their friendship until her death. With reference to the whole of this stanza, Florence Hardy wrote, 'There was never any idea of his letting her go – for he, too, is true and faithful to his friends, but the *poet* wrote that.'

In Death Divided (189–)

The poem was almost certainly written with Mrs Henniker and her aristocratic connections in mind, when Hardy's 'love for her' was 'in its fulness' in the latter half of 1893. Her brother was Lord Houghton, later Lord Crewe.

The Place on the Map

This was first printed as 'A Poor Schoolmaster's Story'. Attempts have been made to prove it autobiographical, but they all seem to founder. For example, Portland cannot be described as 'a jutting height' since the Bill and its approaches are rather unimpressively low. Beeny Cliff in Cornwall is more probable (cf. 'In Front of the Landscape', line 37), but it is difficult to interpret the poem with reference to Emma Gifford and Hardy. The 'wormwood of the whole' has a very different significance from the filling of 'the wormwood cup' in 'Where Three Roads Joined'. The last line of the fifth stanza ran 'Under superstition's hideous control' when first printed, and this verse is reminiscent of Hardy's comments on Tess's shame when she is pregnant (TD.xiii).

In a broadcast talk on 3 January 1973, Dr Robert Gittings showed that the only fine hot Indian summer from 1865 to 1875 was in the year 1865. He has recently suggested that the poem may relate to Horace Moule, who was a schoolmaster at Marlborough from 1865 to 1868, and the father of an illegitimate child by a girl in his father's parish. If this link is valid, the season, place, and viewpoint of the poem may all be part of a fictional disguise. The poem seems to reflect the more romantic, anti-conventional Hardy (cf. 'A Christening', p. 80), producing a story calculated to contribute to the promotion of a more rational attitude towards 'the position of man and woman in nature, and the position of belief in the minds of man and woman – things which everybody is thinking but nobody is saying' ('Candour in English Fiction', Orel, 133). See 'A Confession to a Friend in Trouble' (1866).

The Schreckhorn

For the occasion when the thought of the poem first occurred to him (in Switzerland), see Life, 293. Leslie Stephen was a mountaineer and literary critic. As the editor of The Cornhill Magazine he accepted Far from the Madding Crowd and The Hand of Ethelberta for serialization. Hardy was chosen to witness his renunciation of Holy Orders in 1875. He said that Stephen's 'philosophy was to influence his own for many years, indeed, more than that of any other contemporary' (Life, 100, 105–6).

A Singer Asleep (March 1910)

ness, promontory. *fulth*, fulness. *orts*, fragments. *chines*, clefts, ravines.

The poem was begun at Bonchurch in the Isle of Wight, where the poet Swinburne was buried. Hardy was unable to attend his funeral. He had read *Poems and Ballads* with enthusiasm in 1866, and remained a devoted admirer of Swinburne's poetry, which shocked Victorians by its fierce revolt against prudishness and Christian theology. See *Life*, 270, 344–5, 349.

she the Lesbian, Sappho, who was born on the island of Lesbos *c.* 650 B.C. Of her lyrical poetry, only two odes and fragments remain. Classical tradition holds that, spurned in love by Phaon, she threw herself into the sea from a promontory on the island of Leucas.

A Plaint to Man (1909–10)

phasm, lifeless (phantom) image. *blown*, blooming.

Hardy had studied the Positivist writings of Auguste Comte (1798–1857) at various times in his formative years as a thinker. Comte held that since nothing about God is knowable, man's religion and aims should be centred in the evolution and progress of the human race. For him the golden rule was Altruism (a word he coined, and which became a keystone in Hardy's philosophy; it appears also as 'Charity' or 'loving-kindness' – a love of one's own kind). The MS title is 'The Plight of a Puppet', the implication being that God, the creation and projection of man (ll. 4–12) is what man makes of him. In this fantasy, therefore, a non-existent God pronounces Hardy's message, perhaps the most important he ever uttered. Progress will come when men realize that they must depend on their own resources, and not on any help which is 'visioned' or imagined to come from Providence. It will depend on the elimination of self-seeking and the promotion of unrestricted altruism and brotherhood.

Beneath the deicide eyes of seers, in the eyes of those who see the truth and reject the idea of God.

God's Funeral (1908–10)

foreborne, carried in front.

The poem is remarkable for the fairness of its presentation; some of its lines show deep feeling for a vanished faith. The third verse gives three different impressions of God: the first anthropomorphic, the second vaguely glorious, the third as the Supreme of angels.

man-projected Figure. As in the previous poem. *jealous*, quick to punish; 'for I the Lord thy God am a jealous God' (Exodus, xx. 5). The next lines give the evolution of the concept of God through the Old Testament to the New. *Darkling*. An allusion to Arnold's 'Dover Beach'; see the passage quoted on p. 53. *those who wept in Babylon*, the children of Israel in exile (cf. Psalm cxxxvii). *Whither will wanderers turn . . . ?* In 'Stanzas from the Grande Chartreuse' Arnold describes the seekers after a new faith as

> Wandering between two worlds, one dead,
> The other powerless to be born.

positive gleam. The Positivist creed, first expounded by Comte; its goal is the continuing welfare and progress of mankind, through altruism and education ('loving-kindness' and 'scientific knowledge' in the Apology to *Late Lyrics and Earlier*). For Hardy's comment on this 'new religion' and the reason for the head-shaking of the mourners in the poem, see *Life*, 146.

Spectres that Grieve

This fantasy shows the spirits of those adversely misrepresented by historians returning to earth to claim justice on the eve of the New Year.

'Ah, Are You Digging on My Grave?'

Though the poem owes something to A. E. Housman's 'Is my team ploughing?' (Hardy's favourite poem in *A Shropshire Lad*), its structure is different. Housman's consists largely of varied questions to which the answers are apparently reassuring; Hardy's unfolds irony upon irony, as if the truth were at the centre of a Chinese box of related questions, variations of one, in fact. Hardy's is a blending of the satirical and whimsical; the ending of Housman's comes with tragic finality.

Self-Unconscious

sherd, shard, fragment of broken earthenware.

Hardy recalls a visit to St Juliot when he was too self-engrossed, too full of plans for the future, to see the reality around him. Years later, when 'all that mattered has passed away' (including his wife), he is able to see what he really was, what ought to have been revealed to him then, and how differently he ought to have acted. It is a 'mere derision', a satire of circumstance that 'God, the Elf' (the 'whimsical god . . . known as blind Circumstance' in *WT*. 'Fellow Townsmen, viii) had given him this knowledge too late. The ending seems portentously vague. Does it refer to neglected Love, or to the undying sorrow which resulted from that neglect?

The Discovery

Hardy recalls his first visit to Cornwall. The fires were actual (*PBE*.ii). 'Funeral pyres' has an ominous suggestion.

crude, rough, harsh, inclement – a contrast to 'Love-nest'. *her my heart*, her whom my heart. . . .

Tolerance

Another recollection of Emma Hardy. He is glad that he refrained from asserting himself when crossed, even though he was disdained for his tolerance.

Before and After Summer (1910)

A parallel seems to be implied with fair prospects in life and their stealing away unobserved.

At Day-Close in November

The metre suggests a lighter mood than that of the previous poem.

June time, the prime of life. Hardy was just forty-five when he moved to Max Gate. 'Some two or three thousand small trees, mostly Austrian pines, were planted around the house by Hardy himself' (*Life*, 173). Hence the thoughts of Marty South (*W.* viii; see 'The Pine Planters').

The Year's Awakening (February 1910)

The theme is 'They know Earth-secrets that know not I' ('An August Midnight'). The double repetition of the question at the end of each verse expresses its persistence and Hardy's appeal for an answer.

belting. An exact metaphor. Hardy had long been interested in astronomy. *zodiac . . . Ram.* Reminiscent of the description of spring at the opening of Chaucer's 'Prologue' to *The Canterbury Tales.* During the year the sun appears to move through the twelve equal divisions or Signs of the Zodiac, which are named after their most prominent constellations. It passes from the Fishes (*Pisces*) into the Ram (*Aries*) about the middle of March. *vespering,* singing its evensong. *merest rote,* working according to natural laws.

Under the Waterfall

Rather in the style of Browning (with one ridiculous rhyme), the poem presents Emma Hardy's recollection of an incident which took place when she and Hardy were picnicking in the Valency valley. His sketch of Emma Gifford trying to retrieve the glass is dated 19 August 1870. See *SR.* 57 or *Life,* 71, and *PBE.* xxviii.

Whenever . . . I never miss . . . fugitive day. Similar associations are found in Marcel Proust; cf. the translation *Remembrance of Things Past,* vol. xii by Stephen Hudson, London, 1944, pp. 219–21. *chalice.* The word has a sacramental connotation (cf. 'lovers' wine').

POEMS OF 1912–13

Veteris vestigia flammae (epigraph to this section), the traces of old love (Virgil, *Aeneid,* iv. 23). The implication is that Hardy's love was renewed by regrets – not to mention Emma Hardy's written reminiscences (*SR*) and his return to Cornwall in March 1913. Like George Eliot's Amos Barton, 'now he re-lived all their life together, with that terrible keenness of memory and imagination which bereavement gives'. There could be no pardon, he felt, for his inadequacy and the selfishness of his indifference in their later years. Regret and romantic memories mingled to create the inspiration for 'many poems' at the end of 1912 and in the early part of 1913. 'To adopt Walpole's words concerning Gray, Hardy was "in flower" in these days, and, like Gray's, his flower was sad-coloured' (*Life*, 361).

The series is not quite an elegiac whole. Whether one looks at it from the time or place point of view, it remains rather miscellaneous at certain points, as one would expect in the circumstances. Many more related poems were to follow. The last three, 'The Spell of the Rose', 'St Launce's Revisited', and 'Where the Picnic Was', were transferred to the group in 1915.

The Going (December 1912)

The opening poem in the series touches all its aspects, bright and dark, past and present. Emma Hardy died on 27 November. For some time she had lived in a pair of comfortable attics on one side of Max Gate, and Hardy did not know how ill she was at the end (see *Life*, 359–60 and *ORFW*. 154–5). The poem is developed on an alternating verse-structure, and its lyricism is remarkably close to speech.

Your Last Drive (December 1912)

Mrs Hardy had been on a visit beyond Puddletown to her friend Mrs Wood Homer (cf. *Life*, 359 and *ORFW*. 154). On the way she passed near Stinsford Church and her burial-place. Hardy does not spare himself, recalling particularly his censure of his wife. The last four words reflect different aspects of their relationship, but the final note is 'blame'.

The Walk

The 'difference' is created by the sense of emptiness when Hardy returns to Max Gate.

hill-top tree. Not Culliford Tree (see p. 259). Probably on Conygar Hill, to which 'the gated ways' led on the cross-country walk south from Max Gate to Winterborne Came and beyond.

Rain on a Grave (31 January 1913)

There is ample evidence that Hardy expected to be buried at Stinsford. He was buried in Poets' Corner, Westminster Abbey; at the same hour, 'the heart of this lover of rural Wessex was buried in the grave of his first wife among the Hardy tombs under the great yew-tree in the corner of the churchyard' at Stinsford (*Life*, 448).

daisies . . . loved beyond measure. Hardy had been reminded that they were Emma's first memory (*SR*. 3). 'I am longing to see daisies again, I love them', she wrote at the beginning of March 1902. *part of them.* Cf. 'Transformations'.

'I Found Her Out There'

Dundagel, Tintagel Castle (associated with Tristram and Iseult). In *PBE*.xxi Hardy quotes 'grim Dundagel throned along the sea' from 'The Quest of the Sangraal' by the Cornish poet and unconventional parson R. S. Hawker. *dipping blaze . . . fire-red.* Cf. *SR*. 48, 50. Such was Emma Gifford's complexion that she was called 'The Peony'. *Lyonnesse.* The traditional belief is that part of the Lyonnesse associated with King Arthur is sunk beneath the sea off the north coast of Cornwall. *heart of a child.* Emma Hardy's love of nature, of flowers and animals, for example, never changed. She did not lose her youthful zestfulness. She was so *living*, Hardy used to say (*Life*, 73).

Without Ceremony

What seems at first no more than a prosaic subject is translated into the poetry of felt experience.

Lament

Each verse follows the same pattern of light and shade.

cell. Cf. Gray's Elegy: 'Each in his narrow cell for ever laid,/The rude forefathers of the hamlet sleep.' *Candlemas*, 2 February, the feast of the purification of the Virgin Mary.

The Haunter

Here the supreme irony of these poems is voiced: now that she is dead, Hardy wishes for Emma's presence 'More than he used to do'. Indirectly, the poems say that she is never far from his thoughts.

The Voice (December 1912)

The movement of the verse is the most significant feature. The first three stanzas maintain a throb of excitement (except for a period of suspense and uncertainty at the beginning of the second, and a slighter one at the beginning of the third); yet the effect is a diminishing one as the feeling of uncertainty grows. The broken first line of the final stanza suggests stumbling, eager steps. The last three lines have each a sustained rhythm which conforms with the continuity of features in the setting (the thin oozing sound of the wind being long drawn-out) and, above all, of the woman still calling (though with not quite the insistence heard in the movement and repetition of the opening line).

the town, Launceston. Hardy was driven from the railway station to St Juliot. The 'air-blue gown' indicates the summer of 1870 (*Life*, 78).

His Visitor (1913)

The ghost of Emma visits Max Gate, and finds changes which make her wish not to return.

passing the mail-train. The London-Dorchester line runs about a quarter of a mile below Max Gate. *contrasts*. Between what is and what used to be.

A Circular

The poem is not inspired by any deep feeling, but affords an example of the significance Hardy attached to the wry irony of things. To most poets, the subject would have seemed alien and commonplace. In 1877 Hardy wrote, 'There is enough poetry in what is left, after all the false romance has been abstracted, to make a sweet pattern' (*Life*, 114).

A Dream or No (February 1913)

This poem links the Max Gate poems in the series with those which are based on Cornwall. So remote was Hardy's love that it seems like a dream. St Juliot stands above the valley in which the Valency runs to the coast at Boscastle. Beeny Cliff is to the north-east of this village. Since Hardy refers to it as 'Castle Boterel' in 'At Castle Boterel', 'Places', and *A Pair of Blue Eyes*, Bos may be Bossiney Haven to the

south-west. 'Self-Unconscious' shows that it had poignant associations
for Hardy. For the end of the third stanza, see *Life*, 104.

After a Journey

'I believe it would be said by people who knew me well that I have a
faculty . . . for burying an emotion in my heart or brain for forty years,
and exhuming at the end of that time as fresh as when interred', Hardy
wrote in 1917, doubtlessly with some of the poems of 1912–13 in mind,
though the single instance he gives is 'In Time of "the Breaking of
Nations" ' (*Life*, 378). 'After a Journey' was written on revisiting
Pentargon Bay (immediately below Beeny Cliff), though the journey
refers to his return to Cornwall on 6 March 1913, 'almost to a day,
forty-three years after his first journey' there (*Life*, 361). The poem
matches action, sound, and spirit with exquisite movements.

nut-coloured hair . . . rose-flush. 'They may recall her golden curls and
rosy colour as she rode about, for she was very attractive at that time',
Hardy wrote to the rector of St Juliot in August 1913, after hearing that
some of the parishioners remembered Miss Gifford.

A Death-Day Recalled

Behind this poem lies the tradition of the pastoral elegy that the death
of one for whom the poet grieves is mourned by Nature; it persists in
Shelley's *Adonais*. For Hardy, Nature is indifferent to human fate.
Targan is Pentargon Bay.

Beeny Cliff

In a letter to Clement Shorter, Hardy stated that that Beeny Cliff only
partly suggested the 'Cliff without a Name' (*PBE*.xxi–xxii), which
was 'a composite one'. For another recollection of Emma's riding, see
PBE.vii. The poem falls into two parts, the scene in 1870 followed by
thoughts of 1913 in the last two verses. Each verse is a unit in itself.
The second, for example, is devoted primarily to sounds, with fine
onomatopoeic effects; the third, to scene changes depicted with admirable verbal choice and economy. Had the underlying metrical pattern,
with its pause in the middle of each line, been adhered to rigidly, many
of the effects would have been weakened or destroyed. The rhythm
changes continually, and often subtly, to suit the sense. In context, the

stress-strength of 'bulks', for instance, contributes more to one's impression of Beeny than any other factor. The opening lines give a glorious sense of exhilaration, in contrast to the last two, where the hesitation before 'elsewhere' is more expressive than words. The alliteration does more than enhance the verse; much of it is creative, from the formidable 'bulks old Beeny' to seemingly distant waves, 'engrossed in saying their ceaseless babbling say'.

in a nether sky. The impression is created by the height of the viewpoint, and partly because the horizon between sky and sea is not distinct. *weird*, associated through legends with mystery and romance.   *nor knows nor cares*. A link with the previous poem.

At Castle Boterel (March 1913)

When reaching the main road above the harbour approach, Hardy looked back at the old ascent towards the village of Boscastle, and recalled walking up there with Emma Gifford in the March of 1870 – perhaps when she and her sister Helen Holder accompanied him to Penpethy quarries (*Life*, 75).

Primaeval rocks. Compare Knight's thoughts in terms of geological time, *PBE*.xxii.

Places (March 1913)

Reference is made to Emma's birth at Plymouth ('the Three Towns', i.e. Plymouth, Stonehouse, Devonport) and to her fearless riding at Boscastle. The poem may have been begun at Plymouth, but 'Here/ Upon Boterel Hill' suggests it was finished elsewhere, since Hardy returned home from Cornwall via Plymouth.

Saint Andrew's. See *SR*. 11–12. The tune is that played to the old metrical version of Psalm cxiii. *beneaped*, vapid, to no purpose (as of a ship grounded by a neap tide).

The Phantom Horsewoman (1913)

rose-bright. See the note to 'After a Journey'.

The Spell of the Rose

The ghost of Emma alludes in the manor-hall fiction to the building of Max Gate, where Hardy never planted the rose of love. Not long before her death she planted a rose. In 1918 it had grown luxuriantly, and the attention Hardy gave it (*ORFW*. 183) probably started the train of thought which led to the poem.

couched . . . mis-vision . . . me. As if the cataract (of the eye) which misrepresented me had been removed.

St Launce's Revisited

Hardy's train-journeys to Cornwall in the early 1870s ended at Launceston. Like the previous poem and the next, this was added to the original series for the second edition of *Satires of Circumstance* (1915); it would be better placed after 'A Dream or No'.

Groom and jade, the 'Horse and man' Hardy hired for conveying him to St Juliot.

Where the Picnic Was

The 'urban roar' (cf. 'the roar of London', *Life*, 171) confirms that the two who were the guests of the Hardys were the poets Henry Newbolt and W. B. Yeats, who visited Max Gate to present Hardy the gold medal of the Royal Society of Literature on his seventy-second birthday (*Life*, 358). It will be seen therefore that the poem was written in the winter of 1912–13. The 'hill to the sea' has suggested Ridgeway; another suggestion is Culliford Tree. From both there are excellent views of Portland and the countryside. Yet it seems impossible to explain the lines 'And the sea breathes brine/From its strange straight line/Up hither' with reference to either. The horizon is too remote, and it has no particular strangeness. The only unusual straight line to the sea in the area is Chesil Bank, which stretches from Portland more than twenty miles north-west. Its peculiarity (apart from its straightness) is in the size of its pebbles, which steadily diminishes from Portland onwards. The Chesil Bank link with Portland is seen as a straight line from Culliford Tree, which seems to have been known to the Hardys as a picnic spot (Kate Hardy's diary shows that she picnicked there).

A site nearer the sea, however, appears to be clearly indicated; and it may be that the Hardys took their guests on a more extensive tour. To the west of Abbotsbury, for example, at a point high above Chesil Bank, its most striking stretch appears as a straight line running near the mainland in the direction of Portland with water on either side of it.

MISCELLANEOUS PIECES

The Wistful Lady

This was surely suggested by Hardy's thoughts of his first wife after his marriage to Florence Dugdale in February 1914.

The Woman in the Rye

The poem could conceal a wish that came to Hardy before Emma died.

The Cheval-Glass

Probably occasioned by the memory of Emma Hardy's 'pale-faced form' in a mirror, as she brushed 'her hair's bright bands'. A cheval-glass is a long mirror which can be swung within an upright frame to reflect the whole person.

The Re-Enactment

darkled, became more obscured (as it grew darker). *wist*, knew.

An imaginary story arising from Hardy's return to St Juliot in 1913. The gown and brown locks recall Emma Gifford; cf. *Life*, 69 and 'A Dream or No'. For the piano see *PBE*.iii. In the 'predestined sorrowers' Hardy is thinking of himself and Emma in their last years of 'division'. The 'month of winter' is March, when Hardy first visited St Juliot and returned to it.

Her Secret

The poem could be related to 'An Imaginative Woman' (*LLI*).

'She Charged Me'

This may be based on the memory of an accusation by Emma Hardy, but 'the Cupid's bow' and the 'play of slave and queen' seem more imaginary than real.

The Newcomer's Wife

The story seems to originate from what Hardy heard or read of persons drowned in Weymouth harbour; see *WB*.I.vii (at 'Budmouth').

A Conversation at Dawn (MS, autumn 1910)

The scene suggests the Isle of Wight. The wife is convinced that she is married to her secret lover in the eyes of God, despite the irony of circumstance which makes her a slave to marriage laws. The husband's heartlessness recalls Lord Uplandtowers (*GND*. 'Barbara of the House of Grebe').

A King's Soliloquy (May 1910)

cark, trouble, burden.

Edward VII, son of Queen Victoria, died in May 1910, after a reign of less than ten years. His spirit is imagined looking back over his life, and realizing the limitations of his power. This was controlled by circumstances or Chance. 'That' refers to 'the Cause of Things' or Immanent Will. The poem resulted from Hardy's watching 'from the Athenaeum the procession of the removal of the King's body to Westminster, and the procession of the funeral from Westminster three days later' (*Life*, 350). In 'book and bell' there is a reference to the Mass Service.

The Coronation (1911)

The fantasy is all the more amusing when it is remembered that Hardy contrived a holiday in the Lake District with his brother to escape 'the millions' flocking to London for the Coronation (of George V in Westminster Abbey on 22 June 1911), and refused to write an ode which Clement Shorter requested for the occasion (see *ORFW*. 145, 148 and *Life*, 355). The comments on the Coronation preparations which disturb the monarchs buried in the Abbey reflect events and qualities commonly associated with them: Mary Stuart's execution, Henry VIII ('Hal') and his six wives, the 'saintliness' of Edward the Confessor, the murder of Richard II in Pontefract ('Pomfret') Castle, Charles II's ready way with the ladies. . . .

Rimmon. A false god (II Kings, v), referring to Henry VIII's defiance of the Pope. *catafalque*, a temporary structure representing a tomb in a funeral ceremony.

Aquae Sulis

interlune, the period when the moon is invisible. *baldachined*, canopied.

The Romans called Bath 'Aquae Sulis' from Sul, the British goddess of the waters or springs who was worshipped there. Remains of her temple may be seen near the Roman Baths. Close at hand is Bath Abbey, the Gothic structure alluded to in the poem. Hardy imagines Sul rising and asking the Christian God why this edifice was built. The anthropomorphism of this humorous scene reinforces the concluding view that all religions are man-made and mortal. Compare *D*I.I.vi:

> A local cult, called Christianity,
> Which the wild dreams of the wheeling spheres
> Include, with divers others such, in dim
> Pathetical and brief parentheses.

joys of man, Paganism. Compare the discussion of the conflict between Hellenism and Christian tenets in *JO*.v.v and vi.ii. *Jumping-jack . . . Jumping-jill*, puppets; cf. 'A Plaint to Man' (p. 99).

Seventy-Four and Twenty

Though it does not represent his views, the poem was probably written when Hardy was seventy-four; cf. the third verse of the original ending (Purdy, 168):

> For I am sick of thinking
> On whither things tend,
> And will foster hoodwinking
> Henceforth to the end.

The Elopement

quiz, eccentric. *freak*, play tricks with.

That night . . . bureau. At a hotel. *as it wins all women at last.* Though the story is fiction, this was probably Hardy's view; compare Sue Bridehead (*JO*).

'I Rose Up as My Custom Is'

All Souls' Day (2 November) is celebrated by the Catholic Church, prayers being said for the souls of the departed. It was believed that souls in purgatory returned to their homes on the evening before this day. This superstition is merged in Hardy with old pagan beliefs of Celtic origin which are traditionally associated with Hallowe'en (31 October), the evening before All Saints' Day. The ghostly visitation and departure, to the accompaniment of neighing nightmares, screeching vampires, and flying harpies, form a dramatic framework to amusing impressions of the traditional poet. The woman who speaks had been his comrade, not his wife. She prefers to be conventionally and socially fulfilled (compare the last poem), as she is with her unromantic husband.

chanticleer, poet or songster (usually a cockerel).

A Week

Though Hardy's first visit to St Juliot (Monday to Friday) does not fit the poem, the simile at the end ('As wing-clipt sea-gull for the sea') suggests that he had this visit in mind. The Friday verse indicates his departure. To create a crescendo throughout, he begins with the assumption that the girl had been known earlier.

vill, village or mansion; probably the latter here.

Had You Wept

This dramatic lyric seems to be composite in origin. The 'tidings' may be imaginary; the 'division' suggests Emma Hardy; the 'large and luminous eye' recalls Florence Dugdale (cf. 'After the Visit'). For a parallel, see a passage near the end of *TD*.xxxvii.

Bereft, She Thinks She Dreams

A 'nightmare' that has lasted for days.

In the British Museum

Hardy identified the scene as the Elgin Room. Whether it ever contained a stone from the Areopagus or Hill of Mars where Paul preached (Acts, xvii. 16–29) or not, the sincerity of the poem cannot be doubted. Even if the speaker confused the Areopagus with the neighbouring Acropolis, the thought that the stone could have echoed Paul's voice is Hardy's inspiration. In attributing it to a humble (rather than ignorant) man, his implication may be that the imaginative sense of wonder is stifled by unrealized information. It may reach as far as T. S. Eliot's

> Where is the wisdom we have lost in knowledge?
> Where is the knowledge we have lost in information?

In the Servants' Quarters

A realistic elaboration of the story of Peter's denial before the Crucifixion. See Mark, xiv. 66–72.

The Obliterate Tomb

hackered, uttered with chattering teeth. *garth*, churchyard. *shards*, fragments of stone.

The story seems scarcely worth the telling. It may have been suggested by Hardy's resolve to visit the tombs of the Giffords in Plymouth when he was returning from Cornwall in 1913. This he did in 1916 (*THN.* 80).

'Regret Not Me'

gipsying, on picnics.

One of Hardy's most lyrical poems, it moves lightly in accordance with the character and spirit of the speaker in life. Not surprisingly, it was a favourite with A. E. Housman.

The Recalcitrants

The title was considered for *Jude the Obscure*. The pair may be Sue Bridehead and Jude. Cf. 'The Conformers' and the end of 'The Elopement'.

the prime . . . brazen god, in primitive times before people had learned not to worship images. *current fames . . . abide the names.* Conventional values which demand observation of the letter rather than the spirit of moral codes; cf. the epigraph of *Jude*, 'The letter killeth' (II Corinthians, iii. 6).

Starlings on the Roof

First printed with the sub-title 'Moving House, Michaelmas'.

The Moon Looks In

The Sweet Hussy

The Telegram

The yachts riding mute at anchor, the fair moon 'fulling', and the giddy folk strutting up and down the parade suggest a general indifference to the double tragedy of the bridegroom and his bride.

The Moth-Signal

thwartly smitten, crossed.

Egdon Heath and the tumulus near the house indicate that the poem recasts a scene in *The Return of the Native*, when Wildeve is trying to lure Eustacia Vye out. Here her husband Clym Yeobright sits reading. Cf. *RN*.iv.iv and v (the knoll with its clump of fir trees).

Seen by the Waits

The waits are the musicians and carol-singers on their Christmas rounds.

The Two Soldiers

The drama seen re-enacted by one soldier in the face of the other near the tomb of the 'strange' woman remains a mystery. Had they both betrayed her, or had she betrayed each of them?

The Death of Regret

A letter by Florence Hardy shows that the original subject was a cat found strangled in a rabbit snare on Conquer Barrow near Max Gate. It was buried near a sycamore tree 'in our garden here. My husband thought the poem too good for a cat, and so made it apply to a person.'

In the Days of Crinoline (MS, July 1911)

Sometimes Hardy's justification for telling a story was that it really happened (Edmund Blunden, *Thomas Hardy*, 1958, pp. 246–7). He seems rather partial to jokes against parsons.

The Roman Gravemounds (November 1910)

When the drive at Max Gate was made, five Roman soldiers or colonists were decapitated (Archer, 37). The cat was Kitsy, buried in the Hardy pets' cemetery. A letter to Mrs Henniker suggest that this was the cat strangled on Conquer Barrow: 'I might possibly have saved her life if I had known where to look for her' (*ORFW.* 142).

The Workbox

scantling, remnant.

This narrative-dramatic poem in ballad verse imbues what was probably a simple story of unfaithfulness in love with mystery.

The Sacrilege

rafted, disturbed, upset. *fay*, luck, fortune. *goodman*, husband.

Like 'A Trampwoman's Tragedy' this poem has two characteristics of the old ballad: it tells a sensational tale, and it employs regular repetition (ll. 1 and 3 and the refrain-like alternations of line 2). Both belong to the 1820s and to Outer Wessex. Dunkery Beacon is the highest point on Exmoor in north Devon. Priddy, in the Mendips, was famous for its fair. The cathedral is at Wells in Somerset; and the felon's trial took place at Taunton, the county centre. The fourth verse should read, 'She heavily raised her sloe-black eyes.'

The Abbey Mason (November 1911)

embodying, taking shape. *quoin*, corner.

'Being interested at this time in the only Gothic style of architecture that can be called especially and exclusively English – the perpendicular style of the fifteenth century – Hardy made a journey to Gloucester to investigate its origin in that cathedral, which he ascertained to be in the screen between the south aisle and the transept . . .' (*Life*, 357). The poem was dedicated to the memory of John Hicks, the Dorchester architect to whom Hardy was apprenticed before working in London and whom he subsequently assisted. Hicks died in 1869. The tradition that the Perpendicular style began at Gloucester under Abbot Wygmore (d.1337) has been disproved. The part played by Nature in Hardy's fanciful explanation is of special interest; he probably knew that Sir Joseph Paxton had obtained his architectural ideas for the Crystal Palace from observing plant structure.

parpend ashlars, hewn stones, each of which is fixed across from one side of the wall to the other. *sizing*, (probably) assuming large proportions. *knife the . . . knot*. Compare 'cut the Gordian knot', solve a difficult problem. *cusping*, projecting points. *Prime*, (eccl.) the first hour of the day, six o'clock or sunrise. *ogive*, the diagonal groin or rib of a vault, two of which cross each other at the centre. *Templates*, horizontal beams across archways, etc., for taking the pressure. *Staunton and Horton*, successors of Wygmore. *spandrels*, triangular spaces between the outer curves of arches and the rectangular moulding enclosing them.

The Jubilee of a Magazine

This was *The Cornhill*, which reached its fiftieth anniversary in 1910. Hardy had contributed *Far from the Madding Crowd* and *The Hand of Ethelberta* to it when it was edited by Leslie Stephen. Features of the new cover design by Godfrey Sykes are referred to. The main idea is that (as Hardy wrote in 1900) 'material growth' is 'out of all proportion to moral growth', technical to humanitarian; cf. *Life*, 389 or *ORFW*. 185.

seedlip, a box or basket in which corn was carried for hand-sowing. *steel-roped plough*, drawn to and fro by two traction-engines, one at each end of the field.

The Satin Shoes

Hardy identified the scene for this pathetic ballad as Higher Bock-hampton. The church would be Stinsford, to which a 'lane' and 'grass-path' led from the road.

Exeunt Omnes (2 June 1913)

kennels, gutters.

Hardy emblematically expresses his feelings on his seventy-third birth-day that he should still survive when so many he knew had passed away. It should be noted that *Satires of Circumstance* was originally planned to conclude with this poem and the next (see p. 90).

Thoroughfare . . . highway. The details show that Hardy is thinking of the fair at Dorchester; cf. 'After the Fair' (p. 76).

A Poet (July 1914)

A tribute to Emma Hardy and Hardy's new wife Florence.

doffed this wrinkled gear, died, left (put off) this ageing body.

SATIRES OF CIRCUMSTANCE

These are dated 1910 in the MS (Purdy, 164). Hardy described them as 'caustically humorous', said they had been issued 'with a light heart before the war', but felt that he was expected to republish them, though they were out of harmony with the remainder of *Satires of Circumstance* as a whole (*Life*, 367). They were produced from notes made about 1890 (*ORFW*.146), and their irony is obvious. Their realism or humour often inclines to the cynical. Of the fifteen, all but VIII, XII, XIII, and XV appeared in *The Fortnightly Review* in April 1911, together with a twelfth which was discarded for its stark brutality. See 'On the Doorstep' (p. 264).

I. At Tea

II. In Church

III. By Her Aunt's Grave

IV. In the Room of the Bride-Elect

mollyish, weak, yielding.

V. At a Watering-Place

The scene suggests Weymouth.

VI. In the Cemetery

VII. Outside the Window

It has been suggested (see *The Colby Library Quarterly*, Sept. 1965) that this poem is based on a vignette of Blanche Amory in Thackeray's *Pendennis* (lx):

She and her ma's always quarrelin' .... When a visitor comes in, she smiles and languishes, you'd think that butter wouldn't melt in her mouth: and the minute he is gone, very likely, she flares up like a little demon, and says things fit to send you wild ... Mr. Soppington was a goin' to propose for her, and actially came one day, and sor her fling a book into the fire, and scold her mother so, that he went down softly by the back droring-room door, which he came in by; and next thing we heard of him was, he was married to Miss Rider. Oh, she's a devil, that little Blanche. ....

VIII. In the Study

IX. At the Altar-Rail

The town is probably Dorchester, the second rendezvous being in the Borough Gardens by the curving Albert Road (Bailey, 338).

X. In the Nuptial Chamber

XI. In the Restaurant

XII. At the Draper's

XIII. On the Death-Bed

XIV. Over the Coffin

XV. In the Moonlight

Hardy was familiar with Shelley's moon imagery; it is often associated with the 'shadow of white death'. The 'corpse-cold moon' reflects the feelings of the workman who realizes too late that the woman he ought to have loved is dead. It seems most probable that Hardy wrote this disguised poem to link these sketches with the more serious poetry of *Satires of Circumstance*, but chiefly (through the transference of the series in the second edition) to end the volume on a note of deep regret which was far more appropriate and candid than the tribute to Emma Hardy in 'A Poet' with which he planned to end the first edition.

5

Moments of Vision

THIS volume was first published in November 1917, three years after *Satires of Circumstance*. With the subsequent addition of 'Men Who March Away' there are 160 poems in this collection. Most of them were written in the war years, a high proportion of them being so personal that Hardy could not have contemplated drawing attention to himself by publishing them, except in volume form. Even this embarrassed him. 'I do not expect much notice will be taken of these poems', he wrote; 'they mortify the human sense of self-importance by showing, or suggesting, that human beings are of no matter or appreciable value in this nonchalant universe.'* As could be expected of a poet approaching his eightieth year, most of the poems are reminiscent; many are inspired by the memory of Emma Hardy. The 'finale' leads up to her death and his own; he could not expect to publish another volume of poetry.

Moments of Vision

There are moments of insight when the truth about ourselves is flashed upon us as if by a mirror. In times of regret and sorrow, we see things differently; we see truths which are hidden or veiled in our ordinary, everyday lives. Perhaps at the hour of our death, the mirror may catch our last thoughts and reveal them elsewhere. The poem suggests that Hardy was less rationalistic than he had been, and that his psychological musing turns into a tacit admission of supramundane possibilities. At the end of 1920 he wrote, 'I have no philosophy – merely what I have often explained to be only a heap of impressions, like those of a bewildered child at a conjuring show' (*Life*, 410).

* *Life*, 378. Compare his comment on Frank Harris's assertion that man could make of life what he would: '*ephemeridae*, we men! Flies, summer-flies, with but a day to live!' (F. Harris, *Latest Contemporary Portraits*, London, 1927). See *TD*. xxxii (second paragraph) for a poetical translation of this image.

The Voice of Things

On 7 March 1913, the day after Hardy set off to revisit Cornwall, Florence Dugdale wrote, 'He says that he is going down for the sake of the girl he married, and who died more than twenty years ago.' Earlier she had written of Emma Hardy's 'bitter denunciations' of him, 'beginning about 1891 and continuing until within a day or two of her death'. (Hardy read them over and over again, until Florence was afraid that he would end by believing them.) The three stanzas present Hardy's happiness during his second visit to Cornwall in 1870; the change which occurred approximately twenty years later (in a fictional setting); and his feeling, on his return to Cornwall (in 1913 or 1916) that there is no forgiveness for his failure to seek reconciliation with Emma.

The waves huzza'd. Cf. 'The Wind's Prophecy' and *HE*.xlv. For the association of love and the sea in Hardy's memory, see *RN*.v.vi. *Lammas-tide*, 1 August, a harvest festival day in the early English Church. *the Confession.* Made in the hope of forgiveness for things 'done' and things 'left undone'.

'Why Be at Pains?'

Though dramatized as the appeal of a sailor in a particular setting, the lyric's meaning is general, emphasizing the uncertainty of the future.

'We Sat at the Window'

Rain on St Swithin's day (15 July) has been traditionally believed to presage much rain to come. In July 1875, towards the end of their first year of marriage, the Hardys stayed at Bournemouth, before finding lodgings at Swanage (*Life*, 107). Looking back, he realizes that an opportunity of getting to know each other better had been wasted as the unpropitious rain came down.

Afternoon Service at Mellstock

Hardy's recollections of services at Stinsford are found in several places; cf. *Life*, 10. The scene occurs in *DR*.xii.8. For the concluding thought, compare 'Night in the Old Home'.

one-voiced, with one voice (spirit). *Tate-and-Brady.* Until the second half of the nineteenth century, the metrical psalms (versified by Nahum Tate and Nicholas Brady, and authorized in 1696) were commonly sung as hymns.

At the Wicket-Gate

The scene is probably imaginary, arising perhaps from Hardy's memory of his aunt's refusal to consent to his marriage with her daughter Martha 'on the grounds of its being against the laws of the church', as Martha's brother told his son (*Dorset*, no. 23, 1972, p. 39). There were no meadows around the church at Puddletown where the Sparks family lived, nor is it likely that members of the family would walk past the Hardys' home and proceed to Stinsford Church in order to express their opposition to the match in this dramatic fashion.

In a Museum

Written after a visit to Exeter in 1914 or 1915 (*Life*, 364, 370), this shows Hardy's scientific imagination at work. Sound waves like light waves travel through space, and Hardy is lost in wonderment at their multiplicity in 'the full-fugued song of the universe unending'.

Apostrophe to an Old Psalm Tune
(13 August 1916)

Hardy first sang it when he was in the Stinsford choir.

a temple. This suggests a city church, e.g. St Mary's, Kilburn, London (*Life*, 38). *Monk*, William Henry (1823–89), professor of music, and organist at several London churches. He is best known as musical editor of *Hymns Ancient and Modern* and composer of the tune to 'Abide with me'. *one who evoked you often*. Probably Emma Hardy, who played at St Juliot Church and loved to revive old memories at the piano. *Your raiser ... borne off*. This could allude to the death of Emma. *late outsetter*, Monk, who had died in 1889; 'outsetter' is 'setter-out' or musical arranger. *scathed*, hurt, afflicted. *Endor*. For the calling up of Samuel's spirit by the witch of Endor, see I Samuel, xxviii, 3–20. *belligerent fire*. A reference to the First World War, 1914–18.

At the Word 'Farewell'

This is a recollection of Hardy's departure from the rectory at St Juliot. He described it as 'literally true' (*ORFW*. 179), but was uncertain whether it referred to his first or second visit (*Life*, 75).

Plan . . . weave. Cf. 'The Convergence of the Twain' and the wide web of cause-effect (*W*.iii). *the scale might have turned.* As in 'By the Fireside' which Hardy marked in the copy of Browning's poems given him by Mrs Henniker:

> Oh, the little more, and how much it is!
> And the little less, and what worlds away!
> . . .
> Friends – lovers that might have been.

First Sight of Her and After

The day which seems to the lover to be the beginning, or the end, of his romance is probably that spent by Hardy travelling home from St Juliot in March 1870.

The Rival

Probably a fancy based on Hardy's earlier love of Emma.

Heredity

Compare Hardy's note (*Life*, 217): 'The story of a face which goes through three generations or more, would make a fine novel or poem of the passage of Time.' This was the germ of *The Well-Beloved*.

'You Were the Sort that Men Forget'

It is doubtful if Emma Hardy was 'the sort that men forget', but she seems to be the subject of the poem. Hardy dwells with pity on the inner reality and her failure to communicate it.

She, I, and They (1916: MS, 1 August)

The poem conveys Hardy's thoughts on being childless and on the likelihood that there would be no direct descendant in his family:

Mary Hardy had died a spinster in 1915; Henry Hardy remained a bachelor; and Kate was a spinster. The phrase 'their sturdy line' suggests one family. As Hardy and Katharine were not 'the last' of their family, and the poet would hardly speak of his richer ancestors as 'unsurpassed', the scene must be largely fictional. Even less could the two be Hardy and either of his wives, both of whom had a number of near relatives.

Near Lanivet, 1872

Another poem described by Hardy as 'literally true'. Lanivet is near Kirland, Bodmin, where Emma Gifford's father lived. The incident happened during Hardy's fourth recorded visit to Cornwall (see 'The Seven Times', p. 197); and a note of his indicates that the handpost was on the (old) St Austell road. It had arms (almost certainly wooden and no longer in existence), against which Emma rested her own in her weariness. The stone Celtic cross at Reperry junction is out of the question; even if it were in its present position in 1872 (and this is very doubtful), it was armless, hardly three feet high, and mounted on a bank which is difficult to climb. The site must have been further north, one mile east of Lanivet, where the 'crossways' Hardy remembered after more than forty years consists of two neighbouring T-junctions. It is a mistake to read a crisis in the situation. Emma's figure against the handpost, and her inclined face, evoked a picture of the Crucifixion. For Hardy in retrospect the scene became a symbol of the unhappiness she was to suffer with him.

In the running of Time's far glass, many years after. The image is that of an hour-glass.

Joys of Memory

brume, fog.

Obviously a contrast to the above. The day recalled is 7 March 1870, when Hardy journeyed to Cornwall and met Emma Gifford for the first time.

To the Moon

Copying Architecture in an Old Minster

tale, number. *passager*, bird of passage.

Hardy never lost his interest in architecture, and occasionally did professional work (church restoration) after he had taken up writing as a profession. He lived at Wimborne from 1881 to 1883, and knew the minster well. The tomb references are actual; the Saxon king is Ethelred, elder brother of Alfred the Great, who succeeded him. There are allusions to the contemporary war in 'ail-stricken mankind' and a 'trouble-torn' world.

To Shakespeare (14 February 1916)

The poem marks the tercentenary of Shakespeare's death, and was written in response to Israel Gollancz's invitation to contribute to *A Book of Homage to Shakespeare*. Unlike most memorial poems, it is realistic in vision and presentation. It owes much to 'Others abide our question . . .', the sonnet in which Matthew Arnold stresses the baffling nature of Shakespeare's genius and his ordinariness as a man.[17]

tower, of the church at Stratford. *published on thy passing-bell*. A stroke for each year.

Quid Hic Agis? (1916; probably August)

The words 'What doest thou here?' occur in a story of the prophet Elijah (I Kings, xix), which was a great favourite with Hardy. The poem is a memorial to Emma Hardy. In the first section he recalls sitting across the aisle from her at St Juliot when the chapter was read in August 1870; in the next, reading it himself (probably in August 1872) to the congregation in the same church (cf. *Life*, 156–7 and *PBE*. xix). Finally he thinks of the tablet which he had designed as a mural memorial to her in St Juliot Church (and of the prolonged war), and feels like Elijah: 'O Lord, take away my life . . . I, even I only am left.'

sands were heaping, the sands of Time. *drought with me, with her*. The image (from the August drought in the first section) has a Biblical connotation; in the Old Testament (as in Eliot's *The Waste Land*) the desert and drought denote suffering, deprivation, and God's disfavour. *men say*. Hardy must have been informed (cf. *Life*, 361) that the tablet had been placed in St Juliot Church. The poem was published in

August 1916, and Hardy and his wife Florence went to Cornwall to inspect the memorial the following month (*Life*, 373).

On a Midsummer Eve

Hardy thinks of Emma and old superstitions connected with this evening. One of them was that if certain rites were followed, one's partner for life would be seen at midnight (*W*.xx, *JO*.III.viii). Ghosts of lovers would also appear. Hardy imagines that, by chance, three actions take place which make him see and hear his beloved; the first seems to be a preliminary rite, with the moon an adjunct to success. It may have been a local superstition. Violet roots and parsley were used to create a fumigation which would 'cause a man to see visions in the air'.

Timing Her

vair, squirrel's fur.

Lalage Acland was the daughter of the curator of the Dorset County Museum; she often brought messages or documents from her father to Hardy when she was a young girl (Bailey, 356). The poem conveys a fictitious excitement, occasioned by a name which was that of the Latin poet Horace's favourite mistress (*Odes*, I. xxii).

Before Knowledge

Even if true lovers eventually meet, Chance does not order the circumstances perfectly. How much happier the lover would have been in times of hardship and deprivation could he have known his prospective good fortune! The poem is to some extent a variant of Browning's 'Never the time and the place/And the loved one all together!' The 'closing lines' which intersect recall 'The Convergence of the Twain'.

The Blinded Bird

The blinding described by Hardy had been practised to make the bird sing. The virtues which comprise 'charity' (I Corinthians, xiii) are all to be found in this suffering bird and in Tess Durbeyfield (see *TD*. xxxiii, xxxvi). The view that Hardy was thinking of Tess when he wrote this poem is strengthened by the last line, which recalls the subtitle of the novel, 'A Pure Woman'. He often thought of her in terms of bird imagery; in the fell clutch of circumstance she was like a bird in a springe (xxxi) or a bird in a clap-net (xliii).

'The Wind Blew Words'

The belief here expressed is based on Hardy's view that 'the discovery of the law of evolution' had 'shifted the centre of altruism from humanity to the whole conscious world collectively' (*Life*, 346; see also 224). The tree, animals, and human beings without distinction of race or colour, are selected to represent the whole range of life.

huge distress . . . self-slaughter. This suggests that the 1914–18 war was being waged when the poem was written. Man was adding on a vast scale to the slaughter of the natural world (cf. 'The Mother Mourns'). Hardy's final thought is similar to John Donne's: 'No man is an Island, entire of itself. . . . Any man's death diminishes me, because I am involved in Mankind; And therefore never send to know for whom the bell tolls; it tolls for thee.'

The Faded Face

weeted, knew.

The Riddle

The contrast lies between Emma Gifford of Cornwall, looking westward over the sea, and Emma Hardy, facing eastward in her grave at Stinsford (according to the order of Christian burial).

The Duel

The first speaker is the Earl of Shrewsbury who was killed by the Duke of Buckingham in 1688. In the Countess of Cardigan's *My Recollections*, 1909 (p. 124) Hardy read how the daughter of the second Earl of Cardigan, Anne Brudenell, in the guise of a page, held the Duke's horse while he slew her husband.

At Mayfair Lodgings

In December 1894 Hardy was in London on publishing business, 'and stayed at a temporary room off Piccadilly, to be near his club [the Savile]. It was then that there seems to have occurred, according to what he said later, some incident of the kind possibly adumbrated in the verses called "At Mayfair Lodgings".... He watched during a sleepless night a lighted window close by, wondering who might be lying there ill. Afterwards he discovered that a woman had lain there dying, and that she was one whom he had cared for in his youth, when she was a girl in a neighbouring village' (*Life*, 267). Once again Hardy is found regretting a 'lost prize'. His explanation of the last stanza was that the tragedy might not have happened had the girl he 'had rated rare' married him (Collins, 24). The idiomatic 'for good' in poetry is remarkable for its period, and far less questionable than its rhyme 'unadieu'd'.

To My Father's Violin (1916)

purfling, decorative inlay. *con*, examine.

Hardy's father had played the violin in Stinsford Church many years before the old 'quire' was disbanded in 1841 or 1842 (*Life*, 9–13). For his 'luting a measure', see *Life*, 15, 23–4.

the Nether Glooms and *Mournful Meads*, the classical underworld where the spirits (shades) of the dead lived. Hardy stated this was 'a Virgilian reminiscence . . . of Acheron and the Shades' (*Life*, 410).

The Statue of Liberty

The sculptor of the statue questions the cleaner. The tragic irony between the latter's proud illusions and the reality of his daughter's shame is obvious. More important is the irony of a conception of liberty where circumstances compelled a girl to 'dens of vice'. For a parallel, see the passage on London which ends, 'O richest City in the world! "She knew the rules" ' (*Life*, 214).

The Background and the Figure

Almost certainly a memory of Emma Hardy.

The Change (January–February 1913)

bale, mischief, harm, evil.

The week 'Enringed with a purple zone' (Thomas Gray's 'purple light of love') was that of Hardy's first visit to Cornwall (cf. 'A Week'). The 'deodar' grew in the rectory garden at St Juliot, and the white owl haunted the neighbouring trees. For the idea of 'the mocker' and 'the mocked', see 'The Prophetess'. The poem was probably written after reading Emma Hardy's reminiscences of her early life; cf. *SR.* 59–60:

> I had two pleasant changes – one to stay in Bath. . . . And I went as country cousin to my brother in London, and was duly astonished, which gave him even more pleasure than it did me. I was rather bewildered with the size and lengths and distances, and very much embarrassed at getting in an omnibus . . .

Whether the meeting at the railway station is imaginary or based on experience is not known,[18] but Hardy's belated love and contrition (on the wrong side of death) finds full expression at the end of this poem. The title, it will be seen, had a double meaning for Hardy. The first is 'change' as it was used by Emma; the second, the overtones the word suggested to the spirit of the guilt-ridden poet.

Sitting on the Bridge

The opening suggests that the girls had walked past the barracks and through Dorchester to Grey's Bridge. Perhaps the 'ridge' is 'Top o' Town' at the upper end of High West Street. It is not implied that the Fifth Regiment which was rumoured to be coming was Irish. The coincidence is that an Irish lancer passed while they sang 'Take me, Paddy, will you now?'

The Young Churchwarden

It is clear from a manuscript deletion that the poem recalls a Sunday evening service on 14 August 1870. A note by Hardy in his prayer book indicates that this was at Lesnewth on the other side of the Valency valley from St Juliot. The churchwarden may have been the farmer who (according to Florence Hardy) had been nearly 'secured' for Emma, and whom the latter refers to as 'disappointed' (*SR.* 59). The opening line of the last stanza was clearly intended to give the impression that the poem was 'personative' rather than personal. Perhaps Hardy's poetic imagination led to exaggerated feelings, but essentially the poem reflects one of his moods during the period 'When Love's viol was unstrung'. His use of a conventional view of life-after-death rounds off the irony, which is reinforced by the repetition in the last stanza of all the rhymes in the first.

'I Travel as a Phantom Now' (1915)

The poem shows a more positive and sensible attitude than the desire for the return of 'nescience' in 'Before Life and After'. Perhaps it is related to Hardy's depression at the course of the war, and to meeting Mrs Henniker in London (*ORFW*. 168–70).

Lines to a Movement in Mozart's E-Flat Symphony

strawberry-tree, arbutus. *ratheness*, eagerness.

The verses open and close with the same words throughout; further repetition will be found in the corresponding line-openings (with two slight variations in the last verse, though the sense-pattern remains unchanged); and the fourth lines are notable for the fivefold alliterative stress of disyllabic words. The times recalled are probably autobiographical. The last three could refer to Emma Gifford in Cornwall, the pinnacled tower being St Juliot Church, the dance taking place at the rectory or school (cf. 'The Dream is – Which?'). If all four refer to one person, as seems unlikely, it could be Florence Dugdale, for (to judge by a letter signed by Hardy, but written by her, from Carlisle) she accompanied him and his brother to the Lake District in June 1911, when he was anxious to avoid the Coronation crowds. As the poem was begun in November 1898, the first verse may have been added or substituted at the revision stage. According to Florence, the symphony was one of Hardy's 'very favourite' ones. The MS shows that 'Movement' was originally 'Minuet'.

'In the Seventies'

misprision, error, people in error. *lamp-worm*, glow-worm.

The text from the Vulgate (Latin) Bible (Job, xii. 4) runs, 'I am as one mocked of his neighbours'. Hardy remembers his confidence when he gave up architecture for writing, and how acquaintances including Horace Moule (cf. *Life*, 33) doubted the wisdom of his decision. Hardy believed with Swinburne that 'Save his own soul [man] hath no star'

(*Life*, 345). Fortunately Emma Gifford encouraged him to remain a writer after a period of failure, during which he had to resort to architecture at various times for self-support.[19]

The Pedigree (1916)

Hardy's interest in his family pedigree was extensive, but the subject of the poem is more general: the question of hereditary influence (cf. 'Heredity' and 'Discouragement'). The moonscape is remarkable, the old moon resembling the eye of a 'drifting' dolphin (far more kinetic and visually apt than 'dying' in the first edition) 'seen through a lapping wave' of 'green-rheumed' cloud. The old moon casts a spell, and fantasy takes charge. The genealogical tree which the poet is studying becomes so confusing that it appears as the face of a magician directing his attention to the window. The window has become a mirror, and in it he sees his ancestors in dwindling perspective, all with the same features. He realizes that the first were his 'fuglemen', responsible for all his actions. Thereupon, as if it had achieved its wry purpose, the page resumed its normal features, as did the window with its moonscape.

fuglemen, leaders of the file, whom they copied (in military training), directors, controllers; cf. D1. Fore Scene:

> So may ye judge Earth's jackaclocks to be
> Not fugled by one Will, but function-free.

I am I . . . alone. Cf. W. E. Henley, 'Invictus':

> I am the master of my fate:
> I am the captain of my soul.

His Heart

At several points the widow's dream seems to have been devised with Emma and Hardy himself in mind.

vermiculations, patterns resembling the tortuous tracks left by worms.

Where They Lived (MS, October 1913)

Clearly based on Hardy's return to the rectory at St Juliot in March 1913.

The Occultation

That of Hardy's 'irradiate soul' must refer to the clouding of his happiness with Emma. (The 'starry thoughts' of 'In the Seventies' were not disappointed.) The concluding question seems to be answered to some degree in the next poem.

Life Laughs Onward

All the sites seem to be connected with Emma: Plymouth, her grave at Stinsford (daisies her favourite flower), and the terrace in the rectory garden at St Juliot or by the river at Sturminster Newton, which Hardy revisited in June 1916 (*Life*, 373).

The Peace-Offering

More than any others, the last three lines express Hardy's haunting regret that he had not relented towards his wife when she made a move towards conciliation.

'Something Tapped' (August 1913)

The moth at the window and Emma's death recall Wessex folklore. See *LLI*. 'The Superstitious Man's Story'.

The Wound

The image in this autobiographical poem repeats that of *TD*.xxi. For the 'crest' (and the wound) see 'When Oats were Reaped' (pp. 217–18).

A Merrymaking in Question

Life seems a dance in prospect, but death calls the last tune, the church-yard providing an ironical *danse macabre*.

'I Said and Sang Her Excellence'

If, as the footnote indicates, this poem was written by Rushy Pond, this does not give it significance with reference to actual people. It seems an early piece of work not unrelated to 'Heiress and Architect'

('Where nothing frosts the air', 'dim old hall/Dream-built'). The flattering and fickle lover describes 'her excellence' in terms of 'the very She' he later meets. Here we seem to be near the Well-Beloved theme (*Life*, 286). The singer is rather like Fitzpiers (cf. *W*.xvi, xxviii).

A January Night

The incident occurred at Tooting in 1879 (*Life*, 124). The troubles which began there relate mainly to Hardy's illness (*Life*, 145ff.) and have no link with this poem.

A Kiss

Compare 'In a Museum'.

The Announcement

The MS note 'January 1879' indicates the time of the visit. Hardy identifies the scene as Higher Bockhampton. As he was then at Tooting, he probably heard the story from his parents. See Bailey (370) for a possible identification.

The Oxen (1915)

Christmas Eve is commonly associated with the supernatural in Hardy's prose and poetry. The legend of the poem, which Hardy heard from his mother, is referred to in *TD*.xvii. There is a poignancy in his wish that the old comforting Christian beliefs were true.

The Tresses

The Photograph

Hardy identified the scene as Max Gate. There is no clue to the date of the poem or to the identity of the person then 'living or dead'.

On a Heath

The conclusion suggests an autobiographical interpretation. The heath is almost certainly 'Egdon', the 'town-shine' coming from Dorchester. The meeting is probably romanticized; it seems improbable that Hardy would expect his girl friend to walk across the heath in 'dark weather' to rendezvous with him near his home. Was she Tryphena Sparks or the unknown woman of 'At Mayfair Lodgings'; and is there any personal link between this poem and the last? It was Kate Hardy who told Florence Hardy that the engagement ring which Hardy gave to Emma Gifford had been intended for a country girl. (The story was recorded by Irene Cooper Willis, who heard it from Florence; Miss Willis informed Evelyn Hardy that it came from Kate.) Hardy identified 'another looming', the 'one stilly blooming', and the 'shade entombing/All that was bright of me' as one person (Collins, 24-5). The reference therefore is to Emma Gifford and the nearness (in time) to Hardy's first visit to St Juliot. The last lines allude to the darkest periods in their marriage (cf. 'In Tenebris', etc.).

An Anniversary

The scene is in the eweleaze (opposite the park at Kingston Maurward) through which ran the path used by the Hardys to and from Stinsford Church (and Dorchester). Whatever the anniversary, it seems to have taken Hardy to his old home. The poem's central interest is the difference brought by the intermediate years. The 'garth' is the churchyard at Stinsford; the white stones include those marking the graves of Hardy's wife (d.1912) and his sister Mary (d.1915). The theme of human death and decay is reinforced by impressions of the tree and of the enshrouding moss on the wall. See 'Looking Across' (p. 146).

'By the Runic Stone'

Whether Hardy uses 'Runic' accurately seems very doubtful. In *W.* xliv he mentions symbols of 'runic obscurity'.

When he wrote the poem, he probably knew from Alfred Pope's *The Old Crosses of Dorset* (London, 1906) that the three stones in the neighbourhood of Higher and Lower Bockhampton (including the original of the 'Druidical stone' to which he referred in *RN*.III.iii) were much too modern to be termed 'Runic', not one of them being pre-medieval.

'Two who became a story' has suggested Hardy and Emma and *A Pair of Blue Eyes*. Hardy, however, opposed the view that he and Emma entered to any great extent into the personalities of the hero and heroine of that novel (*Life*, 73-4). The 'she in brown' recalls Emma Gifford in

March 1870, but Hardy's programme during the three short days of his visit was too full to allow time for the experience of the poem (*Life*, 74–5). The fact that he remembered most vividly the metamorphosis of the 'young lady in brown' of March 1870 into the 'young lady in summer blue' the following August (*Life*, 78) does not preclude the possibility of her appearing in brown in the summer of 1870 (or 1872) during his second (or fifth) visit to Cornwall.

There are many stones in that county which could have been described as 'Runic' by non-specialists in the 1870s. The oldest of these in the St Juliot area stands high up on a site with a wonderful view towards Tintagel; from 1860 to 1889, however, it stood in a farmyard, where it was used as a pivot stone for a threshing-machine. Further off, there was a similar stone 'with capitals and minuscules', which served as a gatepost on the Trevillet estate. Nothing is known to suggest Hardy's interest in either of them. The case for the latter is presented by Evelyn Hardy in *The London Magazine*, April-May 1972. Hardy sketched St Nectan's Kieve, a picturesque waterfall in a wooded valley below Trevillet, in October 1871, but the scene of the poem is clearly a summer one.

The 'transport' of talking 'in such a place' implies something of special importance in the situation of the stone. Was it at Tintagel Castle (cf. *Life*, 91)? Was it the Worthyvale stone by a stream below a slight cliff and a grassy bank in a secluded spot some distance from Slaughter Bridge near Camelford? Members of the Royal Institution of Cornwall (I am informed by Kenneth Phelps) made an excursion there on 9 August 1870, the day after Hardy's arrival at St Juliot. As the party lunched at Boscastle before their visit, it is not unlikely that news of the stone reached Hardy at the rectory. At the time it was associated with King Arthur's traditional last battle at Slaughter Bridge. The inscription is in large legible Latin, however.

In addition to the sketch of St Nectan's Kieve, the New York Public Library has an impressive one by Hardy of a stone pillar at St Juliot. It is a Celtic cross which stands just within the southern perimeter of the churchyard and near entrance steps up a steep bank above a meadow sloping down towards the Valency valley. Emma and her brother-in-law Mr Holder may have called this 'the Runic stone'; even in 1975 an inquiry came to an authority on the subject from a Cornish writer who referred to one of these 'wheel-head' crosses as 'a Runic stone'.

The 'die' which cut into their 'encompassment' (restricted their freedom still further) seems to allude to the engagement of Hardy and

Emma. Agreement on this may have been reached as they sat on the steps by the Celtic cross; it was a quiet, sunny spot, sufficiently near the rectory for them to sit and talk regardless of time. The event may have occurred in August 1870, before the church-restoration began. How much the old church meant to Hardy for romantic reasons as well as architectural is acknowledged (*Life*, 79); it is clear in his poems and sketches, one of the exterior particularly. It is significant too that Emma Hardy links the growth of their affection with professional visits to the church (*Life*, 70–71). If the engagement was delayed until August 1872 (which seems hardly probable),[20] the restoration for which Hardy was greatly responsible was complete. The place had a special significance, and the sketch of the Celtic cross and scene beyond suggests personal associations which he wished to preserve.

The last lines of the poem seem to refer to the lives of Hardy and Emma rather than to the story of *A Pair of Blue Eyes*. Their history was becoming known to the world through the publication of 'Poems of 1912–13' and *Moments of Vision* (1917). It should be noted that 'Two who became a story' did not appear before 1919.

The Pink Frock

passed, died.

Marcia, Lady Yarborough, 'a woman very rich and very pretty', was the lady of this poem, 'though it should be stated that the deceased was not her husband but her uncle' (*Life*, 264). Chosen for its exactness and pleasing sound, 'accordion-pleated' exemplifies Hardy's preference for non-traditional imagery.

Transformations

Hardy identified the scene as Stinsford churchyard. The 'fair girl' whom he 'tried to know' was Louisa Harding (see *Life*, 26 and 'Voices from Things Growing in a Churchyard'). In these poems we have a rationalist view of physical 'immortality'. It is found in Emily Brontë's poetry and in the *Rubáiyát of Omar Khayyám*:

> I sometimes think that never blows so red
> The Rose as where some buried Caesar bled;
> That every Hyacinth the Garden wears
> Dropt in its Lap from some once lovely Head.

In Her Precincts

A dream fantasy, based on Hardy's recollections of dancing at Kingston
Maurward with Julia Augusta Martin's niece, or reflecting the feelings
of the hero of The Poor Man and the Lady (cf. 'An Indiscretion in the
Life of an Heiress') towards the heroine at 'Tollamore House'.

The Last Signal

One of Hardy's walks from Max Gate was along the path starting on
the opposite side of the road to Winterborne Came, where William
Barnes preached. His rectory was on the Wareham road. The poem
records Hardy's sight of the coffin turning into this road from the
rectory, to be taken along a by-road 'athwart the land' to the church
and graveyard. At the time Hardy was on his way to the funeral. For
his knowledge of Barnes, the Dorset poet, see Life, 28, 161, 175–6, 183
and his obituary notice of him (Orel, 100–106). It has been pointed out
that Welsh and Irish characteristics in Barnes's poetry are included in
Hardy's memorial verses: the former in the repetition of three con-
sonantal sounds in two parts of a line, before and after the caesura
(notably in the third line of the first stanza); the latter in the 'union' or
rhyming of the last syllable of a line with one in the middle of a line
('road . . . abode').

The House of Silence

The 'phantom' is Hardy at Max Gate; 'the last of its race' refers to his
childlessness and that of his unmarried brother and sisters. He lives less
in his surroundings than in his imagination, which evokes people,
joyful or sad, at all stages of life; 'its ages seven' refers to Shakespeare's
seven ages of man (As You Like It, II. vii. 139ff.).

Great Things

Like the previous poem, this lyric stresses the joys which Hardy
remembered. The use of 'Weymouth', instead of its Wessex name, is
rather surprising; the third line of the MS runs, 'Vamping down to
Budmouth town'.

Soul, I have need of thee. Based probably on Luke, xii. 20.

The Chimes

The sweet tune played by the bells of St Peter's, Dorchester (see *MC.* iv) and its passing are paralleled in Hardy's happy expectation of marriage and the 'bale' that followed it. For the use of this word with the same associations, see 'The Change' and 'At the Piano'. The last two lines recall 'The Division'.

The Figure in the Scene

Hardy's sketch of the scene is dated 22 August 1870. The hooded figure in the foreground (right) is Emma Gifford, with Beeny Cliff beyond. See 'It Never Looks Like Summer' (p. 147).

'Why Did I Sketch?'

See the previous note.

Conjecture

Emma, Florence, and Mary are Hardy's first and second wife and his sister. The image of a highway for life helps to explain why he begins *The Return of the Native* and *The Mayor of Casterbridge* with wayfarers. The rhymes of the first and last lines are so distant that they sometimes pass unnoticed.

The Blow

oubliette, secret dungeon in which a prisoner could be forgotten.

The 'blow' is a general one ('this foul crash our lives amid'), almost certainly an allusion to the First World War. The possibility that it was the work of man is not ignored. Hardy had expressed the view that the First Cause was responsible for events too horrible for human agency in 1878; see 'The Bedridden Peasant' (p. 44).

Love the Monopolist (begun 1871)

The 'airy slim blue form' suggests that Hardy was leaving Emma Gifford at Launceston railway station after his holiday in Cornwall in August 1870 (cf. 'The Voice', p. 105). The date the poem was begun suggests either the May or October 1871 visit (see *Life*, 85 and the note to 'By the Runic Stone', p. 135). The poem turns on 'the pathetic fallacy'.

At Middle-Field Gate in February (c. 1889)

The note that Hardy wrote the poem 'about this time' comes at the end of the 1889 entries (*Life*, 223). The scene and the title suggest that it was written in February. He recalls the young women he saw harvesting when he was a boy; among them, Ann West, whose marriage he remembered from the 'silver frost' of 2 February 1855 (Lennart A. Björk, *The Literary Notebooks of Thomas Hardy*, Göteborg, 1974, pp. 103, 330). Local records confirm an oral tradition that 'Middle Field' is the second of three fields on the eastern side of the road between Lower Bockhampton and Bockhampton Cross.

The Youth Who Carried a Light (1915)

See 'In the Seventies'.

apogee. Although used in its general sense of 'highest point', it is related to the sun, as in astronomy. The 'light' is conceived as dawn and sunshine in the first two verses.

The Head above the Fog

Whether the situation is totally imaginary or not, the poem evokes a lover's excitement. The scene is the Frome valley, possibly between Dorchester and Stinsford (cf. 'The Third Kissing-Gate') or east of Lower Bockhampton (the Valley of the Great Dairies). In *CM*. 'The Romantic Adventures of a Milkmaid' (vii), the 'two trunkless heads' of an approaching pair are seen on 'the white surface of the fog' in this valley (later transferred to Devon). In *TD*.xx 'the summer fog was more general, and the meadows lay like a white sea, out of which the scattered trees rose like dangerous rocks'. In the poem the figure is only 'like to life'; it is recollected, a 'spectre'. The last tryst is wholly imaginary. The poem may have been suggested by an 'evening fog-fleece' in the Frome valley below Max Gate; cf. 'Wessex Heights' (p. 97).

Overlooking the River Stour

This poem and the next two were written after Hardy's visit to River-side Villa, the house where he and Emma lived above the Stour river at Sturminster Newton from 1876 to 1878. Though, in retrospect, he realized that it was the happiest period in their married life, he wondered if he had neglected his wife; he had been preoccupied with the writing of *The Return of the Native*. The descriptive images are remarkably apt, again illustrating Hardy's unconventionality ('Planing up shavings of crystal spray'); and the repetition of the opening lines of each stanza is effective.

The Musical Box

nonce, occasion.

Hardy's remorse and pity may be detected in the image of his wife 'standing shadowed'. For 'Stourside Mill' see 'The Second Visit' (p. 250).

On Sturminster Foot-Bridge

The visual imagery and onomatopoeic effects (to which a reviewer's ridicule prompted Hardy to refer the reader; see *Life*, 301, 390) are unusually successful.

eyot-withies, willows on an island in the river (almost opposite River-side Villa). The footbridge is upstream to the right.

Royal Sponsors

Hardy's *A Group of Noble Dames*, his interest in aristocratic memoirs, and his extensive reading of Horace Walpole's voluminous letters suggest that this story may have a basis in fact. The hollow mockery of the ritual scene is a comment on social pride.

Old Furniture

whilom, formerly. *nut*, bridge.

Hardy is thinking of his home at Higher Bockhampton. Compare D. H. Lawrence's poem 'Things Men Have Made' and the quotation from William Barnes's 'Woak Hill' which Hardy uses with reference to 'old furniture' in *FMC*.lvi, 'all a-sheenen/Wi' long years o' handlen'. The fifth verse recalls 'To my Father's Violin'; in the MS, its second line begins, 'My father's'. The two preceding stanzas illustrate Hardy's close observation admirably.

A Thought in Two Moods

Hardy's thought is of death, 'transformation', and 'dust to dust'. The daisies suggest that Ethleen is a substitute for Emleen or Emma Hardy.

The Last Performance (1912)

Emma Hardy in the autumn of 1912, not long before her death (*Life*, 359). The poem is 'approximately' true; the visit to the town (Dorchester) may be fictional.

'You on the Tower'

This rather striking dramatization embodies Hardy's regret that he had allowed the pursuit of ambition to come between him and shared happiness during his first marriage. He had been 'looking away' (cf. 'The Self-Unseeing'). The thought is more positively expressed in Blake's 'Eternity':

> But he who kisses the joy as it flies
> Lives in eternity's sunrise.

The Interloper

The MS title 'One Who Ought Not to be There' refers to the recurrent 'threat of madness which hung over Hardy's first wife' (Purdy, 200). In a discussion of the poem, Hardy stated that 'insanity' was a better word than 'madness'. Subsequently he added the quotation for the 1923 edition of *Collected Poems* (Collins, 25–6). Emma Hardy's odd behaviour would probably not be regarded as insanity in any form today, yet Hardy's evidence on the subject is the most immediate which remains. He must have realized that he had been given hints of her abnormality almost from the outset: the first scene is by the Cornish coast, the second at Sturminster Newton (see p. 140), the third at a country mansion or in London, the fourth on the lawn at Max Gate.

quaint old chaise. Emma drove with her sister and brother-in-law in a 'very pretty basket-carriage' (*SR*. 48, 58). *pale Form your imagings raise.* This must be Death. *Fourth Figure . . . Furnace,* 'like the Son of God' (Daniel, iii. 25).

Logs on the Hearth (December 1915)

Mary Hardy died on 24 November 1915.

The Sunshade

Seen by Hardy on his visit to Swanage in 1916 (*Life*, 373). He and Emma lodged there 'at the house of an invalided captain of smacks and ketches'; here at the end of 1875 he finished *The Hand of Ethelberta* (*Life*, 107).

The Ageing House

Purdy states that the house is Max Gate. The 'fresh fair head' and 'the head has aged' cast doubt on this view. The first is not appropriate to Emma Hardy at the time Max Gate was new (from 1885); nor would Hardy have allowed the second to remain unchanged after his wife's death if he referred to her. The poem seems to have a general significance, and is typically antithetical.

The Caged Goldfinch

The unfortunate ambiguity of the last line probably explains Hardy's rejection of a third stanza, which appeared in the first edition of *Moments of Vision*:

> True, a woman was found drowned the day ensuing,
>   And some at times averred
> The grave to be her false one's, who when wooing
>   Gave her the bird.

The poem seems to have no overtones; as happened often, Hardy wished to record a strange occurrence.

At Madame Tussaud's in Victorian Years

The poem expresses admiration, and some amazement, that a fiddler should delight in the music he played for forty years amid a strange company of waxwork figures. Madame Tussaud toured Britain with her waxworks, and did not set up her permanent exhibition in Baker Street, London, until 1835. As the fiddler played there 'four decades of years ago', it seems unlikely that Hardy was thinking of Madame Tussaud's belief that her first fiddler was the Dauphin of France, who had not died in 1795 but escaped in disguise. Or did Hardy assume that she established her Baker Street exhibition years before 1835? (See Bailey, 390.)

The Ballet

Compare 'A Victorian Rehearsal' (p. 265).

The Five Students

The course followed is life. The seasons from spring to winter harmonize with its stages. The action suggests the vigour of youth initially, but does not grow continuously weaker as one might expect. At the end the poet still stalks his course, as if driven or battling on. The students' preoccupation is life (not academic pursuits), and their existence as a group is imaginary. The poem is written to an antithetical design but, as the order of each fifth line could easily be changed without affecting the metre, there is no reason to assume that the sequence is not intended to be chronological.

First 'dark He' dies. This is Horace Moule (*Life*, 405), who committed suicide in 1873; see 'Standing by the Mantelpiece' (p. 249).

The next to die is 'dark She', This is Helen Holder, Emma Hardy's sister and wife of the rector at St Juliot. She died in 1900; cf. 'A Duettist to her Pianoforte'. The idea of the poem probably came from reading Emma's reminiscences of their life at Kirland Manor near Bodmin: 'My sister and I were very noticeable, she dark and I fair' (*SR.* 36).

Then 'fair He' dies. Identifications have been suggested, e.g. the Rev. Caddell Holder, T. W. Hooper Tolbort (see *Life*, 161-2 and Orel, 255), but they do not fit the chronological sequence. He may have been Henry Joseph Moule (d.1904; see Orel, 66-73);[21] he could have been imagined purely to create the pattern in the poem.

The last of the four to die is 'fair She', Emma Hardy.

Two additional MS verses are given by Purdy (201).

The Wind's Prophecy

The poem arose from Hardy's sense of attachment to another woman (cf. 'On a Heath', pp. 133–4) as he journeyed to Cornwall in March 1870, where he fell in love with Emma Gifford, the 'fair She' of this anti-thetical composition. It seems that the pattern of the poem was a greater determining factor than the reality. Tryphena Sparks, for example, did not have a 'city home' which was 'matched of none' (she was a student at Stockwell Training College); nor was her hair 'ebon'. Could Hardy have been thinking wistfully of Martha Sparks, who had been a ladies' maid in London until her dismissal in 1869 (Gittings, 119)? Possibly the 'dark She' of Hardy's imagination in this poem was the Julia Augusta Martin whom he had loved in his boyhood and visited years later at her London home (Life, 18–21, 41, 102). In physical features she was almost certainly the original of Lady Constantine in Two on a Tower, where the contrasting design applies to hero and heroine. The finest features of the poem are in the scenic description. The verse is unusually vigorous.

Huzza . . . multitude. See 'The Voice of Things' (p. 121). ups it . . . downs. Bold but unjustified simplicity of expression. like old Skrymer. Formerly 'like a giant' (cf. Durlstone Head, Life, 108. References to Norse mythology do not occur in Hardy before 1884; cf. WT. 'Interlopers at the Knap' (i), 'which brought a snore from the woods as if Skrymir the Giant were sleeping there'. each pharos-shine. Revolving beams from the lighthouse on Lundy Island; flashes also, probably, from Hartland Point and Trevose Head.

During Wind and Rain

The scenes imagined by Hardy after reading his wife's reminiscences (see SR. 4–6, 14–15, 30–32) are of two of the homes and gardens of the Gifford family, which Emma remembered from her girlhood at Plymouth. Each of the recollections, bright and happy in itself, is seen through the regret which years and death have brought. The last lines of the stanzas, with their theme of wind and rain, autumnal storm and destruction, end with an image of tomb-stones and sorrow; 'Down their carved names the rain-drop ploughs'. For the implications of the title (change and decay as well as affliction) see 'An Autumn Rain-Scene' and the song which concludes Twelfth Night.[22] Hardy visited Plymouth in 1914 to find the graves of the Giffords and what remained of the places associated with Emma's youth.

He Prefers Her Earthly

The poem (like 'Paradox') reveals a striking change in Hardy's views on immortality in his later years. The death of those dear to him had made him less rationalistic and assured on this subject than he had been (cf. 'Her Immortality', 'His Immortality', 'The To-Be-Forgotten'), and more ready to entertain hopes of immortality in the conventional sense of the word. He recalls Emma's riding in Cornwall, and accepts the possibility that her spirit may ride in the heavens or 'firmament'.

The Dolls

Molly Gone

Hardy recalls his sister Mary (d.1915) – in the garden at Higher Bockhampton, their outings, and her singing. They were devoted to each other. She became a teacher, played the organ in parish churches, and displayed proficiency in sketching and portrait-painting.

The outings (stanza 3) are to Weymouth, up White Sheet Hill (beyond Maiden Newton) to Wynyard's Gap (cf. 'The Home-coming' and 'At Wynyard's Gap'). On the second they caught sight of distant hills, Montacute Crest west of Yeovil and Corton Hill north of Sherborne on the one hand, and Pilsdon and Lewsdon to the west.

framework of fir, 'rustic work' for climbing plants. *porch-quoin*, the corner formed by the outer porch at the Hardy cottage. *regarding its face from her home*. Hardy fancies that the star flashes a sign in response as Mary looks at it from her home. It is not certain whether her old home is intended or Talbothays, where she spent her last years with her brother Henry and her sister Kate. *have meetings*. An old thought; cf. 'The Musing Maiden' (1866).

A Backward Spring (April 1917)

Compare Keats, 'In a drear-nighted December'.

Looking Across (December 1915)

Occasioned by the burial of Mary Hardy. In chronological sequence Hardy thinks of his father (d.1892), his mother (d.1904), his wife, and Mary, all buried at Stinsford, which he could see across the Frome valley from Max Gate. The theme is reinforced by continuity of rhyme.

At a Seaside Town in 1869

The scene is Weymouth (see *Life*, 63–4, where Hardy describes the 'gist' of the poem as 'fancy only'). The subject is rather like that of *The Well-Beloved*, but instead of proving to be a Jill-o'-the-wisp, the ideal She dwells completely in the poet's imagination. Contact with the real world, however, destroys her image.

The Glimpse

There is a slight analogy with the previous poem. Here it is the ghost of a maid with red hair which, once seen, never returns. The story seems incredible; Bailey (398) provides one of a 'red-haired beauty whose ghost is said to appear in black velvet and to lure all men who see her to fall in love with her'.

The Pedestrian

vamp, walk.

Hardy identified the scene as 'Coll-Hill' near Wimborne, where he lived from 1881 to 1883. The meeting therefore may be considered an actual one.

slopped, (literally) flowed over (from superabundance). *wind-thridded*, penetrated (threaded) by the wind. *Nox venit*, the night cometh (John, ix. 4). The end of the poem shows that the Biblical allusion to death is intended. *Schopenhauer*, *Kant*, *Hegel*. German philosophers. *fountained bower*. The Greek Muses, who presided over the arts, were associated with fountains or springs.

'Who's in the Next Room?'

The poem was placed next to 'The Pedestrian' because the subject of both is death. The scene for the dialogue here is at Max Gate. Hardy did not expect he had long to live.

At a Country Fair

Hardy thought it 'the sorriest of pantomimes' because it was an emblem of man, endowed with reason and power for good, but continually misled by others or by his passions and weaknesses; cf. his 'hideous self-treason' in 'Thoughts at Midnight'.

The Memorial Brass: 186–

See 'The Inscription' (p. 195).

Her Love-Birds

Whether the parallel in the poem is based on fact or fancy is not known. The long journey 'citywards' is most probably to London (not, as claimed, to Plymouth, which is 'The Marble-Streeted Town').

Paying Calls

One of Hardy's most successful poems, it maintains a perfect simplicity of style and tone, to conceal its underlying irony until the end.

The Upper Birch-Leaves

There is a hint of Emma Hardy's death in 'November'. At the end, Hardy thinks of his own.

'It Never Looks Like Summer' (8 March 1913)

Written at Boscastle on Hardy's visit after the death of his wife. Compare the ending of 'The Figure in the Scene'. Hardy's pencil sketch of the latter has written under it: 'Beeny Cliff, in the rain – Aug. 22, 1870. "It never looks like summer." E.L.G. (on Beeny).' Emma's words are repeated in DR. xv. 3.

Everything Comes

The scene is at Max Gate, which was exposed and cold when the Hardys entered it in 1885. For the trees planted by Hardy, see Life, 173.

The Man with a Past

Apart from the reference to the first appearance of 'insanity' in Emma Hardy (see 'The Interloper', p. 141), it is difficult to identify the blows. The second which struck her could have been their 'division'; the third, her illness when they lived apart at Max Gate. The blow which Hardy suffered is almost certainly her loss and the subsequent realization of his own shortcomings towards her. The poem shows that he regarded Emma as an innocent victim of fate, and was more sorry for her than for himself. It is the title rather than the poem which suggests that he was thinking with hindsight of his own failings.

He Fears His Good Fortune

Though 'beryl-bespread' suggests that Hardy was thinking about his past (cf. 'The Chimes'), the radiance is too sustained to be taken as a reflection of his life before the 'blow' fell.

He Wonders About Himself (November 1893)

This must be the poem referred to in a note of 28 November 1893, 'He views himself as an automaton' (*Life*, 260). At the time, Hardy was making his final plans for *Jude the Obscure*, the hero of which he regarded as 'my poor puppet' (*Life*, 272). Here he wonders whether he is a puppet ('fantocine'), or whether he has the freedom to influence the general Will, the sum total of forces affecting the thoughts and actions of mankind (cf. 'A Commonplace Day'). The idea had been expressed by Herbert Spencer in *First Principles*, a book which acted on Hardy 'like a patent expander': man is 'one of the myriad agencies through whom works the Unknown Cause; and when the Unknown Cause produces in him a certain belief, he is thereby authorized to profess and act out that belief'. It is found also in J. S. Mill's essay 'Theism', where stress falls on support for 'the Religion of Humanity'; thus 'we may be co-operating with the unseen Being to whom we owe all that is enjoyable in life'. The person flatteringly addressed (line 8) is probably Hardy's friend Mrs Henniker, who had sent him photographs of herself (*ORFW*. 34).

Jubilate

The title refers with evident irony to Psalm c, which is described as a psalm of praise. At one point (We are out of it all!') this fantasy is reminiscent of 'Friends Beyond'. The MS had 'Mellstock ridge' for 'the churchyard wall' (line 11).

great breastplate ... Urim and Thummim, Exodus, xxviii. 15–21, 30. The Urim and Thummim were objects on the breastplate which the High Priest wore for the declaration of Jehovah's will. *theatre scenes*. The comparison recurs in the penultimate verse. *Eden New*, a hymn tune. *in Little-Ease*, on earth, in this life.

He Revisits His First School

wanzing, wasting away. *quarried*, with diamond-shaped panes. *conned*, learned.

This is the school at Lower Bockhampton which Hardy entered when it was opened in 1848. 'Here he worked at Walkingame's Arithmetic and at geography, in both of which he excelled, though his handwriting was indifferent' (*Life*, 16). The following year he was sent to a school in Dorchester.

'I Thought, My Heart'

I wis, to be sure (*wis* could be 'know').

Though undoubtedly arising from Hardy's recollected experience, these verses do not seem to carry personal feeling. The thoughts are too unqualified, the poetic idea is too romantic, and the movement too light, to suggest that they derive from agonizing over the past.

Fragment

Here is the theme of *The Dynasts*, that eventually awareness of human suffering will reach the Immanent Will. Hardy is less absolute and pessimistic than in 'God-Forgotten'. The last lines approximate in thought to the view expressed by Sue Bridehead (*JO*.vi.iii) 'that at the framing of the terrestrial conditions there seemed never to have been contemplated such a development of emotional perceptiveness among the creatures subject to those conditions as that reached by thinking and educated humanity'.

Midnight on the Great Western

Hardy may have seen such a boy and wondered what were his thoughts. The poem, however, is philosophical; its subject could be summed up from 'Lines':

> O wondering child, unwitting Time's design.

The journey is life; the past and the future are uncertain. Yet the implications of 'past' and 'world unknown' extend beyond life on earth. Hardy wonders if the boy, like Wordsworth's in 'Intimations of Immortality', remembers pre-existence:

> . . . trailing clouds of glory do we come
> From God, who is our home:
> Heaven lies about us in our infancy!

The boy is a mystery to Hardy. In JO.v.iii he appears as Little Father Time. Yet the past which he remembers is anything but heavenly:

> A ground swell from ancient years of night seemed now and then to lift the child in this his morning-life, when his face took a back view over some great Atlantic of Time, and appeared not to care about what it saw.

Since the story of Jude revolves round 'a doom or curse of hereditary temperament' (Life, 271), Hardy seems to suggest that the child has inherited a depressed outlook. The factual descriptions of the boy of the poem and the boy of the novel have much in common; and it would be interesting to know which was written first. In Jude the boy is travelling on a train due to arrive at 10 p.m. It would be easy to interpret symbolically the midnight and 'third-class' of the poem.

Honeymoon Time at an Inn

deedily, intently, busily. *conned*, examined, pried into. *reft*, deprived. *outleant*, lying there. *or ever*, before.

The grimly generalized incident depends on the superstition that the breaking of a mirror spells bad luck; cf. D2.v.iii. The old moon, in contrast to the conventional moon as a symbol of romance at 'honey-

moon time', seems to bode ill with its 'deformed decay'. The Spirits
Ironic and the Spirits of Pity are borrowed from *The Dynasts*. The
stanza pattern suggests that Hardy could not complete the design as he
planned. In each verse the fifth line repeats wholly or in part the first;
ll. 2 and 6 rhyme; ll. 3 and 4 rhyme in the last two verses only. Elsewhere there are three third lines which rhyme.

like a moth. This is a visual moonlight image, not a premonition of
death.

The Robin

The verse movement conveys the diminishing happiness of the bird
until it is released from 'the Frost's decree'. See p. 51.

'I Rose and Went to Rou'tor Town'

'Rou'tor Town' is Bodmin, Cornwall, named after Row or Rough
Tor, one of the highest points on Bodmin Moor. Emma Gifford's
father lived at Kirland Manor near Bodmin. He expressed a snobbish
disapproval of Hardy as his son-in-law (possibly in strong terms when
he was in his cups), and some at least of his objections seem to have
been transferred in a modified form to Elfride's father (*PBE*. ix). The
MS of the novel indicates that she had been in love with a farmer (cf.
'The Young Churchwarden', p. 129), 'so much better' than Stephen's
family. In this crisis, like Emma Gifford, she remained loyal to her
lover when he was slandered (cf. Collins, 26), and Hardy may have
remembered this in 'A Woman's Trust'.

The stanza is that of 'When I set Out for Lyonnesse', but the two
poems form a deliberate contrast in spirit. The Rou'tor poem may be
exaggerated to this effect. It is Emma Gifford who leaves her home at
St Juliot in the early morning for Bodmin. The reference to St Benet's
Abbey near Lanivet and the poem 'Near Lanivet, 1872' indicate
August of that year as the time of the setback (see *Life*, 90–1). Yet how
much of the poem can be accepted literally must remain conjectural.

The Nettles

The collocation of this and the previous poem makes one wonder
whether Hardy's mother objected to his marriage, as Mrs Yeobright
did to Clym's, when he gave up his profession in the city (*RN*). The
mother is not Mrs Jethway (*PBE*); her son died unmarried.

In a Waiting-Room

bagman, commercial traveller.

The most remarkable feature of the poem is the subject. A radiance is shed on the 'fly-blown' picture in the 'squalid room' by children's imaginative vitality and hope. The 'beauty of association is entirely superior to the beauty of aspect' (see *Life*, 120–1). 'To find beauty in ugliness is the province of the poet' (*Life*, 213). 'Others find/Poesy ever lurk where pit-pats poor mankind!' (*D*2.III.i).

The Clock-Winder

The real subject for Hardy is the drawing near of death. The last sixteen lines were a late addition. They are less convincing than the sounds of the church clock, which are admirably reproduced.

a drying Dead Sea, a diminishing interval of life that offers no solace (like the undrinkably salt Dead Sea).

Old Excursions (April 1913)

With the exception of 'Casterbridge', all the names of the places Hardy visited with Emma are actual.

climb up there. Probably to Ridgeway on the Weymouth road. Cerne (Abbas) and Sydling (St Nicholas) are to the north of Dorchester. For Sydling, the MS gives Sutton Mill (at Sutton Poyntz, which contributed much to the setting of 'Overcombe Mill' in *The Trumpet-Major*).

The Masked Face

wight, creature, person. *ken*, knowledge, understanding.

Hardy's image of Life is not memorable. For the entrance and exit doors, compare 'Midnight on the Great Western'; for the title, see 'The Last Chrysanthemum'.

In a Whispering Gallery

lacune, empty space.

The gallery runs round the base of the dome in St Paul's Cathedral. For Hardy's momentary belief in transcendent things, compare 'He Prefers Her Earthly'. The spirit is that of St Paul; see I Corinthians, xv. 51–5.

The Something that Saved Him

The ending recalls Browning's 'Childe Roland to the Dark Tower Came'. Hardy looks back on his sufferings and depression (cf. 'In Tenebris'), and wonders what it was that saved him or kept him going, when he seemed driven into a cul-de-sac of despair. For winter, see 'The Caged Thrush Freed and Home Again' (p. 51).

whirls . . . laved me. Compare the opening of Psalm lxix. *Cit and clown*, the city-dweller (in London) and the countryman.

The Enemy's Portrait

The story seems to have various moral implications; it illustrates man's failure to carry out his intentions, his self-deception, and the dubiousness of evidence.

Imaginings

rolling wheels, carriages. *stressed*, severely restricted.

On the Doorstep (January 1914)

A typical poem of contrasts, but probably no more than the product of a fancy which struck Hardy as he was setting out from Max Gate for a walk after Emma's death.

Signs and Tokens

Hardy's hints on the characters of the speakers create a dramatic framework to local superstitions which he obviously felt worth preserving as an important element in the 'record of a vanishing life' (Orel, 46); cf. 'Premonitions' (p. 230). All the signs here were supposed to foretell death. The last dame does not fear death because she has nothing to lose; she takes the previous speaker to task for faltering when she relates that trotting does have been heard round her domicile ('in the lane' ?).

Paths of Former Time (1913)

Recollections of walks with Emma Hardy in the Frome meadows between Max Gate and Stinsford.

The Clock of the Years (1916)

griff, claw.

The subject is Emma Hardy; the epigraph is from Job (iv. 15).

At the Piano

Whether the 'cowled Apparition' hints at 'insanity' or death is not clear, though the lines –

> But the maid saw no bale,
> And the man no monition

– suggest the former. Hardy is thinking in general terms of the days before Emma suffered from bouts of mental illness, but the picture in the first stanza may be identical with that he had in mind when he wrote *PBE*.iii.

The Shadow on the Stone (begun 1913, finished 1916)

For the Druid stone at Max Gate, see *Life*, 233–4. There is a hint of the legend of Orpheus and Eurydice at the end of the poem.

In the Garden (1915)

Hardy did not reject superstitions altogether, it seems; sometimes he was a rationalist, sometimes not (*Life*, 369–70). The sundial, near which he and his sister Mary leaned, was at Talbothays, where she died on 24 November 1915. It bears the initials MH – HH – KH (Mary, Henry, and Kate Hardy, who all lived at Talbothays), and is dated 1914.

The Tree and the Lady

Probably written with Emma Hardy in mind.

donned . . . bravery . . . greenth, put on my new splendour of green; 'greenth' is analogous to 'blooth', an old form of 'bloom'. *Arcturus*, one of the brightest of the northern stars. *Nor'lights*, the Northern Lights or Aurora Borealis.

An Upbraiding

Written as if from Emma Hardy.

The Young Glass-Stainer (November 1893)

The date of the composition seems to confirm a link with *Jude the Obscure*. In the novel Sue Bridehead designs or illuminates Church-text scrolls; Jude thinks it a 'sweet, saintly, Christian business', but privately Sue reads Gibbon and likes statuettes of Venus and Apollo. At Wardour Castle she prefers paintings by Lely and Reynolds to the devotional pictures which hold Jude's attention. He studies to enter the Church, but gives up this career for Sue. Much in the novel may be regarded as a dramatization of the conflict between conventional Christianity and Hellenism.

Looking at a Picture on an Anniversary
(spring 1913)

Hardy met Emma Gifford on 7 March 1870. The MS of the poem gives 'March 1913'. Although the poet addresses her picture, Hardy was in Cornwall on the 1913 anniversary of their first meeting (*Life*, 361).

rainbow-rays. Cf. 'Her Apotheosis', 'To Outer Nature', and 'On a Fine Morning'. The first use of the iris-bow image by Hardy to express the idealizing effect of love is found in *W*.xvi. Hardy sent Browning a copy of *Wessex Tales* as a birthday greeting in May 1888; as a result Browning may have read *The Woodlanders* and used the same image in the Prologue to *Asolando* (1889).

The Choirmaster's Burial

The story is told by Michael Mail, who played the tenor-viol (see 'The Paphian Ball'). The burial is that of Hardy's grandfather, the 'William Dewy' of the legendary Mellstock 'quire' in which Michael Mail played. 'As if the superintendence of the Stinsford choir were not enough distraction from business for Thomas Hardy the First', he would assist other choirs; it was his 'custom to assemble the rather perfunctory rank-and-file of the choir at his house'; his 'death having been quite unexpected . . . there could be no such quiring over his grave as he had performed over the graves of so many, owing to the remaining players being chief mourners' (*Life*, 10, 12, 13). Hardy's grandfather died in January 1937, wintry weather being given in the poem as the reason for the omission of the 'quiring'.

psalm . . . Mount Ephraim, the metrical version of Psalm xcvii, played to the tune 'Mount Ephraim', according to one of the Hardy music books (Bailey, 415).

The Man Who Forgot

Hardy is thinking of the summer-house in the rectory garden at St Juliot; he had never revisited Cornwall during his first marriage. Cf. 'Where They Lived'.

While Drawing in a Churchyard

The vision of the buried as 'Enlarged in scope' is reminiscent of 'Friends Beyond' and 'Jubilate'. For all three the scene is 'Mellstock' churchyard with its old yew tree. The poem alludes to Wordsworth's 'A slumber did my spirit seal':

> No motion has she now, no force;
>   She neither hears nor sees;
> Rolled round in earth's diurnal course,
>   With rocks, and stones, and trees.

'For Life I Had Never Cared Greatly'

haply, perchance.

The opening is consistent with Hardy's views: compare a childhood experience and its re-affirmation on his eighty-sixth birthday (*Life*,

15-16 and 'He Never Expected Much'). The conclusion, however, seems too vague and optimistic to square with Hardy and his later outlook. If the uncloaked star alludes to Swinburne's 'save his own soul [man] hath no star' (*Life*, 345), and connotes dedication to the truth, it could hardly be said to *illumine* Hardy's later 'pilgrimage'; nor was he likely to forget 'the rough highway'.

POEMS OF WAR AND PATRIOTISM

Most of these poems were written during the First World War of 1914-18. Hardy loathed, and agonized over, war (cf. 'The Man he Killed' and the role of the Pities in *The Dynasts*),yet he was no pacifist: 'when I feel that it must be, few people are more martial than I, or like better to write of war in prose and rhyme' (*ORFW*. 85). See *Life*, 365-6.

'Men Who March Away' (5 September 1914)

This was Hardy's response to the appeal made to writers at a meeting three days earlier in London, to which he was summoned 'at the instance of the Cabinet' (*Life*, 366-7). It was published in *The Times* on 9 September.

His Country (1913)

cot, cottage. *denizenship*, citizenship.

History seems to show that this conception of the brotherhood of man (cf. 'A Plaint to Man') has waxed and waned since the poem was written.

England to Germany in 1914 (autumn 1914)

Hardy quotes one of the jingoistic slogans which was used ostensibly to justify massive war by a self-righteous appeal to God.

On the Belgian Expatriation (18 October 1914)

meted, fixed, regular.

Prompted by the arrival of Belgian refugees in England.

Land of Chimes. An allusion to famous carillons in Belgian churches and cathedrals.

An Appeal to America on Behalf of the Belgian Destitute (December 1914)

Printed in *The New York Times* and other American newspapers. Hardy
wrote in response to an invitation sent on 9 December (*MGC.* p. 103,
letter 1906).

The Pity of It (April 1915)

Hardy believed that 'the group of oligarchs and munition-makers
whose interest is war' had 'stirred' the German people 'up to their
purposes' (cf. *ORFW.* 166, 177). As an example of how the kinship
between the Germans and the English was still to be heard in the
English language, he drew attention to Grammer Oliver's use of
''Ch woll' (*W*.xvii).

In Time of Wars and Tumults (1915)

In Time of 'the Breaking of Nations' (1915)

'I believe it would be said by people who knew me well that I have a
faculty . . . for burying an emotion in my heart or brain for forty years,
and exhuming it at the end of that time as fresh as when interred. For
instance, the poem entitled "The Breaking of Nations" contains a
feeling that moved me in 1870, during the Franco-Prussian war, when
I chanced to be looking at such an agricultural incident in Cornwall.
But I did not write the verses till during the war with Germany of
1914, and onwards' (*Life*, 378; cf. 78–9).

couch-grass. As this coarse grass spreads rapidly, it is removed from arable
land and burnt at the end of the cropping-season. The old horse in the
scene Hardy remembered was harrowing the field in the Valency
valley below, to remove such weeds and prepare the soil for the next
sowing.

Cry of the Homeless (August 1915)

A forced, rhetorical poem compared with the previous. It was written
at the request of Henry James and first printed in *The Book of the*

Homeless (ed. Edith Wharton) to raise money for the Belgian refugees. Readers who are surprised at Hardy's maledictions should remember that the Belgians were innocent victims of unprovoked aggression; compared with vengeance threatened in the Bible (e.g. Jeremiah, li, from which 'the breaking of nations' was taken), they are moderate and finally humane.

Before Marching and After (September 1915)

Frank William George, the son of Hardy's second cousin, was killed at Gallipoli in August 1915. In April, before going on active service, he had visited Max Gate (*Life*, 370, 371), which provides the setting of the poem. He was dear to Hardy and his wife Florence, and it was their intention to leave Max Gate to him.

'Often When Warring' (1915)

In D2.IV.v the soldiers of opposing armies are seen drinking and shaking hands across a brook during a lull in the battle of Talavera.

Then and Now (1915)

The reference to Rama (Matthew, ii. 16–18) emphasizes the slaughter of the innocent.

A Call to National Service (March 1917)

This rather Wordsworthian sonnet was written in response to an appeal from the National Service Department at a time when the Allies were hard beset in France as a result of Russia's military collapse.

The Dead and the Living One (1915)

Described by Hardy as 'a war ballad of some weirdness' (*Life*, 372). The impact of the final irony is driven home with a crescendo of iteration.

A New Year's Eve in War Time (1915–16)

Just before its appearance in *The Sphere*, Hardy informed Mrs Henniker that the incident happened 'not so long ago' at Max Gate (*ORFW.*

175). The 'Young Unknown' (the New Year) was fraught with the disasters of continuing war in Europe. This theme is reinforced by the protracted sound of the wind in the pines which is heard at the opening, echoed at the end of each verse, and renewed at the end.

gable-cock, weathercock on the gable.

'I Met a Man' (1916)

The speaker is imagined to have returned with 'shining face and eye', after hearing the Creator soliloquize on the War, as Moses returned after communion with Jehovah on Mt Sinai (Exodus, xxxiv. 29). The Imperialists are compared to gamblers who promote the bloody sport of cock-fighting; they 'pit' men in war to the death ('main' is a cock-fight).

my malign compeer. Hardy accepts a view discussed by J. S. Mill that God may have been unable to prevent Nature's defects and internecine warfare because the powers of Evil were too strong. Lacking omnipotence, he needs the co-operation of humanity ('Theism' in *Three Essays on Religion*, 1874). *mistake . . . I made with Saul*. Saul was reproved by Samuel because, in attacking the Philistines, he had 'not kept the commandment of the Lord'. The reference is strange, because Saul was next accused of disobeying the Lord in not utterly destroying the Amalekites (I Samuel, xiii, xv.).

'I Looked Up from My Writing'

This strange poem suggests that Hardy believed he could do something to ameliorate the lot of mankind by his writing. He asks the question in 'He Wonders About Himself', and it is apparent in his preface to *The Woodlanders*. Now he asks what is the value of any effort in a world which seems mad. It is typical of Hardy's fantasy that he imagines the moon peering at him and putting the question.

FINALE

This consists of two personal poems, the first relating to Emma Hardy, the second to himself.

The Coming of the End

The poem commemorates stages in Hardy's life with Emma: their courtship in Cornwall; Sturminster Newton; the removal to Max Gate; Emma's refusal to visit Hardy's mother (on Sunday afternoons, *Life*, 442); her sudden death.

afar from the crowd. Cf. 'Far from the madding crowd' (Gray's 'Elegy'). Hardy had written 'afar in the west'.

Afterwards

Hardy thinks of the coming of his own end. Once again, it is obvious that he did not expect to live long enough to achieve another volume of poetry. He hoped he would be remembered for his sensitive observation (his interest in 'the full-starred heavens' should not be overlooked) and for his altruism, which included all living creatures. See *AHC*. 182–3 and the references to 'cruelty to birds and animals' in *ORFW*.

May month . . . leaves like wings . . . silk. Cf. 'the May month when beech trees have suddenly unfolded large limp leaves of the softness of butterflies' wings' (*W*.xlvii). *dewfall-hawk.* Generally called the 'nighthawk' by Hardy. In *CM*. 'The Romantic Adventures of a Milkmaid' (iii) he may have had the same scene in mind: it is moonlight, and the night-hawk is heard 'from the bough of an isolated tree on the open hillside'. Cf. *RN*.iv.vii.

6

Late Lyrics and Earlier

THE most accurate statement on the chronology of these poems is provided in the first paragraph of the 'Apology'. Irrespective of this preface, *Late Lyrics and Earlier* is the longest of Hardy's eight collections of poetry, though it contains only 151 poems. Its range of subjects made R. L. Purdy describe the volume as in many respects 'the most representative of Hardy's whole career'. The period of remorse and emotional stress seems to be at a distance, and a lighter kind of lyric comes to the fore, not always designated as 'song' but written as if for music,[23] and relatively detached, even when based on recollections of Emma Hardy.

APOLOGY

Perhaps this title was chosen with Sidney's *Apologie for Poetry* in mind. Hardy defends his position as a poet, particularly against the charge of pessimism, and discusses the role of poetry in the future. Here he is influenced by Matthew Arnold, but the alliance he envisages between religion and rationality is essentially that of a scientific humanist, rooted deeply in the Positivist humanitarianism of Comte. Some remarks are interposed on the dangers of interpreting tone and intention in verse miscellanies. (Recent history has shown that, with Hardy, a greater one arises from the difficulty of distinguishing between the personal and the 'impersonative'.)

Had Hardy not been recommended to define his views, it is probable that the Apology would never have been written. Most of it came to him when he was seriously ill in January 1922. He sought advice on publishing it, and abridged it, though he was advised not to omit a word. The influence of Wordsworth's preface to *Lyrical Ballads* and of Arnold's critical essays is strong. Hardy's scholarship is reflected also in his quotations and references; they show a familiarity with the writings of Heine, Shakespeare, and Coleridge, the poetry of Wordsworth and Tennyson, *Candide* ('Panglossians'), *Gil Blas*, the life of Shelley, and (above all) the Bible.

Levitical passing-by. See the parable of the good Samaritan: Luke, x. 29–37. *loving-kindness.* Compare 'A Plaint to Man'. Hardy's only hope for the progress of civilization lay in the growth of altruism or Christian 'charity' and the enlightened use of scientific knowledge. *modicum of free will . . . equilibrium.* Hardy believed that man is rarely free to make a rational choice. Material needs, heredity, environmental factors, prejudice, and passion suspend or usurp the sway of reason. There seems to be a parallel for Hardy in these forces and those on which depend 'the balancings of the clouds' (Job, xxxvii. 16). The whole universe, including the human race, is active. Physical and human actions, far removed in space and time, influence the course of present events. Raging storms correspond to dynastic, public, and private turmoils; only rarely is the individual free from pressures, and able to reflect and make a rational choice, just as there is seldom a perfect equilibrium in the universal complex of forces operating at any place and time. See *Life*, 335. *Frederic Harrison*, a Positivist friend of Hardy who was a great Evolutionary optimist. He had reviewed the 1919 edition of Hardy's *Collected Poems* in *The Fortnightly Review*. One heading might serve for every poem, he wrote: 'It is *Memento Mori*.' Hardy does not quote him accurately; see F. Harrison, *Novissima Verba*, London, 1921, pp. 27–34. *a Romanist*, J. M. Hone in *The London Mercury*, February 1922. See Orel, 266 and *ORFW*. 201. *application of ideas to life.* See p. 29. *Mars Hill.* The Areopagus in Athens. See Acts, xvii. 16–31. *keep moving, becoming.* The idea is Arnold's; see *Culture and Anarchy* (I). *witches of Endor.* See I Samuel, xxviii, and compare Hardy on spiritualism in February 1918:

> What a setback this revival of superstition is! It makes one despair of the human mind. Where's Willy Shakespeare's 'So noble in reason' now!

the truth . . . free. See p. 260. *removing those things . . . shaken.* Hebrews, xii. 27.[24] *looped orbit.* Progress is not continuous. After an advance comes a setback which is followed by a further advance. Progress is imagined therefore as a line which creates a series of loops as it moves, judging it as a whole, steadily forward. *forlornly hope.* Hardy's hope had diminished with the 1914–18 war. It made him regret that he had ended *The*

Dynasts on an optimistic note (*Life*, 368). The later poems will show less criticism of a vague ultimate called the First Cause, or collective force known as the Immanent Will, and much more emphasis on the 'unreason' of man.

Weathers

bills, sings.

Artful modulation of the stanza contributes largely to the pleasure given by the contrasting scenes. No particular inn is intended.

hill-hid tides throb. The MS shows that the sea beyond the hills is intended. *on gate-bars*. Cf. 'At Middle-Field Gate in February'.

The Maid of Keinton Mandeville (1915 or 1916)

The poem was probably prompted by a note Hardy recorded on the sweet singing of Miss Marsh from Keinton Mandeville (twenty miles off, in south Somerset) at a concert in Sturminster Newton ('Stower Town', from the Stour river by which the Hardys lived, 1876–8; see *Life*, 118). The song 'Should he upbraid' meant much to Hardy and his wife, since it recalled the beginning of their romance (cf. *PBE*.iii). The music was written by (Sir) Henry Bishop (1786–1855), who had been the musical director of Covent Garden. He was knighted in 1842. Many of his songs, which included 'Home, Sweet Home', remained popular in the nineteenth century.

Summer Schemes

moon, month.

Epeisodia

pressed, hurried.

The 'episodes' are far too general for any biographical reading. The alternation of strong and weak rhymes, the rhyming of the final lines of the stanzas, and the stressed opening of each line, contribute effectively to the general pattern.

Faintheart in a Railway Train

A record of a momentary impulse. The opening inversions are awkward (line 2: 'At ten the sea passed by me').

At Moonrise and Onwards

vill, village. *mew*, place of confinement. *Heath-Plantation Hill*, a hill on the afforested Puddletown ('Egdon') Heath, beyond the Frome valley from Max Gate. The 'vill', like the fire, must be imaginary. *Wan Woman of the waste*, the moon in space. *Lady of all my time*. The moon's waxing and waning, and its measurement of months would remind Hardy that his days were numbered. The idea of the moon as woman runs through the poem; perhaps Hardy recalled the opening lines to the moon-goddess in Swinburne's *Atalanta in Calydon*:

> Maiden, and mistress of the months and stars
> Now folded in the flowerless fields of heaven.

cyme. Either from the French *cime* (summit) or the architectural term (usually 'cyma') as in D1.v.iv:

> Until the topmost cyme
> Have crowned the last entablature of Time.

The Garden Seat

At night, when reddest flowers appear black, Hardy fancies he sees the ghosts of all who had sat on the garden seat where he used to sit with Emma at Max Gate. Its site was considered sacred after her death; nobody was allowed to tidy it up; and eventually the decrepit seat became overgrown.

Barthélémon at Vauxhall

The poem appeared in *The Times* on 23 July 1921, the anniversary of Barthélémon's death in 1808. The scene was one Hardy had often imagined: 'the weary musician, returning from his nightly occupation [at Vauxhall Gardens] . . ., lingering on Westminster Bridge to see the rising sun and being thence inspired to the composition of music to be heard hereafter in places very different from Vauxhall' (*Life*, 414).

Ken, Bishop Ken (1637–1711), the author of 'Awake, my soul, and with the sun', one of Hardy's favourite hymns, which was sung at Stinsford to Barthélémon on Sunday mornings throughout the year (*Life*, 10). *galleried naves*. Cf. 'A Church Romance'.

'I Sometimes Think'

Hardy may allude to his literary efforts to promote imaginative sympathy and altruism (cf. the preface to *The Woodlanders*), to more practical steps taken to relieve the distressed (e.g. refugees and prisoners during the 1914–18 war), and possibly to the support he gave various organizations for a more humane treatment of animals. In a despondent mood, he felt that hardly anyone had taken note, with the exception of his second wife Florence, who believed in him and all he stood for.

Jezreel (24 September 1918)

Hardy wonders whether any of the soldiers entering Jezreel under General Allenby thought of its Biblical associations: the prophet Elijah confronting Ahab; Jehu, who drove furiously; and the notorious queen Jezebel (see I Kings, xxi. 17–24 and II Kings, ix. 16–37). 'It was written very rapidly . . . it being just a poem for the moment. I thought people did not seem to realize that Esdraelon and Jezreel were the same. Well, as to my having any affection for Jezebel, I don't think I can admit that: I have the same sort of admiration for her that I have for Lady Macbeth, Clytaemnestra, and such. Her courage was splendid' (Hardy to Mrs Henniker, *ORFW*. 182).

A Jog-Trot Pair

The gravel-path is in the garden at Max Gate; the pair are Hardy and his second wife Florence (cf. the chronology, 1907–14; p. xviii). Their wedding was sudden, and appears to have been unromantic. The poem has its unintentional humour. The ending accords with that of *Far from the Madding Crowd*, a story which contrasts romantic passion with a more durable love, 'usually occurring through similarity of pursuits', which grows 'in the interstices of a mass of hard prosaic reality' (lvi).

'The Curtains Now Are Drawn' (1913)

The MS note 'Major and Minor' marks the contrast between the verses. They were written with Emma in mind, first during the period of courtship in Cornwall, secondly after her death. For poetic effect, the rectory at St Juliot seems to be imagined near the harbour at Boscastle.

The suggestion in the context of 'jagged', 'surly', and 'sneering' is that, however hostile the circumstances, love is stronger; in the second verse, love survives death. Yet the emphasis on 'dream' has its irony.

'According to the Mighty Working' (1917)

moiling, toil and turmoil.

The title is taken from the Church of England Burial Service. As the poem was written during the First World War, 'Peace' has its distinct meaning. However peaceful the atmosphere or period seems, unseen events are being continuously created. The universe is a bewildering mass of cause-effect relationships, and all that happens is logically traceable (in the abstract) to a First Cause ('the Spinner of the Years' in 'The Convergence of the Twain').

quick-cued mumming, immediate automatic response. *spinner's wheel.* The image of the potter and his wheel for the shaper of events is found in Edward FitzGerald's *Rubáiyát of Omar Khayyám* and Browning's 'Rabbi Ben Ezra'. Hardy's image is of a wheel spinning so rapidly that it is invisible.

'I Was Not He'

In writing this song, Hardy must have remembered that he was not Emma Gifford's first suitor; cf. 'The Young Churchwarden'.

The West-of-Wessex Girl (begun in Plymouth, March 1913)

squired, escorted.

Emma Gifford was born in Plymouth, and lived (until her marriage) in Devon and Cornwall. See *Life*, 66.

Hoe, the promontory overlooking Plymouth Sound. *marbled ways.* See 'The Marble-Streeted Town' (pp. 195-6). *Andrew's.* See 'Places' (p. 107). *As phantom.* The spirit of Hardy's West-of-Wessex girl draws him. *as planned.* Hardy expressed an inclination to go in 1908 (C. J. Weber, *Dearest Emmie*, London, 1963, p. 70).

Welcome Home

The same ironical idea provides the theme of the narrative framework to *LLI.* 'A Few Crusted Characters', where the hero who returns to 'Longpuddle' and soon departs is appropriately named John Lackland (after John, King of England).

Going and Staying

prime, excellent.

The third stanza (which was added) shows a more impartial view than the first or second, which are more typical of Hardy.

Read by Moonlight

The repetition of the line 'By the cold moon's shine' emphasizes the cold reality. Hardy may have been thinking of Emma's letters.

At a House in Hampstead (July 1920)

In March 1920 Hardy joined the National Committee for acquiring Wentworth Place, Hampstead, the house once occupied by John Keats (*Life*, 404). The poem was included in *The John Keats Memorial Volume*, 1921.

Seven famed Hills. Keats was buried in the Protestant Cemetery at Rome (see 'Rome: At the Pyramid of Cestius' (p. 36). This is the pyramid which beckons with marble finger in one poem and keeps uplifted its white hand in the other, to point the way to Keats's grave and Shelley's.) Keats died in lodgings overlooking the Spanish Steps above the Piazza di Spagna in Rome. *wind-wafts.* Made by his ghost. *umbraged . . . tree,* shaded by the mulberry tree in the garden.

A Woman's Fancy

Her Song

cup-eyed, hollow-eyed. *untouched*, did not touch.

Though not accurate in every detail ('summer . . . him as a new-comer'), the song is based on a recollection of Emma Gifford at St Juliot at the time of Hardy's first visit.

A Wet August (1920)

Hardy recalled the August of his second visit to Emma Gifford in Cornwall (*Life*, 78–9).

the light I bore, of love and hope. *waste world*. Shelley, *Prometheus Unbound*, II. i. 126, where light again is associated with love.

The Dissemblers

The pair who deceive themselves are typical rather than individual, though Hardy can be seen in the man and his regret. The daisies recall Emma Hardy.

To a Lady Playing and Singing in the Morning

The last stanza suggests that Hardy recalled his regret at not having shown greater interest in Emma and her singing during their married life.

'A Man Was Drawing Near to Me'

Emma Gifford's reflections in the evening at St Juliot rectory, just before Hardy's first visit in March 1870. The places indicate stages on his final approach by road from the railway station at Launceston. Tresparret seems much more likely than Tresparret Posts, for the road passed Hennett Byre to the rectory; see map, *AHC.* 352.

legends, ghosts. See *SR.* 39–41, 51–2. *pharos-fire*. See 'The Wind's Prophecy' (p. 144).

The Strange House

The piano-playing and the context of the poem suggest that the 'love-thralls' were Hardy and his first wife.

'As 'Twere To-night'

The song is based on Hardy's recollections of falling in love at St Juliot. See 'A Week' (p. 112).

The Contretemps

The poem belongs to the fictional verse Hardy wrote at Weymouth.

A Gentleman's Epitaph on Himself and a Lady

Hardy may have found evidence of such a burial; there is one in 'A Woman's Fancy'.

Weippert's 'First Set', a series of quadrilles composed probably by John Weippert. Of the Weipperts (who lived in England and wrote countless quadrilles from the early years of the nineteenth century until the 1840s), John and John Michael were the most prolific.

The Old Gown

pomped, rode in pomp.

All the recollections could be of Emma; she attended a Royal Garden Party, for example, on 22 June 1907 (*Life*, 335). The 'gown of fading fashion' was that worn on the evening before Hardy's departure from St Juliot in March 1870.

A Night in November (1913?)

Emma Hardy had died one year previously. *at last you knew*. Probably that Hardy loved her.

A Duettist to Her Pianoforte

Emma Hardy recalls playing duets with her sister Helen, wife of the Rev. Caddell Holder, rector of St Juliot.

pleated show/Of silk. On the upper front of the piano.

'Where Three Roads Joined'

The MS indicates that the place was near Tresparret Posts, Cornwall. Here, recalling a view of the sea that seemed eloquent with the ecstasy of their early love, Hardy imagines the spectres of Emma and himself grieving bitterly that they had allowed happiness to slip from their grasp. The thought that the place too grieves for their tragic mischance is an unusual instance of the pathetic fallacy in Hardy, indicating that 'imaginative reason' operates on a different plane from reason itself (cf. *Life*, 147, 369–70).

'And There Was a Great Calm'

The subject is the conclusion of the First World War. The title is from Matthew, viii. 26. The Spirits are to be found in *The Dynasts*. Much imaginative thought is packed into this poem. Abstractions, including the Spirits, are given greater reality through personification, and much detail of scene is evoked. Hardy had been brought an invitation to contribute to *The Times Armistice Supplement*. At first he was inclined to refuse, being unable to write to order. But 'an idea seized him in the middle of the night . . .' (*Life*, 407).

thinned peoples, with populations diminished by heavy and prolonged recruitment, and by the abandonment of towns and villages as the enemy advanced. '*Huns*', a term of opprobrium for the Germans. *boom*, of a heavy gun. *weft-winged engines*, aeroplanes.

Haunting Fingers

The museum of musical instruments is probably the Horniman Museum, London (Bailey, 449). The poem is arranged in five sections, each of three stanzas beginning and ending with a short line. The first two stanzas of each section consist of dialogue between instruments; the third, of narrative.

Phosphor, the Morning Star. *Amphion*, son of Jupiter and such a musical genius that the walls of Thebes sprang up at the sound of his lyre. *contra-basso*, double bass. *dampered*, subjected to a damper, a device for stopping string-vibration. *clavier*, keyboard. *con*, examine closely. *shawm*, medieval instrument of the oboe class. *Cecilian*, church music (St Cecilia its patron). *faced the sock*, played at comedies. In classical drama, actors wore low shoes ('socks') for comedy, but were buskined for tragedy.

The Woman I Met (1918)

weeting, knowing.

For the origin of this encounter with the ghost of a Piccadilly prostitute, see *Life*, 235.

the Lock, a London hospital for those suffering from venereal disease. *our kind of every feather*, people of all kinds, a cosmopolitan crowd.

Forms. Hardy wrote 'Flesh' against this in his copy of *Collected Poems* (Bailey, 450). *wafts as from clay*, odours suggesting a grave and decomposition.

'If It's Ever Spring Again'

Light verses written (as were many of Hardy's later poems, it seems) for music.

The Two Houses

teens, sorrows. *upfetched*, brought up. *inbe*, dwell (be in).

With the main theme (from the old house) compare the fourth paragraph of *W*.iv, ending: 'It was a house in whose reverberations queer old personal tales were yet audible if properly listened for; and not, as with those of the castle and cloister, silent beyond the possibility of echo.'

hide, skin, outer covering. This humour is maintained by the youthful house in 'Your face wears furrows untold' (where 'untold' means 'beyond telling or counting, innumerable'). By contrast, it reinforces what the old house has to say, filling the new one with awe. *Byss* (bottom, foundation), source of life.

On Stinsford Hill at Midnight

Based on Hardy's experience in February 1894 when he was 'walking back to Dorchester from Bockhampton very late – nearly 12 o'clock. A girl almost in white on the top of Stinsford Hill, beating a tambourine and dancing. She looked like one of the "angelic quire", who had tumbled down out of the sky, and I could hardly believe my eyes. Not a soul there or near but her and myself. Was told she belonged to the Salvation Army, who beat tambourines devotionally' (*Life*, 262). The verse is of the Wordsworthian ballad type.

The Fallow Deer at the Lonely House

Deer from the heath still invade the garden in front of the Hardy cottage at Higher Bockhampton. The thought of its loneliness when Hardy's grandparents first occupied it, and the 'garden-plots and orchards' were still 'uncultivated slopes' (see 'Domicilium'), could be the background inspiration of the poem. The contrast between the warmth and glow within and the glistening snow outside is out-weighed by the glow in the eyes of the wondering deer. Those within are unaware of it, yet the fascinating spectacle of curiosity in the deer suggests a natural affinity between man and the animal world (cf. altruism: *Life*, 346–7). There are no overtones of ominous superstition as in 'Signs and Tokens'.

The Selfsame Song

To the personal associations evoked by the song of the bird Hardy links a thought on lines in Keats's 'Ode to a Nightingale':

> Thou wast not born for death, immortal Bird!
>   No hungry generations tread thee down;
> The voice I hear this passing night was heard
> In ancient days by emperor and clown:
> Perhaps the self-same song that found a path
>   Through the sad heart of Ruth, when, sick for home,
>   She stood in tears amid the alien corn. . . .

The Wanderer

The poem concludes with a vagrant's thought that it is fitting to sleep *à la belle étoile*, for soon he will be dead and buried. R. L. Stevenson's 'The Vagabond' may have influenced the poem slightly.

witch-drawn, as if impelled by a power he cannot withstand.

A Wife Comes Back

park-pale, park fencing.

The irony and surprise of the ending soon lose their effect, for the combined themes of love's illusion and the effect of age had become rather hackneyed with Hardy.

A Young Man's Exhortation (1867)

Although its basis coincides with Hardy's customary view of life, the shallow cynicism of this poem is not his. He believed in seeing life as it is, with all its faults, not according to conventional views or as an escapist. He did not believe in the 'preciousness of dreams'. The poem is written stylistically, with deft alliteration and lyrical tautness.

passing. The term is ambiguous; it probably means 'surpassing' as opposed to the passing joys of life. *aspects are within us.* The illusion is exposed in 'The Well-Beloved'. Here the young man exhorts us to take refuge in illusion: 'who seems/Most kingly is the King'.

At Lulworth Cove a Century Back (September 1920)

Hardy's interest in a possible link between Keats and Dorset arose no doubt from the fact that a Keats family lived at Higher Bockhampton. Llewellyn Powys ('Some Memories of Thomas Hardy', Toucan Press, 1969) recorded a conversation in which Hardy said that a family of saddlers named Keats lived at Broadmayne (on the road to Lulworth Cove and near Warmwell) when he was a boy. He had wondered if they were related to the poet, and sometimes 'indulged a fancy' that Keats might have walked over the down to see them when the ship taking him to Italy was driven to shelter in Lulworth Cove. Warmwell Cross is the crossroads near Warmwell. In 'He looks up at a star' Hardy alludes to Keats's sonnet 'Bright star! would I were steadfast as thou art'.

A Bygone Occasion

evened, equalled.

Based on a recollection of Emma Gifford's singing at St Juliot.

Two Serenades

Cassiopeia . . . Seven of the Wain, two constellations, the latter known as Charles's Wain (Waggon) or the Plough.

The Wedding Morning

The brief dramatization hardly succeeds in giving life to a rather hackneyed subject. For 'Carry', compare 'Carrey Clavel' (p. 77).

End of the Year 1912

Hardy is thinking of the death of his wife in November. The six bells are those of Fordington Church ringing in the New Year.

The Chimes Play 'Life's a Bumper' (1913)

Written with the death of Emma Hardy in mind, and with an obvious play on 'Bumper' (first indicative of success, and finally of shock).

'I Worked No Wile to Meet You'

unprimed, not ready. *unrecked*, uncared for. *influent star*. At one time stars were thought to influence character and destiny. *hydromels*, drinks of water and honey, a kind of mead. *Round with the turning sphere*. Cf. Wordsworth, 'A slumber did my spirit seal'.

At the Railway Station, Upway

Upwey (Hardy's Upway) is north of Weymouth.

The prisoner would be on his way to the County Gaol at Dorchester. The irony is hackneyed. Goldsmith (1728–74) has a prisoner in gaol who rejoices in the liberty of the English (*The Citizen of the World*, iv).

Side by Side

distuned, out of tune.

Dream of the City Shopwoman (1866)

garreteer, one who lives in a garret. *list*, listen.

'From Her in the Country' (also written in 1866) is an ironical companion to this.

this eternal wheel refers to the incessant movement and crowding of life in London; cf. *Life*, 131, 137, 171. 'This hum of the wheel – the roar of London!' For its grime, compare 'To a Tree in London'.

A Maiden's Pledge

The Child and the Sage (21 December 1908)

Hardy's views are inconsistent; cf. 'To Sincerity' (pp. 85–6). The question which concludes the poem seems to come from Hardy the perfectionist rather than represent the innocence of a child; and it could be argued that Browning in 'Rabbi Ben Ezra' and *The Ring and the Book* shows a more robust attitude to life, though Hardy, in a letter to Edmund Gosse, dismissed his philosophy as the 'smug Christian optimism of a dissenting grocer'.

Mismet

Hardy reflects 'that curious refinement of cruelty . . . which often proceeds from the bosom of the whimsical god at other times known as blind Circumstance' (*WT*. 'Fellow-Townsmen', viii). Rarely do the two halves meet at the right juncture to form the perfect whole (cf. *TD*.v and *LLI*. 'The History of the Hardcomes'). So it was in Hardy's life and in his novels: Clym and Eustacia, Grace Melbury and Fitzpiers, Tess and Alec d'Urberville, Jude and Arabella, Jude and Sue Bridehead. Compare also 'Fellow-Townsmen'.

An Autumn Rain-Scene (October 1904)

Hardy described this as 'mild' and 'trifling' (*ORFW*. 199). The rain seems to signify what it does in Feste's song at the end of *Twelfth Night*. Hardy's philosophy is different; only the dead are free from. 'Little-Ease' (cf. 'Jubilate').

Meditations on a Holiday (May 1921)

Hardy thinks in turn of the regions he might visit for a holiday, but the thought that those he associated with them are dead deters him (cf. *Life*, 295 and *ORFW*. 65). He associates Tristram and Iseult with 'Lyonnesse' (Cornwall), Shakespeare with Stratford-on-Avon, Wordsworth with the Lake District, Burns and Scott with Scotland, Shelley with London. The 'town street' is Skinner Street, where Shelley fell in love with Mary Godwin, and whence they eloped, accompanied by Claire Claremont, in 1814. The liveliness of the metre is a sufficient indication that the theme is not serious.

An Experience

There is a lack of explicitness in this poem (as in several others) which suggests that Hardy sometimes wrote more for his own satisfaction than for the reader. 'Fetching Her' shows that 'My friend' may be no more than a dramatizing address. Gittings (38-9) believes it refers to

Horace Moule (cf. 'Before my Friend Arrived'). If this is so, Hardy recalls walks and talks with him in the Dorchester region which were exhilarating and unforgettable.

cobwebbed, crazed. Hardy was not 'the subtlest one' at the time; intellectual cobwebs needed removing. His thought was uncoordinated and flawed, 'in pieces' ('crazed' in its earliest sense). He scarcely knew what would be the outcome ('Might pend') of what he had heard.

The Beauty

wanzing, decline. *clam*, become feverish.

Although about London, Hardy's note was not taken from a London paper but from *The Dorset County Chronicle* (as an entry in his notebook shows). For the thought, compare Thomas Carew's 'He that loves a rosy cheek', a poem which Hardy would know from *The Golden Treasury*.

The Collector Cleans His Picture

luthern, dormer-window.

The speaker is William Barnes, the Dorset poet and rector of Winterborne Came. At Max Gate, Hardy lived near him; see 'The Last Signal' (p. 137). The poem is based on a passage in the biography of Barnes by his daughter Mrs Lucy Baxter. This shows that most of the poet's picture-collecting took place before he entered the Church (*The Life of William Barnes*, London, 1887, pp. 151–2). The picture revealed when the 'grimefilms' are removed may be Hardy's fancy. There is some disguise in the poem (the 'soon-reached city', the 'adjacent steeple'; 'steeple' can mean 'church tower', but the church at Winterborne Came is a long way from the rectory). Compounds such as 'artfeat', 'brushcraft', and 'grimefilms' are in the style of Barnes. The epigraph, from the Vulgate, reads: 'Son of man, behold, I take away from thee the desire of thine eyes with a stroke.'

dew-fleece, fleece-like covering of dew.

The Wood Fire

shroff, odds and ends, waste.

Ostensibly about the three crosses on Calvary after the Crucifixion, the poem 'was inspired by the news of the clearance of the wooden crosses on the old Western Front' (in France, after the First World War). It 'brought down on Hardy the allegation of blasphemy, which he very keenly resented' (Edmund Blunden, *Thomas Hardy*, London, 1958, p. 167).

Kranion. Greek for 'the place of a skull' or 'Golgotha' (John, xix. 17).

Saying Good-bye

On the Tune Called the Old-Hundred-and-Fourth

Thomas Ravenscroft's setting to Psalm civ was published in 1621, and was one of Hardy's favourite hymn tunes. The poem is addressed to Emma Hardy, as he remembered her singing in the drawing-room at Max Gate while he worked upstairs in his study.

Old-Hundred-and-Fourth. 'Old' signifies the pre-Tate and Brady metrical psalms. Those by Sternhold and Hopkins (1562) had formed almost the whole hymnody of the Church of England for nearly two centuries. *Sheol*, the world of the dead (Hebrew).

The Opportunity

It is rather typical of Hardy's hindsight over lost opportunities in love that he seems to assume that an offer of marriage from him would have been accepted. In May 1874 he met Helen Paterson, illustrator of *Far from the Madding Crowd* (*Life*, 100). The following August, just before Hardy's marriage to Emma Gifford, she married the poet William Allingham. In answer to Edmund Gosse in 1906, Hardy wrote (Purdy, 220):

> Though I have never thought of her for the last 20 years your inquiry makes me feel 'quite romantical' about her (as they say here), and as she is a London artist . . . you might hunt her up, and tell me what she looks like as an elderly widow woman. If you do, please give her my kind regards, but you must not add that those two almost simultaneous weddings would have been one but for a stupid blunder of God Almighty.

The light measure (which suggests that the ills of Chance have to be shrugged off) is that of Browning's 'Youth and Art' (*Dramatis Personae*), where the theme is the same:

> Each life unfulfilled, you see;
>   It hangs still, patchy and scrappy:
> We have not sighed deep, laughed free,
>   Starved, feasted, despaired, – been happy.

> And nobody calls you a dunce,
>   And people suppose me clever:
> This could but have happened once,
>   And we missed it, lost it for ever.

Evelyn G. of Christminster

Written on the death of Emma Hardy's cousin, Evelyn Gifford of Oxford. She was the daughter of the archdeacon who officiated at Hardy's marriage, and he held her in high regard. She died on 6 September 1920 (cf. *Life*, 101, 397–8, 407). The explanation of 'Christminster' for 'Oxford' is to be found in a rather forced parallel that emerges intermittently in *Jude the Obscure*.

The Rift

The song is too vague in reference to tell whether it has autobiographical overtones. 'We faced but chancewise (we met by chance) after that' suggests that it is fictional.

Voices from Things Growing in a Churchyard

withwind, bindweed, convolvulus.

Hardy records that Walter de la Mare visited Max Gate in June 1921, walked with him to Stinsford, 'and was much interested in hearing about the various graves and in reading a poem . . . just lately written, 'Voices from Things growing in a Country Churchyard'. (Here his memory was led astray by the title of Gray's 'Elegy'.) He then states that Fanny Hurd's name was Fanny Hurden, and that he 'remembered her as a delicate child who went to school with him. She died when she was about eighteen. . .'. Hardy misestimated; she was just over twenty when she died in October 1861. She lived at Higher Bockhampton, and her younger sister Elizabeth was one of the girls Hardy remembered working in Middle Field at harvest time (*Life*, 223, 413-14). The subject recalls 'Transformations', but the metre is more lively, indicative like 'Friends Beyond' and 'Jubilate' of the happiness of mortals who have escaped from 'Little-Ease'. One feature therefore of the double refrain that runs through the poem is 'All day cheerily'. Part of the humour of this fantasy is that each natural 'thing' deferentially overcomes its ignorance of the sex of the person addressed. The repeated 'Sir or Madam' also serves to increase the appeal to readers.

Bachelor Bowring, Benjamin Bowring of Kingston Maurward House (d.1837). His 'feat of change' was delayed because he could afford to be buried in relatively durable oak (a shingle is a board). *Thomas Voss*. He appears in *Under the Greenwood Tree* (I. iv); see *Life*, 92, 214 and 'Winter Night in Woodland'. *Lady Gertrude*. Unidentified, though Hutchins mentions a Gertrude in the Grey family of Kingston Maurward. *Eve Greensleeves*. See Hardy's footnote to the poem. *Audeley Grey*. Like Bowring's, his memorial (to Audley Grey) is in the church at Stinsford – in the north aisle by which the Hardys sat.

On the Way

list, please. *knop*, bud.

The contrast between the neutral tones ('cold listless lustre of a dead man's eye') and the sweet or bright impressions of the lovers is similar to that of 'A Wet August'.

'She Did Not Turn'

The 'table spread' suggests she was expected. There is no evidence that the poem is autobiographical.

Growth in May

neats, cattle.

The scene is near Chard in Somerset. The poem is devalued by its metre, expressions such as 'possessed of the neats' and 'range not greatly', and the failure to produce a climax (rather the reverse) in the association of love with lush pastures (cf. *TD*.xxiv).

The Children and Sir Nameless

Hardy's ironical story of 'Sir Nameless' (a minor Ozymandias) is based on a tradition (referred to in *RN*.i.iii) relating to a battered effigy in the Athelhampton Chapel of St Mary's Church, Puddletown. The historical references are not clear. Hardy said that the effigy of Sir Nameless was 'dated back a hundred years further, to get rid of the doubt about the ruff' (V. Meynell, ed., *Friends of a Lifetime*, London, 1940, p. 291).

At the Royal Academy

foils, leaves.

Compare the note written by Hardy after visiting the Academy exhibition in the spring of 1891 (*Life*, 235):

> They were not pictures of *this* spring and summer, although they seem to be so. All this green grass and fresh leafage perished yesterday; after withering and falling, it is gone like a dream.

Her Temple

A Two-Years' Idyll

At the end of their stay at Riverside Villa, Sturminster Newton (1876–1878), Hardy wrote 'End of the Sturminster Newton idyll', adding later 'Our happiest time' (*Life*, 118). The 'designs smart and tall' were not so much his as Emma's. Her brother had visited them and criticized her for living in so remote a place. She thought she would be 'someone' in London (from a note by Irene Cooper Willis based on talks with Florence Hardy).

By Henstridge Cross at the Year's End

The poem was written during the 1914–18 war, probably near the end. It first appeared under the title of 'By Mellstock Cross at the Year's End' in *The Fortnightly Review* of December 1919. For its inclusion in *Late Lyrics and Earlier* the place was changed, the note added, and the last stanza modified. 'Cross' indicates crossroads, first Bockhampton

Cross in Stinsford parish, then the crossroads at Henstridge, north-west of Sturminster Newton. It will be seen that only the former makes complete sense with reference to Hardy. All the roads taken have led to disappointment. Hardy thinks of his sojourn in London; the decline of collateral ancestors who had owned much property at Woolcombe and Up-Sydling (*Life*, 5, 214–15); his Cornish romance and the death of Emma; finally of the soldiers who marched south for embarkation to the battlefronts. They and their cause are already forgotten by some, and Hardy believes that people who wonder about the purpose of life are out of place in the modern world.

Penance

Perhaps the most dramatic of the poems in which Hardy expresses regret for his neglect of his first wife. The subject is continued in the next, where he looks at her portrait.

'I Look in Her Face'

Hardy looks at a portrait of Emma. For the 'far-off room' at Max Gate, compare 'On the Tune Called the Old-Hundred-and-Fourth'.

After the War

A typical irony or satire of circumstance.

'If You Had Known' (1920)

white-selvaged, white-edged.

The poem (originally in the first person) records the laying of roses on Emma Hardy's grave at Stinsford exactly fifty years after being caught in the rain with her on the cliffs in Cornwall. Hardy remembered his second visit in August 1870; cf. 'The Figure in the Scene'.

The Chapel-Organist

vinaigrette, smelling-bottle.

Hardy chose (ironically) to write this poem in the metre of Browning's 'Abt Vogler'. Both are soliloquies by organists. One rises to 'high philosophy'; the other reveals a scandal. High Street and 'this little chapel down here' could be in any town within convenient travelling distance of 'Havenpool' by rail. The scene could be Dorford Chapel, near the lower end of High East Street, Dorchester.

Old-Hundredth . . . Eaton, hymn tunes. *Tallis . . . Ken.* From Tallis, the tune for the evening hymn 'Glory to Thee, my God, this night', the organist's thoughts turn to Bishop Ken's morning hymn 'Awake, my soul, and with the sun' (cf. *Life*, 10 and 'Barthélémon at Vauxhall').

Fetching Her

outing, going out.

A dramatic lyric with general overtones but reminiscent of Emma Hardy.

'Could I but Will'

Though the usual Hardy overtones are in 'this frozen scene' (cf. 'A Self-Glamourer'), and he feels something deeper than sympathy for the 'unbetrothed', the yearning after perfection in this poem is not to be taken too seriously, as the ending indicates. 'Mid which old friends and I would walk/With weightless feet and magic talk' undercuts the whole very considerably. As in earlier songs, the minor key for the second verse (where the subject is the death of a girl who did not live to enjoy the love she expected) suggests a sadder tone.

She Revisits Alone the Church of Her Marriage

The kind of lyric that escapes notice among the host of Hardy's collected poems. It is one of his most finished. Though tautened with stresses and subject to telling rhyme-scheme and repetition, it keeps close to living language; 'but, anyhow, I made my vow' shows Hardy's readiness to follow Browning in the use of speech idiom. The poem illustrates the imaginative selectivity at Hardy's command in evoking a common emotional experience.

At the Entering of the New Year (31 December, 1914–17)

Hardy contrasts the cheerfulness of New Year's Eve in his youth and the gloomy expectations (better undisclosed) it brings in war-time.

allemands, *heys*, *poussettings*, German dances, country dances, dancing round and round with linked hands. *muffled peal*, of church bells. *mystic*, enigmatical.

They Would Not Come

Occasioned by one of Hardy's visits to Cornwall, probably that of 1916. The verses recall the church where Emma had worshipped, the reading of lessons by her brother-in-law, and picnicking by the sea.

lectioned, read. The lectionary comprises those portions of Scripture appointed for Church of England services. *Shows contingent*. Cf. 'gear of the Present' above. *night wisps*, will o' the wisps, which were supposed to mislead night wanderers in marshy places.

After a Romantic Day

liquid, clear, serene.

Hardy had used a railway cutting for a scene of incipient romance in *L.1.xi–xii*. For him Nature was played out as a Beauty, and the poet's province was to find beauty in everyday things, even in ugliness (*Life*, 185, 213). The 'popular commonplace' is that 'science, steam, and travel must always be unromantic', but the 'poetry of place' depends on the feelings of the beholder.

sheet . . . visions. For the precise metaphor, see 'A Plaint to Man' (ll. 10–12).

The Two Wives

Except for the irony of the last two lines, this is the story of 'Fellow-Townsmen' (*WT*).

'I Knew a Lady'

Another club-story (hardly a 'song'), with a similar irony in the tail.

A House with a History

says, things said.

Compare 'The Two Houses' (p. 172). One of the houses Hardy knew best in London was Lady Jeune's (79 Harley Street).

A Procession of Dead Days

The days recalled as ghosts are associated with Emma Hardy, from Hardy's first meeting her to her death.

the mumbling river, the Valency below St Juliot and towards Boscastle. *the rainbow sign* suggests blessing. It was a token of God's promise after the Flood (Genesis, viii. 21 – ix. 17). Here it probably relates to Hardy and Emma's engagement. *a meteor act*. Their marriage. *I close my eyes*. Hardy probably had in mind Emma's mental illnesses, which caused inevitable sufferings. *I did not know . . . glossed the thrums/Of ivy*. Hardy did not know his wife was seriously ill until the morning of her death (*Life*, 359–60). The morning light caused the hard persistent tufts of ivy flowers to shine. The evergreen ivy, crowning a skull, has been commonly associated with death and immortality. *third hour*. By Biblical reckoning. This indicates that Emma Hardy died between 8 and 9 a.m. According to Rebekah Owen, she died 'about 8 a.m.' (*HLMSq*. 162). The choice of 'third hour' was undoubtedly influenced by Mark, xv. 25: 'And it was the third hour, and they crucified him.'

He Follows Himself

dree, suffering.

In this characteristically dramatized lyric Hardy observes his heart, and finds that it turns to the grave of a friend – a slight disguise for his sorrow over the loss of Emma. The yew-plumes suggest the tree over her grave at Stinsford. Not surprisingly Hardy queried 'love' for 'friend' and 'her' for 'his' in his copy of *Collected Poems* (Bailey, 472).

The Singing Woman

Without, Not Within Her

The poem expresses the effect of Emma Gifford's zest for life on Hardy. 'She was so *living*, he used to say' (*Life*, 73; the same italicized expression is used with reference to Elfride, *PBE*.iv). Her freshness of spirit drove away all his gloom.[25]

bale, and ban, misery and gloominess suggesting a curse. *corn-chaff . . .*

fan. The image comes from Matthew, iii. 12: 'Whose fan is in his hand, and he will throughly (thoroughly) purge his [threshing-] floor, and gather his wheat into the garner; but he will burn up the chaff with unquenchable fire.'

'O I Won't Lead a Homely Life'

At one point, each stanza evokes a snatch of a lively violin tune.

In the Small Hours

The dream-tunes recall those times when Hardy the boy accompanied his father to fiddle at farm-parties. 'Haste to the Wedding' is not surprising, for 'little Thomas played sometimes at village weddings, at one of which the bride, all in white, kissed him in her intense pleasure at the dance' (*Life*, 23); the tune, moreover, is found in the Hardy music books.

The Little Old Table

This is probably the table still to be seen in the Hardy Room at the Dorset County Museum. One can only guess that it was given him by his mother for his boyhood studies at Higher Bockhampton.

Vagg Hollow

Fall, autumn.

A marshy spot traversed by the Fosse Way, the Roman road southwest of Ilchester in south Somerset. The things 'seen' usually took the form of a wool-pack in the middle of the road. As a result (according to the tradition) horses 'stopped on the brow of the hollow, and could only be made to go on by whipping. A waggoner once cut at the pack with his whip: it opened in two, and smoke and a hoofed figure rose out of it' (*Life*, 314). The village of Tintinhull lies to the south of the road.

The Dream Is – Which? (March 1913)

The poem was occasioned by Hardy's visit to Cornwall after Emma's death. Visions of her appear and disappear. The recollected past is dis-

placed by the present reality: the loneliness of Max Gate replaces a
happy scene by the Valency river; winter and old age, their radiancy in
love; and her grave at Stinsford, the country-dances they enjoyed
'around the hall'. The title asks whether the past or the present is the
dream, with perhaps a hint of Shakespeare's

> We are such stuff
> As dreams are made on, and our little life
> Is rounded with a sleep.

The Country Wedding

Michael [Mail] and Reub[en Dewy] were members of the Mellstock
choir (*UGT*), yet 'A fiddler's story' suggests that the tale was one Hardy
heard from his father, and that some of the Stinsford players took part
in the wedding celebrations at Puddletown, walking across the heath
from Higher Bockhampton. The serpent was an instrument played by
a member of the Puddletown choir (*Life*, 10). The bride may have
been a member of the Sparks family (Mrs Sparks was Hardy's maternal
aunt), who lived by 'Mill-Tail Shallow'. The choir had been too
exuberant. Taking precedence in the procession was an irregularity,
and playing loudly outside the church while solemn vows were made
within seemed improper to the bridegroom and a tempting of Providence to the bride. The poem illustrates Puritanical superstition, its
final

> Yes: little fogs were in every hollow,
> Though the purple hillocks enjoyed fine weather

being a reminder of the ill-omens that might have been discerned in the
general gaiety of the wedding.

The rhyme-scheme is interesting. The middle lines of each stanza
rhyme. The first lines of the opening and closing stanzas all have the
same rhyme, as do those of the middle section. Within the same group-
ings the fourth lines rhyme, though the rhyme differs at the end from
that at the beginning.

First or Last

Hardy's songs often voice common sentiments, which are not always
his own.

Lonely Days

forespent, spent (there) previously.

The diary may have been Emma Hardy's, found by Hardy after her death and destroyed because of its harsh and intemperate criticism of him. She was often lonely at Max Gate, not only when he was absent but when he was there. He forgot her birthdays, as Florence Dugdale discovered before she married him. The 'city' found so changed must be Plymouth, where she spent her girlhood, and to which she returned for her father's funeral (*Life*, 228).

'What Did It Mean?'

seise me of, acquire legally.

A Gothic fantasy in which the speaker is a woman convinced that the man she married is haunted by the spirit (or spectre, which she has seen) of his first love. It has an obvious link with Hardy's marriages.

At the Dinner-Table

The Marble Tablet (8 September 1916)

In September 1916 Hardy and his wife Florence went by train to Cornwall 'to see if Hardy's design and inscription for the tablet in [St Juliot Church] had been properly carried out and erected' (*Life*, 373). It had been ordered at Plymouth in March 1913, when he was returning from his first revisitation of scenes with which he became familiar more than forty years earlier on his excursions with Emma Gifford. She was buried at Stinsford, but Hardy wanted her association with the work of the church at St Juliot, where she played the organ, to be remembered.

There it stands. The poem opens in dramatic style, rather like Browning's 'My Last Duchess', where the speaker calls attention to a painting, 'There she stands/As if alive.' *It may stand for.* The second verse includes birth, marriage, and death. Emma was born in Plymouth on 24 November 1840, the same year as Hardy; she lived to find marriage a burden, as he discovered from her diary; and she died on 27 November 1912.

The Master and the Leaves (1917)

treen, trees.

The subject of birth, life, death is continued in another setting. It is something with which Hardy had become so familiar that it occasions no surprise. It seems strange, therefore, that he should have thought it worth while to say as much in this little fantasy.

Last Words to a Dumb Friend (2 October 1904)

Many of the Hardy pets were buried under the trees at Max Gate. In *The Fortnightly Review* (March 1928) S. M. Ellis, describing his visit to Max Gate in 1913, identified the cat as 'Snowdove', and observed that Hardy's 'sense of pain and loss was as sharp as on the first day'. The last lines of the poem suggest that Snowdove had been buried for some time. These verses are some of Hardy's most finished; the initial stress in every line helps to sustain their vigour.

A Drizzling Easter Morning

Though not as satirical, Hardy is as sceptical as in 'Christmas: 1924'. Both his mood and the plight of man (as he sees it) are expressed in the scene. Such harmony is a feature of his novels.

On One Who Lived and Died Where He Was Born

The subject is Hardy's father, who was born in November 1811 at Higher Bockhampton, and lived in the same house until his death in July 1892. As happened in other poems, the facts are altered to produce a pattern (cf. 'The Wind's Prophecy'). His father 'went upstairs for the last time' on 27 April 1892 (*Life*, 247).

Wealth-wantless. For this aspect of Hardy's father, see *Life*, 21. He was much like Giles Winterborne (cf. *Life*, 248 and *W*.xxx).

The Second Night

The hero of this supernatural ballad is a 'man of mystery', 'unresting', doomed 'to wander wide' like the Ancient Mariner. Sparks appear in the dark pupils of Eustacia's eyes (RN.I.vii); here they are the reflections of a 'mad star' that streams in sparks to the sea (proleptically, one suspects, for the heroine). As Hardy's cousin Tryphena Sparks had taught in Plymouth, not far from the scene of the poem, and he, in long retrospect, regarded her as one of his lost prizes (see 'At Mayfair Lodgings' and 'The Opportunity' for others), it would be strange if he did not think of her when he wrote this weird story. There is no evidence that he met her in Plymouth. Whether he found time to visit Cremyll from West Hoe pier when he visited Plymouth after Emma's death is uncertain. He had probably heard her talk of excursions there in her childhood (SR. 9). Its interest for Hardy would have been enhanced had he known (as he probably did from, for example, Emma Sophia Countess Brownlow's *Slight Reminiscences of a Septuagenarian*, London, 1867, to which *The Journal of Mary Frampton* could have called his attention) that Napoleon wished to land at Mount Edgcumbe and enjoy a walk there when he was a prisoner on board the *Northumberland* in Plymouth Sound.

Fair, Beauty. There is no hint here of the 'tresses flashing fair' of 'The Wind's Prophecy'.

She Who Saw Not

The rose-tree (cf. 'The Spell of the Rose') suggests Max Gate and love. The subject of this vague fantasy may be Emma Hardy's inability to understand Hardy's aims and outlook, and her insensitiveness when she 'wounded' him on many occasions.

like the face of Moses. When he came down from speaking to the Lord on Mt Sinai (Exodus, xxxiv. 29).

The Old Workman

As an architect, even practising at times on a small scale with church restoration in his later years (C. J. P. Beatty, *The Architectural Notebook of Thomas Hardy*, Dorchester, 1966, pp. 32–3), Hardy may have met such an old mason. Work on one such restoration coincided with the final planning period for *Jude the Obscure*, the hero of which was also engaged in ashlar work. Hardy's admiration for the workman's pride in fine building recalls the protest of 'A Man', and the substitution of 'Workman' for 'Mason' in the title is significant.

The Sailor's Mother

Based on the story of 'To Please His Wife' (*LLI*). Shadrach Jolliffe of 'Havenpool' married and started a grocery business. His wife was ambitious, and persuaded him to seek a fortune at sea. Ultimately he took his two sons, but not one of them returned. Joanna was so destitute that she accepted accommodation at the house of a friend. The poem is comparable to the end of the story, though the voices are reduced to one.

Outside the Casement

The MS shows that the original title was 'After the Battle'. The sub-title suggests that the poem could have been prompted by an experience which the Hardys observed or participated in, though it was such a common one during the First World War that they may merely have heard of it.

The Passer-By

The poem is not wholly true, though it is based on Hardy's silent 'attachment' to Louisa Harding, who lived at Stinsford Farm, near the church. He did not pass her window every day, except at a distance when he walked along the road to Dorchester during the period of his apprenticeship to the architect John Hicks. He believed she reciprocated his attachment, and one is left wondering whether he cherished the flattering thought that she remained single for his sake (cf. 'My joy, my fate').

'I Was the Midmost'

The poem has some kinship with the 'metaphysical' poetry of John Donne. In childhood Hardy felt, and was made to feel, that he was the centre of his small world. When he fell in love with Emma Gifford, the axis round which he turned like the Earth was extended to a Pole-star which was his 'all-day' centre of interest. Now, in his old age, like many others eager to find a faith, he can discover no centre, no clue to life.

A Sound in the Night

coupled, married.

The origin of the story is unknown. Hardy may have heard of a tradition of this kind when he was working with his father (for the architect, John Hicks) at Woodsford Castle (*Life*, 27). The 'Castle' was a fourteenth-century house on the south side of the Frome valley (the Valley of the Great Dairies in *Tess*) to the east of Lower Bockhampton. If its original name was 'Wyrdesford', from the 'weird' or fateful ford of Rocky Shallow (Bailey, 485), this in itself could be the root of a story which Hardy considered in 1902 (*THN.* 70–71). He knew the area well in his youth, especially when he helped on his father's farm at Talbothays. Down in the meadow, he witnessed the recovery of a drowned boy from the pool below 'Shadwater Weir'. He thought at first it was a girl, and from his memory of this incident the story of *The Return of the Native* originated (Gertrude Bugler, 'Personal Recollections of Thomas Hardy', Toucan Press, 1962.).

plinth-steps, downward sloping slab stones over wall projections just above ground level. *the hatches*, those of the original of 'Shadwater Weir' (*RN*). *the moor*, the low-lying meadows of the Frome valley. *for good-and-all*. Another instance of Hardy's boldness in the use of spoken English in poetry.

On a Discovered Curl of Hair (February 1913)

Found in a green leather locket with a miniature of Emma Gifford; cf 'A Forgotten Miniature'.

your old abode, the rectory at St Juliot in Cornwall.

An Old Likeness

wist it, known it to be.

Michael Millgate thinks that the picture of R.T. is the frontispiece of *A Summer Night and Other Poems* by Graham R. Tomson, a copy of which the author, Rosamund Tomson, sent Hardy in 1891. Her reputation as a poet was considerable at the end of the nineteenth century, and Hardy alludes to her poetry in 'gamut of song'. This identification has much to recommend it, but it assumes that Hardy's condemnation of her in 1893 was forgotten or no longer felt. See *ORFW*. 15–16.

Her Apotheosis

Secretum meum mihi, my secret, mine alone. The words are a marginal comment on Isaiah, xxiv. 16 in the Latin Bible. *iris*. See 'To Outer Nature' (pp. 20–21).

'Sacred to the Memory'

Part of the inscription on the tombstone which Hardy designed for his sister Mary. With the closing line of the poem, compare the last stanza of 'Molly Gone'.

To a Well-Named Dwelling

remark, notice.

Neither the house nor the person to whom it meant so much is known. The thought may have been occasioned by the sight of an old stone house with an appropriately attractive 'title'.

The Whipper-In

Behind this implausible story lies Hardy's inveterate hatred of blood-sports.

A Military Appointment

The musical note 'scherzando' indicates a playful measure. The situation is too much a Hardy commonplace to be taken very seriously.

The Milestone by the Rabbit-Burrow

The milestone on Yellowham Hill, on the road from Puddletown to Dorchester, stands about half a mile across country from Hardy's birthplace. The poem has a double significance. It urges Hardy's Altruism, which includes the animal world (*Life*, 346, 349), and it alludes to the never-never land where all is perfection.

The Lament of the Looking-Glass
Probably a memory of Emma Hardy.

Cross-Currents

The Old Neighbour and the New

Perhaps an imaginary visit to Came Rectory soon after the death of William Barnes, who lived there as rector from 1862 to 1886. 'September' is a poetic licence for the sake of rhyme; Barnes died on 7 October 1886, and was buried four days later. See 'The Last Signal'.

The Chosen
fell, fierce, eager.

The Greek epigraph (Galatians, iv. 24) reads 'Which things are an allegory'. It may be a common experience for the image of the woman who is loved and lost to be associated with the woman who is loved and won. The subject of the poem is much more unusual. It probably came back to Hardy when he was re-reading *The Woodlanders* for a revised edition. In the novel (xxix) Grace Melbury has discovered her husband's infidelities. Fitzpiers had felt affection 'of some sort' for herself and Suke Damson 'simultaneously; and was now again spreading the same conjoint emotion over Mrs Charmond and herself'. Hardy then tells the reader that Grace's deduction was wrong, 'for the love of men like Fitzpiers is unquestionably of such quality as to bear division and transferences. He had indeed once declared, though not to her, that on one occasion he had noticed himself to be possessed by five distinct infatuations at the same time. If this were true, his differed from the highest affection as the lower orders of the animal world differ from advanced organisms, partition causing not death but a multiplied existence. He had loved her sincerely in his selfish way, and had by no means ceased to love her now. But such double and treble-barrelled hearts were naturally beyond her conception.' The realization that Fitzpiers had played the hypocrite to her sickened Grace.

The woman who sickens in the poem is not Grace Melbury. The lover is not the sensualist Fitzpiers nor the 'Visionary Artist in pursuit of the unattainable Perfect in female form' in *The Well-Beloved*. Unlike the former, the latter is sincere. The one is condemned by his conduct; the other is the subject of playful satire. Neither the setting nor the narrative of the poem is realistic; they are more in keeping with the emblematic presentation of a general truth. The 'Christ-cross stone' may suggest another Alec d'Urberville. The unfortunate hero, however, is a type, the victim of his imagination. His grandiose opening words proclaim both the deceiver and the deceived. Like Fitzpiers he is incapable of the highest affection; his 'conjoint emotion' makes him see in the 'composite form' of the sixth woman whatever charms existed for him in the previous five. He cannot love her, for he does not know her as a person. He is guilt-ridden, and doomed to disappointment as long as the spell worked by his imagination lasts. Perhaps the statement which comes nearest to the allegorical meaning of the poem is one Hardy wrote on 28 October 1891, when he was contemplating the plot of *The Well-Beloved* (see the note on 'The Well-Beloved', p. 47). The subject may owe something to Browning's poem 'St. Martin's Summer'.

called a jade. Cf. 'She, to Him' (II).   *mast*, fruit of the beech. (It was autumn in *The Woodlanders* scene.)   *Christ-cross stone*. This recalls Cross-in-Hand (see Hardy's footnote to 'The Lost Pyx' and *TD*.xlv). The settings, though different (one moorland, the other upland) are the same in tone – 'mournful' or 'most forlorn'.

The Inscription (30 October 1907)

Another story given a Gothic ending. Hardy found it in Hutchins (IV. 456) and no doubt in the church at 'Estminster'. The memorial brass is for John Horsey (d.1531) of Clifton Maybank near Yeovil (the home of 'Master John Horseleigh, Knight' in *A Changed Man*) and his wife Elizabeth Turges of Melcombe. Where details of the date of her death could be expected, blanks are left. See 'The Memorial Brass', in which Hardy dramatizes a more modern variant of the story.

maintain the apostrophe good, be true to the inscriptional address 'Of your charyte pray for ye soules of . . .' .

The Marble-Streeted Town

Hardy's footnote indicates that the poem was written at Plymouth. His query suggests that he was there in 1914 as well as on his return from Cornwall in March 1913. The title derives from Emma Hardy's description of the smooth, worn, limestone setts paving Plymouth streets. See *SR*. 10, 70 and, for the 'bandsmen' and 'schoolgirls', 8; cf. 'During Wind and Rain' and 'The West-of-Wessex Girl'.

A Woman Driving

chine, ridge, crest.

The recollection of Emma driving is transmuted into something unearthly. She is seen in Cornwall, first as Hardy saw her, then (a rather preternatural, legendary figure) as others remembered her. Finally, as in 'He Prefers Her Earthly', Hardy wonders if her driving continues in a celestial after-life.

A Woman's Trust

scathless, unharmed, undimmed. *aurore*, dawn.

Hardy dwells on Emma's faith in his genius during his early years as a writer. But for her he would probably have given up writing as a profession (*Life*, 86–7). The poem stresses her childlike confidence and serenity; finally, her absolute faith in his loyalty to her (cf. 'I Rose and Went to Rou'tor Town').

scorn of him by men. Hardy could never forget harsh criticism of his novels by reviewers. One review of *Desperate Remedies* made him wish he were dead (*Life*, 84).

Best Times

Four happy occasions associated with Emma Hardy are selected. They range from love's beginning (scene, in the Valency valley) to her last happy evening, when Rebekah Owen and her sister called at Max Gate (*Life*, 359 and *HLMSq*. 157–62).

calm eve. Mrs Hardy was obviously ill, but Rebekah Owen noticed that she seemed 'better and calmer for talking'.

The Casual Acquaintance

The poem seems to embody the general in the particular: the reinvigoration or encouragement which comes from casual encounters and is not appreciated until one can look back and see things in perspective.

Intra Sepulchrum

typic, typical, conventional. *note*, distinction.

'Within the Tomb' presents the realization by one of a buried pair that, though unusual in their love, unconventional in their ideas, and unique in their lives, they will now be regarded as very ordinary, and undifferentiated from those among whom they are buried.

the tether of typic minds. MS: 'Like other men, and their wives'. *Into blind matter hurled.* A reference to Nature's indifference to man.

The Whitewashed Wall

Written for *Reveille*, November 1918, the Government quarterly for disabled sailors and soldiers, at the request of the editor, John Galsworthy. The means by which a mother's devotion to her absent son is continually renewed recalls Mrs Martin's attachment to the astronomical mural sketches left by her grandson when his career compelled him to travel extensively (*TT*.xxxviii).

Just the Same

On the insignificance of the individual. To himself he is the centre of the universe. He may suffer a blow which changes his outlook completely, but the world goes on as if it had never happened. Hardy repeated the idea on 23 December 1925 (*Life*, 430).

The Last Time

Probably prompted by the recollection of Emma Hardy's sudden death.

The Seven Times

If Hardy was eighty when he wrote the poem, he may have been preparing notes on the early part of his life for Florence Hardy. The first six visits to Cornwall seem to coincide with the six recorded in his *Life* (March and August 1870, May 1871, August 1872, early 1873, and December 1873; he omitted one at least, that of October 1871 (see 'By

the Runic Stone', p. 135). The seventh combines those of 1913 and
1916 after Emma's death.

Life was clogged in me with care. For the effect of Emma Gifford on his
spirits, see 'Without, Not Within Her' (p. 185). Hardy's principal
worries arose from his uncertainty about his future. He had just sent
Macmillan the script of *Desperate Remedies*, a sensational novel which
he hoped would launch him as an author. It had yet to be completed,
and the embarrassingly crude climax was on his mind when he was
asked to visit St Juliot. He had rejected a first request, and accepted the
second with reluctance (*Life*, 65; for his worries about the conclusion
of the novel and his future, see *Life*, 83).

The Sun's Last Look on the Country Girl

This suggests that Mary Hardy had a sunny disposition like Thomasin
Yeobright (*RN*.III.vi); cf. 'Middle-Age Enthusiasms'. After her death,
Kate Hardy wrote, 'We can see now who did so much to keep us
cheerful.'

In a London Flat

The scene may be imaginary, but Hardy is thinking of Emma's death.

Drawing Details in an Old Church

Compare 'Afterwards' and 'Intra Sepulchrum'.

Rake-Hell Muses (189–)

unshame, lack of shame. *intermell*, intermingling (of sorrow and gladness). *fell*, skin. *misprision*, error.

The MS title is 'The Seducer Muses'. The rake-hell's casuistry takes the
form of a Browning dramatic monologue. In the main, the verse is
little removed from speech, though the carefully wrought rhyme-
scheme results in some obvious Hardy neologisms.

gladness . . . knell. As a result of their marriage.

The Colour

Hardy's poem has little originality. The white, red, blue, and black
questions are found in the Wessex folk-rhyme 'Jinny Jones', and the

answers also are repeated by Hardy, including the final twist. See Bailey, 496–7.

Murmurs in the Gloom (22 September 1899)

trow, believe in.

Written when the Boer War seemed imminent and inevitable. On 17 November 1899 Hardy wrote, 'I suppose this unfortunate war with the Boers will come. . . . It seems a justification of the extremest pessimism that at the end of the 19th century we settle an argument by the sword, just as they would have done in the 19th century B.C.' (*ORFW*. 84).

breathing threats and slaughters. As did Saul (later St Paul), Acts, ix. 1. *frowardly*, literally away from the right direction, as opposed to *vawardly* (from 'vanward'), forward.

Epitaph

Compare 'For Life I Had Never Cared Greatly'. The final thought was elaborated a little in 'He Never Expected Much'. Hardy probably wrote 'Epitaph' when he was collecting poems for *Late Lyrics and Earlier* (at the age of eighty-one), and thought this could be his last volume of poetry.

An Ancient to Ancients

wot, knows. *Aïdes*, Hades.

The tone is different: genial, confident, and even sprightly, befitting an after-dinner speech. Looking over the past, Hardy finds much that was enjoyable, though now forgotten or out of vogue. Early beliefs may have lost significance, and the ancients may be tiring, but (he reminds his younger audience) many reached their peak in their latest years. In the end he says something which is true for every generation. The fifth and sixth stanzas have a special interest, since they show some of the literature which excited Hardy in his earlier years. His admiration for Tennyson's poetry may be seen in the quotations (largely from *In Memoriam*) in *A Pair of Blue Eyes*. The faith to which Tennyson had been restored was no longer acceptable, however.

She who voiced those rhymes is dust, Emma Hardy. Before their marriage, she and Hardy read Tennyson together 'in the grounds of the rectory' at St Juliot (*Life*, 78–9); the 'roof-wrecked' bower may have a double reference, the first to the wrecking of Tennyson's religious views by scientific philosophy, the second (more allusively) to the effect of time on the trellised summer-house at the end of the rectory garden.

After Reading Psalms XXXIX, XL, etc. (187–)

list, listen.

Though he had lost faith in the God of Christianity, Hardy turned to the Bible regularly for spiritual sustenance; he prayed, as it were, to the unknown God. What he says about himself, when he began to write poetry ('At my start by Helicon') has its significance with reference, it may be, to poems such as 'She, to Him' and 'Neutral Tones'.

Quoniam Tu fecisti, Because Thou didst it (xxxix. 9). *me deduxisti*, Thou hast led me; cf. xxvii. 11, lxxxvi. 11, cxix. 37. *Me suscepisti*, Thou hast upheld me (xli. 12). *Dies . . . Meos posuisti*, Thou hast made my days (xxxix. 5). *Domine, Tu scisti*, O Lord, Thou knowest (xl. 9). *Quem elegisti*, Whom hast Thou chosen? (lxv. 4).

Surview

Hardy looks back on his life, and considers his lack of charity (particularly, he may have been thinking, towards his first wife). The poem enshrines his highest beliefs.

Cogitavi vias meas, I thought on my ways (Psalm cxix. 59); cf. *Life*, 405. *whatsoever was true . . . just . . . suffereth long . . . Charity*. Philippians, iv. 8 and I Corinthians, xiii. 4–13. See also 'The Blinded Bird'; *TD.* xxxi, xxxvi; and *JO.*vi.iv (on I Corinthians, xiii): 'Its verses will stand when all the rest that you call religion has passed away!' *taught not . . . set about*, did not put into practice what you intended.

7

Human Shows

THIS collection of 152 poems was published in November 1925 under the full descriptive title (which remains unchanged) of *Human Shows, Far Fantasies, Songs, and Trifles*. It is longer than every other volume of Hardy's poetry except *Late Lyrics and Earlier*. As in *Winter Words*, poems of reminiscence and observation (particularly of outdoor scenes) are on the increase. Some of the former were undoubtedly the product of memories awakened by Hardy's interest in notes and letters when he and his wife were jointly engaged in compiling the first part of his life story.

Waiting Both

To the Bishop of Durham, one of Horace Moule's brothers, Hardy wrote on 29 June 1919: 'We were reading a chapter in Job, and on coming to the verse, "All the days of my appointed time will I wait, till my change come", I interrupted and said: "That was the text of the Vicar of Fordington one Sunday evening about 1860". And I can hear his voice repeating the text as the sermon went on . . . just as if it were yesterday' (*Life*, 390–91). The vicar was the bishop's father, in some ways the prototype of Angel Clare's father (*ORFW*. 92). The text is Job, xiv. 14, and Hardy was thinking of its context, the subject of which is death. He had ended *Late Lyrics and Earlier* expecting it; three years later he still awaits the expected change.

A Bird-Scene at a Rural Dwelling

codling, costard, kinds of apples.

The scene recalls early mornings at Hardy's birthplace.

'Any Little Old Song'

A trifle perhaps, but it emphasizes Hardy's imaginative interest in anything with moving human associations.

In a Former Resort after Many Years

The theme is age. In a resort he used to know well, Hardy asks himself how much he knows about the aged and shrunken people he sees. Conversely, what do they know about him, whose mind, once relatively unscored with memories, is now full of memories of the dead?

El Greco, the Spanish painter Domenico Theotocopouli (1541–1614), who acquired the name by which he is remembered because he was born in Crete. *necrologic*, obituary; cf. 'Paying Calls'.

A Cathedral Façade at Midnight

A passage by Hardy (*Life*, 296) shows that the scene – outside Salisbury Cathedral 'under the full summer moon on a windless midnight' – was most beautiful to him; and so it appears in the poem. Then a breeze stirs, as if it were the sighings of regret that the old Christian faith had been displaced as science and rationalism made their steady advance. This regret may be seen in 'The Oxen'. Hardy rejected Christian theology, but not Christian ethics (cf. 'Surview'); he felt that if the gospel of charity or loving-kindness did not survive, there was no hope for the future. All this is memorably presented, from an individual point of view, in Arnold's 'Dover Beach'.

the Universe . . . its centre, Earth. In the pre-Copernican era the earth was thought to be at the centre of the universe, and man the most important part of creation.

The Turnip-Hoer

The opening verse provides a comment not only on the story of the poem but on much in Hardy's fiction and vision of man. Some people learn from experience, and are wise enough to use restraint and self-control; others are a prey to the passions. The division is best expressed in Gabriel Oak and Boldwood (*FMC*). Boldwood's passion is ultimately like that of the turnip-hoer. For the collective folly of men, his 'hideous self-treason', whether self-generated mainly or stirred up by imperialists, see 'Thoughts at Midnight' and *The Dynasts*.

Terminus, a Roman god who presided over boundaries.

The Carrier

St Sidwell's Church, which stood in Sidwell Street, Exeter, was destroyed in the Second World War. The carrier was proceeding eastward out of the city when the towers of Exeter Cathedral disappeared from view.

Lover to Mistress

bysm, abysm, abyss.

The Monument-Maker (1916)

See 'The Marble Tablet' (p. 188). As the tablet was made in Plymouth to Hardy's design, the experience of the poem is imaginary, though it includes an underlying sense of guilt which is real.

planet . . . at its height. Perhaps there is an astrological link between this and the appearance of her 'ghost'.

Circus-Rider to Ringmaster

The MS adds '(Casterbridge Fair: 188-)'. Hardy notes that he went to all the circuses that came to Dorchester while he was living in the town from 1883 to 1885. At one performance 'the equestrienne who leapt through the hoops on her circuit missed her footing and fell with a thud on the turf. He followed her into the dressing-tent, and became deeply interested in her recovery. The incident seems to have some bearing on the verses of many years after entitled "Circus-Rider to Ringmaster" ' (*Life*, 166).

tan-laid, covered with dried bark ('tanbark') as a protective measure.

Last Week in October

This shows (in 'suspended criminal') just a trace of Hardy's penchant for *grotesquerie*; cf. Dairyman Crick's knife and fork 'planted erect on the table, like the beginning of a gallows' (*TD*. xviii).

Come Not; Yet Come!

Hardy may have written this with Mrs Henniker in mind (Purdy, 345–6), possibly in 1895 when she was on holiday in Germany (*ORFW*. 42–3). Or it could have been a late revision of a poem written at that time. Whether Mrs Henniker had visited Max Gate before then is not known, however.

tear. Cf. 'time-torn' in 'A Broken Appointment'.

The Later Autumn (MS, 1921)

Toadsmeat, a poisonous fungus; cf. 'toad-cheese', 'toadstool'. *couch-fires*. See 'In Time of "the Breaking of Nations" ' (p. 158).

'Let Me Believe'

At a Fashionable Dinner

The substitution of 'Lavine' for 'Emleen' seems to indicate that the presentiments or superstitions (thirteen being considered an unlucky number) are connected with Hardy's wife Emma and her death. The poem suggests fantasy rather than actual experience.

Green Slates

The object of Hardy's first visit to Cornwall was the restoration of the church at St Juliot, and it was for this reason that he drove with Emma Gifford and her sister Mrs Holder to inspect the slate quarries at Penpethy (*Life*, 75). See 'At Castle Boterel' (p. 107).

An East-End Curate

Cf. *JO*.iii.i: 'the humble curate wearing his life out in [a] city slum – that might have a touch of goodness and greatness in it; that might be true religion'. 'Dowle' or 'Dow-well' suggests 'Do well', but Hardy is less sanguine than Jude about the effectiveness of 'the ecclesiastical and altruistic life' in a city slum.

cyphering. As the dampers were worn, the strings continued to vibrate, and notes were unduly prolonged. '*Novello's Anthems*'. Published by Vincent Novello (1781–1861).

At Rushy-Pond

substant, real.

The poem seems to be no more than a Gothic fancy, the narrator seeing the wraith of a former love in the image of the moon's reflection in the pond; it appeared just as her face did when she withdrew from his life, her beauty faded. The 'frigid face' of the pond and the parting make one wonder if this is a 'moon' variant of 'Neutral Tones'. Rushy Pond is on the heath, not far from the Hardys' home at Higher Bockhampton. Hardy presents a moon-reflection scene with similarities and other properties when Gabriel Oak realizes how disastrous is the loss of his sheep (*FMC.*v).

in a secret year, a period of secret meetings. 'Year' is given probably to meet the need of rhyme; cf. 'days' below.

Four in the Morning

Although 'this vale's space' suggests Lower Bockhampton, the poem is based almost certainly on observations made by Hardy when he rose early to study or write during the 1867–74 period.

cerule, azure. Compare the early October morning view in *TT*.xviii: 'Far in the shadows semi-opaque screens of blue haze made mysteries of the commonest gravel-pit, dingle, or recess.' *Great Nebula*, the brightest of the nebulae, appearing in the constellation Andromeda. *Pleiads*, Pleiades, a cluster of stars in the region (apparently) of the constellation Taurus. *with eyes of guile*, looking suspiciously. *grisly grin*, the defects of Darwinian nature. *stewardship*. See Luke, xvi. 1–2.

On the Esplanade

The setting is Weymouth Bay. The sensuous quality of the description, like that of the same scene in *DR*.iii.2, suggests that the poem can be associated with Hardy's other fictional Weymouth poems. It leads deliberately up to climax and suspense. Was it intended as part of a narrative, and can it be assumed that some turning-point for the lover would come late that Midsummer Eve according to traditional folklore? Cf. *AHC.* 134.

In its overblow, when its full bloom is over.

In St Paul's a While Ago

enthusiast, self-deluded visionary.

The MS gives '1869' for 'a While Ago'. The description of Paul as an 'epilept enthusiast' shows the influence of the 'higher criticism' on Hardy; cf. 'The Respectable Burgher'. Satirical wit takes an antithetical turn: 'Pondering whatnot, giddy or grave', 'Hebe . . . Artemisia'.

Hebe . . . Artemisia, a woman in the bloom of youth like Hebe the cup-bearer of the Greek gods passes close by a widow in ostentatious mourning attire. Artemisia, queen of Caria, erected the famous Mausoleum to her husband's memory, instituted prizes for the best elegies in praise of him, and died after two years' grief. *Beatrice Benedick*, a pair of high-spirited, teasing, witty lovers like Beatrice and Benedick in Shakespeare's *Much Ado about Nothing*. *strange Jew, Damascus-bound*, Saul (later St Paul). See Acts, ix. 1–22. The iconoclastic climax suggests that the poem belongs to an earlier period, and that Hardy kept it in reserve until he felt it would not provoke a loud outcry. *encircling mart*, the shop and business premises of the streets called 'St. Paul's Churchyard' which surround the cathedral.

Coming Up Oxford Street: Evening

A slight poem which derives from the period when Hardy assisted the London architect T. Roger Smith in designing for the London School Board. The assessment of the city clerk seems to be coloured by one of Hardy's gloomy views of life.

A Last Journey

The scene recalls the realistic style of the Pre-Raphaelite painters.

King's-Stag. South-west of Sturminster Newton, and named after the legend of Blackmoor Vale (*TD.*ii). See the glossary (p. 275) for other places.

Singing Lovers

The MS gives '(in 1869)' as part of the title. See *Life*, 63–4 and the Weymouth note to 'On the Esplanade' (p. 205).

The Month's Calendar

The poem has been associated with Mrs Henniker, the 'one rare fair woman' of 'Wessex Heights'. Its calendrical plan makes it very much an artifact; if it alludes to Mrs Henniker, its conclusion seems to be inconsistent with the evidence of 'Wessex Heights' (cf. ORFW.xxxi–xxxvi).

A Spellbound Palace

The vocal texture of the poem intensifies the contrasting effects. Hampton Court seems to be a refuge or secret place ('asile') for History to dwell, ignoring the 'clamorous clutch' of modern London. In the spell created by the fountain's flow Henry VIII and his minister Cardinal Wolsey are seen passing, 'Sheer in the sun'. Wolsey had Hampton Court built in 1514–16. In the hope of appeasing the king, he presented it to Henry VIII, who added the great hall and other buildings between 1531 and 1536.

passive lapse, a flow so continuous that it seems to be motionless. *insistent numbness*. Cf. the MS title, 'A Sleeping Palace'. *tinkling . . . thin . . . will*. The assonance here (cf. 'within' above) helps to create a sense of continuity and enchantment.

When Dead

The 'To —' casts some uncertainty on the view that this poem presents Emma speaking to Hardy before her death.[26]

resume my old . . . Vast. Though vague, this is clearly remote from Hardy's former rationalism on the subject of immortality. Does he hint at the same idea of existence before and after life in 'Wessex Heights'? See p. 96.

Sine Prole

sine prole, without offspring. *misprision*, scorn, indifference.

Hardy's will of 1922 shows that he did not rule out the hope of an heir by his second marriage, but this poem expresses his reconciliation to being childless. See 'She, I, and They' (pp. 123-4) and 'Before Marching and After' (p. 159). Hardy believed that 'English prosody might be enriched' by adapting verse-forms from Latin hymns (*Life*, 306).

Unlike Jahveh's ancient nation. The Israelites, continually in danger of being over-run and exterminated, looked forward to being as numerous as the sand on the seashore (Genesis, xxii. 17).

Ten Years Since (November 1922)

The anniversary of Emma Hardy's death.

Every Artemisia

See the note to 'In St. Paul's a While Ago' (p. 206). Though the view seems to be that every Artemisia is atoning for the neglect of her husband during his life, there can be little doubt that (with the roles reversed) the dialogue of the poem shows Hardy's realization that he and they had much in common.

The Best She Could (8 November 1923)

Hardy contrives a comment on 'the Frost's decree' from a slight subject.

The Graveyard of Dead Creeds

Religions are regarded as a comforting physic. Hardy seems to have realized that, 'as a matter of *policy*', it was necessary to preserve some of the supernatural theology of orthodoxy to make 'the new religion' of Positivism palatable (*Life*, 146). For his ideas on this new religion, see also *Life*, 332-3. The irony of the message from the spectres of dead creeds is that the purer medicaments are not expected to present the whole truth (which is too much for man to accept; cf. 'He Resolves to Say No More'), but only to make life more 'tolerable'. Religion must remain an 'opiate' to some extent.

wastes . . . fennish fungi. The imagery (probably from Shelley's 'The Sensitive Plant') occurs frequently in Hardy in association with set-backs and sorrows; cf. 'The Mother Mourns' and *AHC.* 165-6. *Catholicons*, universal remedies, panaceas. *caustic.* This probably alludes to the severities imposed by ancient religions.

'There Seemed a Strangeness'

The fulfilment of the Intention (see *Life*, 149) and its revelation to man are imagined.

Men . . . heard . . . seen. Isaiah, lxiv. 4 and I Corinthians, ii. 9. *glass . . . face to face.* I Corinthians, xiii. 12.

A Night of Questionings

For the tradition of the returning spirits, see 'I Rose Up as My Custom is' (p. 112). Five groups are heard, and they all express the view that the world has not changed. The poem is one of Hardy's most pessimistic statements. First come those from their graves by a tottering church (i.e. in a poor parish); then those of high degree from cathedral vaults; then sailors; then soldiers from the battlefields of northern France; lastly criminals.

years the locust hath eaten. Joel, ii. 25. *the circuiteer*, the wind as it made its way round. *Comorin to Horn . . . Wrath*, southern tip of India and that of South America . . . north-west corner of Scotland. *Go down to the sea in ships . . . deep.* Psalm cvii. 23–4. *Ardennes to Dover.* The Ardennes mountains are in France near the border with south-east Belgium. The line north-west from the Ardennes to Dover runs near the main battle-grounds on the Western Front during the First World War. *knave*, contrive by 'knavish tricks'. *white cap your adorning*, when hanged ('stretched'). *lovely deeds or true.* Philippians, iv. 8 (quoted in a note to 'The Souls of the Slain', p. 33).

Xenophanes, the Monist of Colophon (1921)

shotten, worthless, discredited.

Xenophanes was a Greek philosopher who believed that God and the universe were one. He was born at Colophon in Asia Minor, but was banished for his heterodoxy. Here he is imagined speaking, about 480 B.C., in his ninety-second year, from Elea in Italy by the Tyrrhenian Sea. As a monist he addresses the God of the universe, asking the questions which Hardy had often raised. The Years answer as in *The Dynasts*.

Life and Death at Sunrise

Dogbury Gate is a short stretch of the Dorchester-Sherborne road, north of Cerne Abbas, where it climbs between Dogbury and High Stoy, prominent hills in the north Dorset downs. As Hardy sketched Dogbury from 'the Devil's Kitchen' on 10 September 1867, it seems likely that this was the day when he heard of the birth and death on which the poem is based. The scene is cheerful in background and dialogue. There is a hint of Norse mythology in the image of the hills raising themselves like awakened sleepers to look around. Life goes on just the same. Even if John dies, Jack is born ('Jack' is the common variant of 'John'). The theme has a parallel in 'In Time of "the Breaking of Nations" '.

Night-Time in Mid-Fall

The MS title is 'Autumn Night-Time'. The night is so dark and stormy that old folk, being more superstitious, believe that witches ride the winds.

storm-strid, with the storm striding (moving strong and fast) across the sky.

A Sheep Fair

Hardy, it will have been noticed, often places two or more poems together which have a similarity of subject. Here we have another rain scene in a different setting. Six varied winter scenes follow.

Pummery. See 'The Burghers' (p. 11).

Snow in the Suburbs

The MS shows that this was written at Upper Tooting, where the Hardys lived (at 1 Arundel Terrace, Trinity Road) from 1878 to 1881; see *Life*, 147. The verse-movement conveys the actual movements of the scene, and the monosyllabic words of the last line have a satisfying finality in sound, as if the door is heard closing.

A Light Snow-Fall after Frost

holm, holly.

The scene is near Surbiton, London, where the Hardys lived in lodgings (St David's, Hook Road) during the winter of 1874–5.

Winter Night in Woodland

swingels, flails. *thrid*, thread their way across.

The period is that of *Under the Greenwood Tree* or slightly earlier, as the names of members of the 'Mellstock quire' indicate. The view is from the edge of the heath, immediately behind the Hardy cottage. On the left, the 'winding path called Snail-Creep' enters the copse (*UGT*.IV.i). To the right, south of the cottage, stretches Thorncombe Wood. In the middle distance, left of the heath, are the outskirts of Yellowham Wood. The carriers of smuggled spirits are a reminder that Hardy's grandfather (while in charge of the Stinsford choir from 1801 to about 1805) allowed his house to be used as a secret station for the transport of tubs; sometimes he had up to eighty of them hidden away in his house (*THN*. 35).

Ice on the Highway

On Yellowham Hill, following the road from Puddletown to Dorchester.

Music in a Snowy Street

Based on a 'curious scene' in Dorchester on 26 April 1884 (*Life*, 165). Hardy thought there was 'a fine poem' in it.

Antoinette, Marie Antoinette, wife of Louis XVI of France (cf. 'One We Knew'). She was guillotined in October 1793.

The Frozen Greenhouse

The second frost is not literal, but another example of 'the Frost's decree' or life's setbacks. Hardy's first visit to the rectory at St Juliot after his wife's death was in March 1913.

Two Lips

Another poem in memory of Emma Hardy.

No Buyers

A dismal scene which shows Hardy's observation and latent pity. Edmund Gosse described it as a photographic 'street scene in London', and one must assume he learned its location from Hardy.

Turk's-head brush, a round long-handled brush.

One Who Married Above Him

whimmed, followed a whim.

Hardy wrote some dismal Christmas stories; cf. 'What the Shepherd Saw', 'The Grave by the Handpost' (*CM*) and 'The Rash Bride'. The house with the mullioned windows and door frame of Ham Hill stone, with the sycamore roots forming steps up to it, was at Melbury Osmond, where relatives of Hardy's mother had lived. Another description of it, giving most of the same details, is to be found at the opening of the second part of *WT*. 'Interlopers at the Knap'.

Farmer Bollen. A 'Farmer Bollen' is mentioned in *W*.vi.

The New Toy

The remainder of the passengers think – and with reason, Hardy believes – that the child is a cause for wonder. The interest is in the behaviour of the mother, who puts on an appearance of indifference when it cries (as if she is equal to the situation), though her previous petting shows that it gives her great pride and pleasure.

Queen Caroline to her Guests

Hardy's sympathy for Caroline of Brunswick may be seen in *D*2.VI.vi, vii and *D*3.II.iv, IV.viii. When the Prince Regent came to the throne in 1820, she returned from the Continent, where she had lived indiscreetly. Popular feeling caused the withdrawal of the bill to deprive her of the title of Queen and dissolve her marriage. She was refused admission to the Coronation, and committed suicide three weeks later. Hardy's stanza befits her mood, and for the most part it is handled well.

Plena Timoris

'Full of fear'.

in its southing, on its southward course.

The Weary Walker

A symbol of life for one tired of it. Cf. 'Conjecture' (p. 138).

Last Love-Word (189–)

The date has caused the poem to be associated with Mrs Henniker. It could have been written with her in mind; if so, it is largely imaginary (cf. *ORFW*. xxxv).

Nobody Comes (9 October 1924)

Like many of his vignettes, this shows that there were no 'poetical' subjects for Hardy. How many other contemporary poets would have written of the telegraph wire and a car 'whanging' along? The music of the former may be heard. The scene is outside Max Gate.

In the Street

Compare 'Before Knowledge'.

The Last Leaf

The time and the lover's forgetfulness suggest there is a link in this fictional poem with Emma Hardy (d. 27 November 1912).

At Wynyard's Gap

stirred, moved.

Here the road from Dorchester to Crewkerne, beyond Toller Down, descends sharply through the chalk hills before Somerset is reached. Pen Wood and the Yeo river (running north to Yeovil) are to the north-east. Lewsdon Hill and Pilsdon Pen (cf. 'Doom and She', 'Molly Gone') are to the south-west. This short drama shows that Hardy's gift for fiction was not spent.

At Shag's Heath

nighty-rail, nightdress. *weeds*, mourning dress.

A monologue by a traditional betrayer of the Duke of Monmouth This claimant to the English throne, after being defeated at Sedgemoor (6 July 1685) was captured on Shag's Heath near Horton and Holt, north of Wimborne. Accounts of the Duke's capture vary. Hardy's story is romanticized, and owes something to a tradition of Monmouth at Melbury Osmond; see 'The Duke's Reappearance' (*CM*).

A Second Attempt (MS, about 1900)

The thirty years go back to the time when Hardy fell in love with Emma Gifford. He recalls the stages in their love as he had foreseen them then, when he could convey such dreams to her without the medium of words. Then comes the sad realization that it is impossible to relive the past.

'Freed the Fret of Thinking'

blow, bloom.

Compare 'Before Life and After'. Both poems express an atavistic point of view or 'seeming' which is quite inconsistent with Hardy's declaration that he was an evolutionary meliorist. All the hopes he expressed for the future (at the end of *The Dynasts*, for example) depend on the higher consciousness of mankind.

The Absolute Explains (31 December 1922)

fell, skin. *bruits*, makes renowned.

Hardy had been reading Einstein's theories of Relativity and the concept of Time as a 'fourth dimension' in which Past and Future exist in the Present. The Absolute explains it with reference to Hardy and Emma in the past, and then states that the Future remains best unshown.

toothless. It does not devour or destroy the Past. *phasmal*, visionary; cf.

'a gleam . . . gazing sense' (iii). *irised bow*, of love. See 'Her Apotheosis' (p. 193). It is related to Hardy's 'pilgrimages' to Cornwall (ix).[27] *her . . . yon*, Emma Hardy . . . Stinsford churchyard. *others you used to prize.* Cf. *Life*, 25–6, 'Thoughts of Phena', and 'At Mayfair Lodgings'.

'So, Time'

dure, duration.

A further comment on Einstein philosophy. See p. 255.

Thief of my Love's adornings. Cf. 'Amabel', 'She, to Him'.

An Inquiry

Hardy returns to the theme of the Unfulfilled Intention, here with reference to death. The epigraph from the Vulgate Bible reads, 'The sorrows of death compassed me.'

Many years . . . an instant. Cf. Psalm xc. 4: 'For a thousand years in thy sight are but as yesterday when it is past'.

The Faithful Swallow

This seems to be a comment on virtue and worldly expedience rather than on sensibility and sense.

In Sherborne Abbey

One of the family genealogical tables drawn up by Hardy shows that Joseph Pitcher of Melbury Osmond, an ancestor on his maternal side, eloped with Miss Heller of Kay, Yeovil, near Sherborne, in the eighteenth century.

The Pair He Saw Pass

weird-wed, wedded by fate.

Perhaps both Hardy's temperament and experience help to explain why the story of a man legally married to one person but spiritually to another appears in several forms in his prose and poetry. For the idea of marriage by fate or chance, see 'Ditty' and 'I Worked No Wile to Meet You'.

The Mock Wife

A full account of the case, trial, and hanging in Maumbury Rings, the Roman amphitheatre at Dorchester, is to be found in Hardy's article on 'Maumbury Ring' (Orel, 228–30); it is referred to in *MC*.xi. Hardy examined the evidence, and did not think it proved Mary Channing guilty. She had not reached her nineteenth birthday when she died. The mock wife story seems more fictional than traditional.

The Fight on Durnover Moor

The scene is immediately to the east of Dorchester, on the Fordington side of the road over Grey's Bridge. For Pummery Ridge, see 'The Burghers' (p. 11).

Last Look round St Martin's Fair

patroon, patron. *stay*, end.

The ponies ('heathcroppers') and 'the Great Forest' (cf. 'A Tramp-woman's Tragedy') indicate that the scene is near the New Forest. St Martin's Day or Martinmas falls on 11 November.

The Caricature (MS, about 1890)

hit, caused to be 'smitten' with love.

A Leader of Fashion

pipkin, small earthenware cooking-pot.

The MS title is 'The Fine Lady'. In saying, by implication, that she knows nothing of life, Hardy instances some of its common features, including suffering (its 'calvaries'). Cf. *Life*, 224.

Midnight on Beechen, 187–

Hardy climbed Beechen Cliff for the view of Bath in June 1873 when Emma Gifford was staying there (*Life*, 93).

dim concave, the Royal Crescent dimly seen in the distance.

The Aërolite

aërolite, meteorite.

Another version of a hackneyed subject, which runs counter to Hardy's tenor as an evolutionary meliorist.

grin no griefs while not opined, do not appear as griefs except to conscious awareness. *this disease*. See 'Before Life and After' and the note, p. 85. *Normal unwareness*. Cf. 'The Mother Mourns'.

The Prospect (December 1912)

For Emma Hardy's last garden-party at Max Gate, see *Life*, 359 and 387. (The lady who had been made 'the happiest woman in the world' by meeting her future husband near the Druid stone was Mrs Fortescue, wife of the librarian at Windsor Castle; cf. *ORFW*. 181, 184.) The image in the second line of the poem is apt; Hardy thinks he is ready for the grave. Sound and movement in the second stanza accord with the sense.

Genetrix Laesa

For the subject, compare 'The Sleep-Worker'. Mother Nature does not know the defects of her plans, what 'malversations' mar her 'ministry'. Her deeds fall short of her dream. So it appears to man, and why should he 'Crave to cure, when all is sinking/To dissolubility'?

The Latin title means 'The Wounded Mother'. The metre is that used by Adam of S. Victor (Purdy, 240) in *Sequences from the Sarum Missal* ('Sarum' is the old name for Salisbury). See *Life*, 306 and 'Sine Prole' (pp. 207–8).

concordia discors. From Horace, *Epistles*, 1. xii; cf. *The Dynasts*, After Scene, 'chordless chime of Things'.

The Fading Rose

With memories of Emma Hardy; cf. 'The Spell of the Rose'.

When Oats were Reaped (August 1913)

There were cornfields behind Max Gate. Hardy had walked beyond the crest of the hill (cf. 'The Wound', where the setting seems to be the same) and could see Stinsford Church beyond the level stretch of the Frome valley. Perhaps Emma Hardy had uttered the wounding words on the same route.

Louie (July 1913)

Hardy's date for the poem must be wrong; Louisa Harding died on 12 September 1913, at the age of seventy-two. She had lived in Dorchester, but was buried at Stinsford near her old home. The 'elect one' is Emma Hardy; the scene is Stinsford churchyard. See 'Transformations', 'The Passer-by', and 'To Louisa in the Lane'.

'She Opened the Door' (1913)

The critical turn in Hardy's recollection of Emma comes with the change of tense at the end.

'What's There to Tell?' (190–)

The Harbour Bridge

cutwater, wedge-shaped base of the bridge pier.

The poem (ending with the indifference of the universe to human lives) has a fictional trend, which suggests that it was written with other poems at Weymouth in 1869.

black as char, as if sketched in charcoal.   *cut black-paper portraits*. A similar description is found in *UGT*.i.i. The silhouette portrait was common, especially at resorts like Weymouth, before the days of the cheap camera.

Vagrant's Song

burns, streams. *Che-hane*, I am safe (cf. 'Ich' in 'The Pity of It').

Farmer Dunman's Funeral

their one day, their only day of the week.

The Sexton at Longpuddle

The Harvest-Supper
ballet, ballad.

Interest in one of Hardy's memorable boyhood experiences was probably reawakened when he began the record of his early years for his *Life*. He revisited the barn near the old manor at Kingston Maurward in 1924. The harvest supper he had witnessed three-quarters of a century earlier was 'among the last at which the old traditional ballads were sung'. The ballad he remembered best (concerning 'the parrot, and cage of glittering gold') was variously called 'The Outlandish Knight', 'May Colvine', 'The Western Tragedy', etc. See *Life*, 18–20, 426. The ballad metre is appropriate for a supernatural narrative which has its parallel in a number of the old ballads.

At a Pause in a Country Dance

The parenthetical note suggests that Hardy could have heard the story of the couple with reference to, or during, one of the Christmas-New Year parties at which he and his father fiddled (*Life*, 23–4). 'The Dashing White Serjeant' was a lively tune; the 'Longpuddle' choir 'blazed away' at it 'like wild horses' (*LLI*. 'Absent-Mindedness in a Parish Choir').

six-eighted, played to six-eight time. *cuckoo-father*, the man who cuckolded the husband (from the cuckoo's habit of laying its egg in another bird's nest).

On the Portrait of a Woman about to be Hanged (6 January 1923)

Written three days before the hanging of Mrs Edith Thompson. She and her lover were convicted for her husband's murder. Her love story and correspondence (used in evidence) were much in the press, and created public sympathy. In charging the Prime Cause with guilt for her Clytemnestra spirit, Hardy is consistent with his presentation of 'the rages/Of the ages' in *The Dynasts*; yet his case does not seem to square with his criticism of man for his 'unreason' and 'hideous self-treason' ('Thoughts at Midnight'). The first thought is the result of sympathy; the second, of impatience. See *Life*, 221.

Clytaemnestra was unfaithful to her husband Agamemnon while he was engaged in the Trojan war. She and her lover murdered him on his return. *Sowed a tare.* Matthew, xiii. 24–30.

The Church and the Wedding

The Shiver

Hardy's fictional story of a premonition includes a memory of his early departure for his first visit to Cornwall. 'One of far brighter brow' recalls Emma Gifford, but 'sea-goddess' suggests the lover's insincerity.

'Not Only I'

Written with Emma Hardy in mind.

drives and rides . . . red. Before her marriage (*SR.* 48). *the Call.* On Doomsday or the Day of Judgement, 'for the trumpet shall sound, and the dead shall be raised incorruptible, and we shall be changed' (I Corinthians, xv. 52).

She Saw Him, She Said

For superstitions indicative of the man's imminent death, see 'Premonitions' (p. 230) and *LLI.* 'The Superstitious Man's Story'. The moon links this poem with the next.

Once at Swanage

cusps, points (architecture), horns. *weirdsome,* fateful. *demilune,* half-moon.

The Hardys lived at Swanage in 1875–6. They walked 'daily on the cliffs and shore'. He noted an evening scene: 'Durlstone Head roaring high and low . . . the new moon, and a steady planet' (*Life,* 108). In the poem, the moon casts a spell, as if 'I and she' were fated.

The Flower's Tragedy (MS, about 1910)

teen, sorrow.

Compare Clym Yeobright's discovery after his mother's death (*RN.*v.ii).

At the Aquatic Sports

An observation of human nature, perhaps at Weymouth.

crab-catchings, mistakes by rowers which throw a crew out of rhythm and so hamper the boat that they provide an amusing spectacle.

A Watcher's Regret

J. E. has not been identified.

Horses Aboard

The band and the 'fighting afar' suggest the Boer War rather than the First World War; cf. 'Departure', 'The Colonel's Soliloquy', and *Life*, 303.

The History of an Hour

The poetry resides in the simile, which occurs in Hardy's novels.

The Missed Train

Probably a memory of one of Hardy's return journeys from Cornwall. The 'visions then vast in me' are not so much those of 'In the Seventies' as those inspired by love; cf. 'The Occultation'. The last three words seem to have no explicit reference; 'days of allure' is rather an infelicitous phrase, obviously fashioned for the rhyme.

Under High-Stoy Hill

Who were the three who predeceased Hardy and climbed High Stoy with him is not known. The poem may present a distant memory which came to Hardy when he made his last visit to the hill in 1922 (*Life*, 417). Climbing 'from Ivelwards' shows that the party had followed minor roads from the Melbury Osmond-Melbury Bubb region, where some of Mrs Hardy's relatives lived. The four could have been Hardy's parents, Hardy, and his sister Mary, returning by horse-conveyance from the Melburys, and following the road from the vale along the shoulder of High Stoy to Dogbury Gate.

At the Mill

'Yalbury Brow' suggests that the mill was at Puddletown (and the remains of one could be seen there in 1969). The market would be at Dorchester. It is not known whether this gruesome event took place in Hardy's lifetime; he had several relatives in the village, and the story would remain unforgotten for a long period.

home-along. A common expression in Dorset (and Hardy) for 'homewards'. *borne*, brought forth, born.

Alike and Unlike

There is an allusion here to the great 'division' between Hardy and his wife during their last twenty years or so (cf. 'The Voice of Things', p. 121). He was aware of it in May 1893 when they were travelling to Dublin at the invitation of the Lord-Lieutenant of Ireland. There he met Mrs Henniker, the Lord-Lieutenant's sister and hostess. The Hardys travelled by rail to Holyhead, stopping at Llandudno and driving round Great Orme's Head. See *Life*, 254-6 and *ORFW*.xxxii. In the poem Emma is imagined speaking. For the relationship between mood or outlook and the appearance of external things, compare 'The King's Experiment' (p. 58).

The Thing Unplanned

This is the kind of poem that inevitably raises the question whether it is imaginary or autobiographical. Even more speculative is 'the thing better'. The detail of the setting (the bridge, the meadow rills, the thatched post-office) suggests Lower Bockhampton, though 'ridge' is a convenient rhyme rather than a disguise. The juxtaposition of this poem and 'Alike and Unlike' makes one wonder whether Mrs Henniker would have consented to write *poste restante* during a marital crisis at Max Gate. Mrs Hardy did not care for Mrs Henniker, and it is significant that only two of the latter's letters to Hardy from 1893 to 1912 have survived (see *ORFW*.xxxi–xxxiii, xxxvi–xl). If this is the background to the poem, 'the thing better' was to continue the correspondence. It was broken only by Mrs Henniker's death.

The Sheep-Boy

A scene from Rainbarrows, three adjacent tumuli overlooking the heath near Higher Bockhampton. The most prominent of the three is the focal point in *The Return of the Native*. The 'concave of purple' heather is on the southern side. The mist comes up from the sea over the south downs by Poxwell (the 'Oxwell' of *The Trumpet-Major*), covering Draats-Hollow (so called from the air currents which are common there) and Kite Hill to the north-east near Puddletown. Such a fog in the woods to the west of Kite Hill is described in *FMC*.xlii.

pillar of cloud . . . Israelite, which led the children of Israel out of Egypt (Exodus, xiii. 17–22). Did Hardy assume it was raised by Moses?

Retty's Phases

For the old draft of 22 June 1868, see Purdy, 242. Hardy may have thought the footnote on an old custom as worthy of preservation as the song itself. The 'Vale' is the 'valley of the shadow of death' (Psalm xxiii).

A Poor Man and a Lady

It is not known when the poem was written, but 'it was intended to preserve an episode' in Hardy's first, unpublished novel, *The Poor Man and the Lady* (see *AHC*. 15–17). As far as Edmund Gosse could remember ('Thomas Hardy's Lost Novel', *The Sunday Times*, 22 January 1928), the novel ended in a church scene, where the lady, after being angry, confessed that she loved the architect (and radical) hero.[28] The poem is a dramatic monologue, showing Browning's influence, particularly in the appeal to God at the end.

town campaigns, social engagements in London. A rather bitter, satirical note may be observed, as if the engagements were operations in which she sought to impress the opposite sex. *the bell that tolled*, seeming to end his marriage hopes.

An Expostulation

Masquings and the cosmetic patch suggest a period not far removed from the end of the seventeenth century. 'Your lines' has the same connotation as in Psalm xvi. 6: 'The lines are fallen unto me in pleasant places; yea, I have a goodly heritage; 'rare' means 'splendid', as in the seventeenth century.

To a Sea-Cliff

For Durlston Head, see the note to 'Once at Swanage' (p. 220).

Between them lay a sword. Cf. George Meredith, *Modern Love* (i), where the husband and wife lie motionless after a quarrel:

> Like sculptured effigies they might be seen
> Upon their marriage-tomb, the sword between;
> Each waiting for the sword that severs all.

The Echo-Elf Answers

The MS shows '(Impromptu)'.

Cynic's Epitaph

This appeared in *The London Mercury* with 'Epitaph on a Pessimist'. There is a difference: the cynic is certain that goodness will not prevail, and does not wish to live again; the pessimist wishes he had never been born.

A Beauty's Soliloquy During Her Honeymoon

con, examine and judge.

Based on Hardy's observation, no doubt, at the hotel. The phrase 'this cargo of choice beauty' might be used humorously or sarcastically, but does not befit the speaker, whose reflections take a more dramatic turn at the end.

Donaghadee (August 1914)

Correspondence between the Hardys and the St. John Ervines (who were staying at Donaghadee when the poem was written) shows that Hardy improvised the poem on the name of the village (in County Down, Northern Ireland), and that it was prompted by a letter he received from a stranger at Donaghadee on 'some book of mine'. The 'impromptu' reveals Hardy's familiarity with Irish songs.

He Inadvertently Cures His Love-Pains

For 'sweet agonies', cf. *TD*.xxv: 'torturing ecstasy . . . "pleasure girdled about with pain" '.

The Peace Peal

Rung at St Peter's, Dorchester, on Armistice Day, 11 November 1918. An amusing fable, with the seriousness of the moral in the last line.

Lady Vi

In *The Poor Man and the Lady* Hardy satirized the upper classes (see *Life*, 58 for some of Alexander Macmillan's critical advice. Rotten Row is mentioned, and this particular scene was adapted for inclusion in *PBE*.xiv.) The poem is based partly on such recollections, but its attack is not so much on society as on blood-sports.

arm-embowments. Cf. 'The Face at the Casement'. *big-game killing*. Mainly in Africa; cf. Sir Blount Constantine, a cruel husband (*TT*). *many a wend*, numerous twists and turns.

A Popular Personage at Home (1924)

sill, threshold of the door.

Lady Cynthia Asquith suggested a poem about the Hardys' dog. She had seen its extraordinary behaviour at table (cf. *ORFW*. 162).

Inscriptions for a Peal of Eight Bells

Hardy's interest in church bells and bell-ringing may be seen at the end of *Desperate Remedies*, and in his visit to the belfry of St Peter's, Dorchester, to hear the peal on New Year's Eve, 1884 (*Life*, 169–70). Probably all the names and dates are imagined; the MS shows that he tried 'Payne' and 'Scryne' before choosing 'Brine'. The timbre of the bell can be heard in 'So that in tin-like tones I tongue me'.

canon, cannon, the part of the bell by which it is hung.

A Refusal (August 1924)

dict, preaching. *horner*, adulterer. *gablet*, gabled niche.

A petition, signed by a number of statesmen and writers (including Hardy) had been published in *The Times* urging the erection of a memorial tablet in Poets' Corner, Westminster Abbey, to Lord Byron on the centenary of his death. The proposal was rejected by the Dean. The poem reaches an ironical climax with reference to Shelley and Swinburne, the two English poets to whom Hardy had been most consistently devoted.

Epitaph on a Pessimist

In Wessex names 'Stoke-Barehills' is Basingstoke. In his letters, Hardy refers to Stoke Poges (where the poet Thomas Gray was buried) as 'Stoke'. There was also Stoke-sub-Hamdon near Yeovil, well known to Hardy for its Ham-hill building-stone. Stoke-on-Trent, better known to readers generally, need not be discounted. The epitaph exists in many forms, all deriving from the Greek.

The Protean Maiden

Compare 'The Well-Beloved'.

A Watering-Place Lady Inventoried

Hardy's analysis and rhymes suggest an ambivalent attitude and a light-hearted composition.

The Sea Fight (1916)

Captain Prowse was in command of the *Queen Mary* when it was sunk in the battle of Jutland on 31 May 1916. Hardy's interest stemmed principally from knowing Captain Prowse's sister, Mrs Cowley, wife of the vicar of Stinsford.

Down went the. . . . A reminder of William Cowper's 'On the loss of the Royal George'.

Paradox

For Hardy's greater open-mindedness on the subject of immortality (based on his own emotional experience rather than on scientific reasoning), compare 'He Prefers Her Earthly' (p. 145). He is thinking of his sister Mary, who died in 1915.

The Rover Come Home

This arose from a passage on Bob Loveday, the miller's son, immediately on his return home. Though he 'had been all over the world from Cape Horn to Pekin, and from India's coral strand to the White Sea, the most conspicuous of all the marks that he had brought back with him was an increased resemblance to his mother, who had lain all the time beneath Overcombe church wall' (*TM*.xv).

Canso Cape to Horn, Nova Scotia to the southern tip of South America. *Comorin . . . Behring's Strait.* From the tropical southern point of India to the Arctic strait between Asia and Alaska. (For 'India's coral strand' in the quotation above, see R. Heber's 'From Greenland's icy mountains' in *Hymns Ancient and Modern*.)

'Known Had I'

Though some link with Emma Hardy may be seen, the general situation is imaginary.

The Pat of Butter

The places mentioned suggest that the agricultural show took place at Yeovil when the Hardys lived there in the summer of 1876. The Yeo river runs on the eastern side of the town; the Coker rill, to the south. Netherhay and Kingcomb are further south, the first, north-west of Broadwindsor, the second, east of Beaminster.

Bags of Meat

The title and the description show how far poetry had moved with Hardy towards the ordinariness of life. The MS suggests that the market was at Wimborne, where Hardy wrote *Two on a Tower*. If he

intended the poem to have a humane influence, he failed in the sentimental flicker of the last two lines.

The Sundial on a Wet Day

quiz, question.

The sundial was most probably in the rectory garden at St Juliot, and
'He' is the sun.

Her Haunting-Ground

The opening of this dramatic lyric resembles Henry Vaughan's 'And
do they so? Have they a sense/Of ought but influence?'. There can be
little doubt that Hardy had his first wife Emma and St Juliot in mind;
she was buried 'far away' at Stinsford. Her tomb was not slighted,
though she had been (Hardy felt) in her later years, and she had never
been very happy in Dorchester.

A Parting-Scene

Travel by train gave Hardy glimpses of the 'poetry of life'; see, for
example, 'In a Waiting-Room' and 'The New Toy'.

Shortening Days at the Homestead

Like shock-headed urchins. Hardy's imagery is often anthropomorphic;
'pollard willows' sprout rapidly and thickly after being 'beheaded'.
the cider-maker . . . press. Cf. *W.*xxv. The scene may be in Blackmoor
Vale, 'Pomona's plain'.

Days to Recollect

One of the most lyrical of Hardy's dramatic poems, it addresses Emma
Hardy, recalling a walk towards St Alban's Head in the autumn of
1875 when they lived at Swanage, and contrasting it with the day of
her death. The description indicates when the seventh instalment of
The Hand of Ethelberta (as it appeared in *The Cornhill Magazine*,
January 1876) was written, for in it (xxxi) we find a description of
ladies' dresses 'sweeping over the hot grass and brushing up thistle-
down . . . so that it rose in a flight from the skirts of each like a comet's
tail'.

To C. F. H.

The Hanburys bought the Kingston Maurward estate at Stinsford during the First World War. Through his first marriage, they were related to Hardy, who was a godparent at the christening of their daughter Caroline Fox Hanbury in September 1921. His gift to 'his little godchild' was the manuscript of this poem in a silver box (*Life*, 414).

chance and change. Two important features in Hardy's tragic vision of life. With them he began his first volume of poetry.

The High-School Lawn

Hardy's detail on uniform colours made the school recognizable, no doubt, when the poem appeared, but it has not been identified.

The Forbidden Banns

For another instance, without such a sequel, see *RN*.i.iii.

The Paphian Ball

weirdsome, fateful, casting a spell.

Another legendary story of the Mellstock Quire, with the carol-hymn 'While shepherds watched' once again magically defeating the spirit of revelry as Christmas Day begins (cf. 'The Dead Quire'). The choir's round lay from Higher Bockhampton over the heath past Rushy Pond to isolated farms, then in Lower Bockhampton, and on by the river-path to Stinsford itself. An MS note states that the poem was composed 'several years ago'; 'but being cast in a familiar medieval mould was not printed till now [Christmas 1924], when it has been considered to have some qualities worth preserving'. It illustrates the triumph of Christianity over Paganism (a theme reflected in Milton's 'Ode on the Morning of Christ's Nativity'). The pagan quality of the ball is represented in the image of the dark tumulus Rainbarrow, 'like a supine negress' breast'. The miracle of the singing is not explained. For lack of evidence to the contrary, perhaps it can be assumed in a supernatural context that the choir did their usual round while imagining they were elsewhere. Wherever they went, they found at the end of their 'experience' that they were at the same spot on the heath as when it began.

Clyffe-Clump. See 'Yell'ham Wood's Story', (p. 89). *Paphian*, of Paphos in Cyprus. Its inhabitants, according to Lemprière's classical dictionary, were 'very effeminate and lascivious'.

On Martock Moor (1899)

deep-dyed, steeped in guilt.

Hardy may have changed the setting to Martock (north-west of Yeovil) because the dismal and rather unromantic ballad was based to some extent on actuality. The MS shows 'On Durnover Moor', i.e. below Fordington, on the eastern side of Dorchester. The 'Weir-water' could be by 'The Ten Hatches' (cf. *MC*.xli and 'Before my Friend Arrived').

knowing/By rote each rill's low pour. See the description in *MC*.xli.

That Moment

The poem seems to be autobiographical, referring to words uttered by Emma, for which Hardy in retrospect felt she was not responsible. The first title was 'The Misery of that Moment'.

Premonitions

Betty is Betty Privett of 'The Superstitious Man's Story' (*LLI*), and the superstitions are connected with the death of her husband.

went heavy, seemed unusually heavy to the ringer.

This Summer and Last (1913?)

The 'corn-brown curls' show that Emma Gifford is the main subject; cf. 'her corn-coloured hair abundant in its coils' (*Life*, 73). 'Yester-summer' may seem to refer to the previous year, but Emma is remembered in her pre-marriage days; the 'alert brook' is the Valency.

'Nothing Matters Much'

Judge Benjamin Fossett Lock was one of Hardy's friends. He was born in Dorchester in 1847, and died at Bridlington, near Flamborough Head, in 1922. Hardy remembered his saying, 'Nothing matters much'. It represented one of his common views (though not the only one; cf. *TT.* preface and 'Great Things').

In the Evening

On the death of another distinguished Dorchester friend. The poem is a revision of a tribute paid by Hardy in *The Times* (see Edmund Blunden, *Thomas Hardy*, 1958, p. 266 for the text). Sir Frederick Treves began in very moderate circumstances. After attending William Barnes's school in Dorchester, he went to the Merchant Taylors' School in London, leaving at eighteen to qualify in medicine at the London Hospital. After acting as a consulting surgeon to the Forces during the Boer War, he became Surgeon Extraordinary to Queen Victoria. His fame spread as a result of operating successfully on Edward VII in 1902. He wrote several medical texts and a number of other books, including one on Dorset and another, *The Country of 'The Ring and the Book'*, on the Italian background to the story of Browning's great dramatic poem. First President of the Society of Dorset Men (1904–7), he was succeeded by Hardy (1907–9). For the latter's note on Treves, see *Life*, 423.

Aesculapius . . . Hippocrates. Aesculapius, the Greek god of medicine; Galen, a Greek physician of the second century A.D., and a voluminous writer on medicine and philosophy; Hippocrates, born in Cos (an island in the Cyclades) and the most celebrated of Greek physicians, is reputed to have saved Athens from the plague, and to have died (*c.* 361 B.C.) at the age of ninety-nine, free from all disorder of body and mind.

The Six Boards

They represent all sides of a coffin.

Before My Friend Arrived

The subject of death is continued. Hardy thinks of the time when he sat on Ten Hatches Weir (cf. 'On Martock Moor', p. 230), after hearing of his friend Horace Moule's suicide at Cambridge. He looked across at the tower of St George's, Fordington, of which Horace's father was vicar, and then began a sketch of the grave which had been prepared in the churchyard, and which one imagines he had visited. Hardy attended the funeral the next day (*Life*, 96). See 'Standing by the Mantelpiece' (p. 249).

Compassion (22 April 1924)

Hardy in his later years became more actively engaged in promoting the humane treatment and slaughter of animals. See *AHC*. 182–3 and the *ORFW* index, 'cruelty to birds and animals'. The poem was written at the request of the Royal Society for the Prevention of Cruelty to Animals.

Ailinon! . . . But may the good prevail. From Aeschylus, *Agamemnon*, 120ff.

'Why She Moved House'

Tragedian to Tragedienne

After counterfeiting death in a tragedy, an elderly actor contemplates his own death.

The Lady of Forebodings

Cf. 'Mother's notion (and also mine) – that a figure stands in our van with arm uplifted, to knock us back from any pleasant prospect we indulge in as probable' (*THN*. 32).

The Bird-Catcher's Boy (21 November 1912)

The narrative, founded on Hardy's dislike of caging birds (cf. Orel, 252) and his association of Christmas and the supernatural, seems entirely unconvincing.

like those in Babylon. Psalm cxxxvii. *Durdle-Door*, a rock which projects into the sea, forming a natural archway west of Lulworth Cove.

A Hurried Meeting

The night-hawk plays the role of the Spirit Ironic (as at the end of *W*.xx). Hardy offended upper-class readers with a similar story in *DR*.iii.1 and xxi.3.

crossing South, crossing the Equator to live in the Southern hemisphere for a time.

Discouragement (1863–7)

The MS date may be correct, '1865–7'; no other poem appears to have been written at Westbourne Park Villas before 1865. This is Hardy's most explicit complaint against the injustices of birth and heredity. Nature is considered to be the mere tool of an unknown Lord (cf. 'Doom and She'). Hardy seems to have been impressed by *Hamlet*, I. iv. 23ff:

> So, oft it chances in particular men
> That, for some vicious mole of nature in them,
> As in their birth, wherein they are not guilty,
> Since nature cannot choose his origin. . . .

He instances looks, 'hap of birth' (class, income, opportunities), and physical propensities. His novels show how much he had these in mind when turning the tragic spotlight on those to whom chance had given little choice. His first novel, *The Poor Man and the Lady* (1867–8), was heavily charged with class satire; his last, *Jude the Obscure*, depends much for its tragedy on heredity and lack of educational opportunities.

naturing Nature. Not in the philosophical sense of Coleridge's phrase in his lecture 'On Poesy or Art', but 'nature which produces the natures of people'. *frost*. A key image in relation to Nature's defects and man's handicaps; see 'The Caged Thrush Freed and Home Again' (p. 51).

A Leaving

One MS of the poem has the title 'A Last Leaving'. This and the 'journey afar' suggest Emma Hardy's funeral journey. So little room was there for vehicles at the front of Max Gate that Hardy could have watched as the first car moved off. It is true that the sun shone when the coffin was lowered into its grave at Stinsford (Bailey, 573), but there may have been rain when it left Max Gate. Or the rain and the watching may be poetic licence. The alternative suggestion (Emma Hardy's last outing; see 'Your Last Drive', p. 103) is not borne out by the MS title and the ominous note in the last line of the poem. The reversed rhyme-scheme is noteworthy: the first line is repeated at the end, the second line rhymes with the last but one, and so on.

Song to an Old Burden

Once again Hardy nears the end of a volume with the thought that he has outlived his span. This is the old 'burden' or motif; cf. 'Looking Across'. He thinks of happiness in the past, but, as those he chiefly associates with it are dead, he asks why he should expect it to continue. The opening verse alludes to his boyhood (cf. 'The Self-Unseeing'), with references to his father (the fiddler) and grandfather (the 'cello player) buried together at Stinsford. The second and third verses recall his early happiness with Emma Gifford/Hardy.

'Why Do I?'

Hardy's 'apology' for continuing to write poetry. He asks whether he writes it merely as a pastime, and answers that he will continue to write as long as he lives in a world of pain. In this he may have been influenced by Hugo's preface to *Les Misérables*.

8

Winter Words

THIS volume was published posthumously in October 1928. Despite
the ostensible uncertainty of the blank in the 'introductory note', there
can be little doubt that Hardy hoped it would be published on his
eighty-eighth birthday, since he began the work of assembling the
poems shortly before his final illness in January 1928. Further revision
was intended, and the final order was not settled. There are indications
that some of the 105 poems might have been discarded for others
(Purdy, 262). It is interesting to see that he could still find unpublished
poems from various periods, even two which were written about sixty
years earlier.

In his last years Hardy seems less prone to blame some ultimate Cause
for the plight of man. *Winter Words* ends significantly with one of the
poems which express his disillusionment with the human race for its
'hideous self-treason'; he could see that the Second World War was
almost inevitable. The title chosen for the volume recalls 'The Darkling
Thrush', and indicates how far removed Hardy ultimately was from
the buoyant young man who read *The Revolt of Islam* with the inspired
faith that, if Winter comes, Spring cannot be far behind. It is a little
surprising therefore that he should have thought it worth while to
protest in his introduction against the 'licensed tasters' or reviewers
who had carelessly pronounced his last volume of poetry 'wholly
gloomy or pessimistic'.

In saying that the poets of ancient Greece did not die young, Hardy
was thinking of writers such as Aeschylus, but much more of the
contrast between Hellenism and 'the ache of modernism'* which had
engaged his attention in some of his major novels ever since he read
Walter Pater's *Studies in the History of the Renaissance* (1873). He
presented it first in *The Return of the Native* (III. i):

* The phrase occurs in *TD*.xix. For the Greek poets, cf. *Life*, 384.

What the Greeks only suspected we know well; what their Aeschylus imagined our nursery children feel. That old-fashioned revelling in the general situation grows less and less possible as we uncover the defects of natural laws, and see the quandary that man is in by their operation.

The statement seems both exaggerated and incomplete. The implications of 'the quandary that man is in' extend beyond Darwinism and the Unfulfilled Intention to include Chance and the conventions of society, as may be seen in *Jude the Obscure*.*

Hardy's final remarks reiterate what he had written in his preface to *Poems of the Past and the Present*, in his 'General Preface to the Novels and Poems' for the Wessex edition of 1912 (Orel, 48–9), and elsewhere (e.g. *Life*, 410–11). He had learned the danger of being too positive, had declared that his views were but 'seemings', and come to the conclusion that experience extends beyond the bounds of rational apprehension.

The New Dawn's Business

Hardy was eighty-seven when he began arranging poems for his last volume. Appropriately he begins with a poem on time and age, with an ironical reference to his survival.

heathy ledge. Of 'Egdon Heath', clearly visible from Max Gate. *killing . . . bringing to birth*. Cf. 'Life and Death at Sunrise'. *debt . . . bed and*

* The essay to which Hardy was indebted in Pater's Renaissance studies is that on Winckelmann. Can the modern artist 'represent men and women' in the 'bewildering toils' of natural forces (which are universal and 'woven through and through us' like a 'magic web') in such a way that we are inspired with 'at least the equivalent for the sense of freedom'? 'Natural laws we shall never modify, embarrass us as they may; but there is still something in the nobler or less noble attitude with which we watch their fatal combinations.' Hardy realized the web which was for ever weaving through the universe (cf. 'The Lacking Sense', p. 41, and the Apology to *Late Lyrics and Earlier*, p. 163); and it was his custom to present men and women in 'the fell clutch of circumstance'. The nobility of his tragic characters is variable rather than doubtful; he believed that 'The business of the poet and the novelist is to show the sorriness underlying the grandest things, and the grandeur underlying the sorriest things' (*Life*, 171). Yet it seems impossible that he could give a ready consent to Pater's conclusion: 'Who, if he saw through all, would fret against the chain of circumstance which endows one at the end with those great experiences?' There were times when Hardy believed philosophically (unlike Browning) that life was not worth the purchase. Such an attitude was apt to colour the presentation of his tragic figures; in such a mood he saw Jude as his 'poor puppet' (*Life*, 272).[29]

board. Cf. 'Those who died before 1914 are out of it, thank Heaven – and "have the least to pay" according to the old epitaph' (*ORFW.* 196). Hardy alludes to a poem by Francis Quarles (1592–1644) which may be seen in various forms in English burial-places, e.g.

> Our life is but a winter's day:
> Some only breakfast and away;
> Others to dinner stay, and are full fed;
> The oldest only sups and goes to bed.
> Large is his debt who lingers out the day;
> Those who go the soonest have the least to pay.

Proud Songsters

Part of life's cycle is seen with both wonder and scientific detachment.

Thoughts at Midnight (part written 25 May 1906)

Its special interest is that Hardy places the blame for the failures of civilization not on the Will or any other abstraction but on people, their 'unreason' and 'hideous self-treason'. He seems to be much more pessimistic than in 'A Plaint to Man'.

'I Am the One'

train, procession. *scathe*, harm.

An ideal picture of a person who is natural. He does not make birds and animals start with fear; he is not bitten with curiosity about burials; and he is at one with the stars. Cf. 'Wagtail and Baby' (p. 88).

hollowed spot, place where a grave has been dug.

The Prophetess

'The Mocking-Bird' was a song Emma Hardy used to sing (*MGC.* 177, letter 4093). The mockery lies in the last words of the song:

> Pretty warbler, wake the grove
> To notes of joy, to songs of love.

Hardy's second verse was added to make this evident.

A Wish for Unconsciousness

The Bad Example

More explicit than the original by Meleager (in J. W. Mackail, *Selected Epigrams from the Greek Anthology*, London, 1911).

To Louisa in the Lane

Louisa Harding; cf. 'The Passer-by' (p. 191) and 'Louie' (p. 218). The Harding family were too proud to encourage a friendship between her and Hardy; hence, perhaps, the beginning of his poor-man-and-the-lady complex. The 'hollow of the lane' is on the road from Stinsford to Bockhampton Cross, near the point where Hardy often took the path across the fields to Higher Bockhampton.

Love Watches a Window

The saint's figure reminds the lady of her former lover.

The Love-Letters

No satisfactory identification has been found.

An Unkindly May

Although Hardy revised the poem on 27 November 1927 (*Life*, 444), this does not imply that it is an early one. The 'white smock-frock' and the addition of '(1877)' to the MS title suggest that the scene was remembered from the period when the Hardys lived at Sturminster Newton.

Unkept Good Fridays (Good Friday, 1927)

Though the date changes each year, Good Friday in Holy Week is regarded as the anniversary of the Crucifixion (to which Hardy refers in 'mockeries', 'bloody sweat' – from the Church Litany – 'sepulchres', 'cross and cord'). He thinks of the 'Christs of unwrit names', all those who suffered horribly and died for their faith in times of persecution.

The poem seems to be the outcome of one of the Positivist beliefs, that in the cause of humanity Jesus was but one of many Messiahs or Redeemers. This view is expressed by Frederic Harrison in *The Positive Evolution of Religion* (1913).

The Mound

This brief lyric is so dramatic and imaginatively detailed that it is apt to suggest autobiography. It may be based on a situation Hardy heard of in his earlier years, or it may be wholly imaginary. The mound by the tree is obviously much smaller than the wooded eminence in Hardy's illustration to 'In a Eweleaze near Weatherbury'. Whether there is a link between 'simpleton' and *Jude the Obscure* (originally 'The Simpletons') is doubtful, though the refusal of the woman to be 'bound/ For life to one man' has a parallel in Sue Bridehead. Pupil-teacher regulations combined with what is known of Tryphena Sparks's up-bringing and career make any suggested link between her and the poem seem wildly improbable.

Liddell and Scott (1988)

Hardy owned a copy of their famous Greek lexicon (1843). In com-piling it, they made use of the Greek-German lexicon by Franz Passow (1819–24).

mused on a college living. Dr H. G. Liddell, after being head of West-minster School, became Dean of Christ Church, Oxford, in 1855. *Donnegan.* James Donnegan was the author of an earlier Greek-English dictionary (cf. *LLI.* 'A Tragedy of Two Ambitions', i). ἄατος ... ἀαγής, the two opening words of the dictionary. ὠώδης, the word with which it concluded.

Christmastide

Compare 'A Nightmare, and the Next Thing.'

the Casuals' gate, the entrance for tramps and paupers (not for regular or permanent inmates) to the Union or workhouse on Damers Road, Dorchester (where Fanny Robin is imagined to have died, *FMC*.xl, xlii).

Reluctant Confession

shards, pieces.

Expectation and Experience

lew, shelter.

Aristodemus the Messenian

outshown, shown forth, manifested.

This brief and sensational drama was adapted from the account of the war between the Messenians and Spartans by the Greek historian Pausanias. The Messenians, after being forced to retreat to the mountain stronghold of Ithome, sent for advice to the oracle at Delphi. They were told that they must sacrifice a virgin. Accordingly Aristodemus offered his daughter. . . . The hendecasyllabics (lines of eleven syllables in classical metre)are not always dramatic, especially in 'Thus and now it adumbrates', 'I'll make the asseverance first'.

intact one, virgin. *Aépÿtids' renowned house*, renowned descendants of Aepytus. *Euphaes*, King of the Messenians. Hardy makes the sacrifice by Aristodemus more imperative at this point, since he has been proclaimed successor to Euphaes (six years in advance of its occurrence, according to Pausanias).

Evening Shadows

cyst, hollow, grave.

As he watches the evening shadows, Hardy reflects that, though there is nothing in the indifferent scene to suggest it, those cast by Max Gate will still appear when he is buried, just as those cast by Conquer Barrow will last long enough to have seen both the adoption and the rejection of the Christian creed. (For this last thought, cf. the note on 'Aquae Sulis', p. 111.) The poem has no Shelleyan-Platonic implications to the effect that man and his ideas are but as passing shadows. Hardy's thought is scientific and historical (like that of the Spirit of the Years): in one sense, life and religions are less than shadows.

The Three Tall Men

One of Hardy's humorous ironies.

The Lodging-House Fuchsias

Mrs Masters was probably the wife of the captain with whom the Hardys lodged at Swanage (cf. *Life*, 107-8 and *HE*.xxxi, at the end of which the fuchsias appear). In the novel, which Hardy completed there, he was called 'Mr Flower', perhaps to commemorate his wife's regard for her fuchsias.

The Whaler's Wife

This is the kind of story that Hardy would at one time have told in prose. The small town may be Bridport, where an inn called 'The Five Bells' may still be seen.

anyway buried her. The colloquial parenthesis ('anyway') is appropriate to the narrator.

Throwing a Tree

It first appeared in *Commerce* (Paris), Winter 1927-8, with a misleading note to the effect that it was the last poem Hardy wrote. The original title 'Felling a Tree' suggests that the subject was prompted partly by William Barnes's 'Vellèn the Tree'. The process Hardy describes with obvious interest is more modern, but the conclusion shows regret like Barnes's

> Zoo the gre't elem tree out in little hwome groun'
> Wer' a stannèn this mornèn, an now's a-cut down.

Perhaps Hardy watched the scene while on a visit to Hermann Lea at Linwood, Ringwood, after the latter had left the Hardy cottage at Higher Bockhampton (see 'Silences', p. 243).

The War-Wife of Catknoll

In the register of baptisms at Melbury Osmond which Hardy consulted to trace his maternal ancestry, there is an entry he would note. It concerns the private baptism of a boy whose mother was the wife of a soldier who had been out of England more than two years (Bailey, 586). Hardy changed the time and place: from 1817 to the period immediately after the First World War, and from Melbury Osmond to Chetnole, less than two miles away.

Concerning His Old Home

One of Hardy's moods is explained by a note written at the end of May 1922. He found his old home and garden 'shabby'. It became increasingly painful to visit it, and 'often when he left he said he would go there no more'. His last visit was in 1926; he was accompanied by Mr Hanbury of Kingston Maurward, and his motive was to have 'the Hardy house' tidied up and made more secluded (*Life*, 415, 433). The poem reflects a crescendo of interest from 'never' to 'night and day'.

Her Second Husband Hears Her Story

Probably one of the sensational stories that came to Hardy from gossip or the local newspaper.

Yuletide in a Younger World

still small voices . . . fire-filled prophets. See I Kings, xix. 12 and Jeremiah, v. 14.

After the Death of a Friend

doff, take off. *outrun*, run out of.

The 'grey claimant' is Death; 'this worm-holed raiment', the body.

The Son's Portrait

The germ of this story of disloyalty to the memory of a husband killed in the 1914–18 war is to be found in JO.1.xi.

Lying Awake

Hardy thinks of the Morning Star still visible in the east, the beeches which he can see at the front of Max Gate, a meadow in the Frome valley, and the Stinsford churchyard beyond, with the Hardy graves awaiting him under the yew.

The Lady in the Furs (1925)

The original title ('The Lady in the Christmas Furs') and the fact that the poem was first published at the beginning of the 1926 Christmas season indicate the direction and implications of Hardy's satire. Like 'Christmas: 1924', it turns ironically on the traditional association of Christmas with peace and goodwill. Peace for Hardy was not limited to mankind; his altruism included the whole animal world. His criticism extends to the exploitation of workers. No authority can be found for the view that Hardy had any particular lady in mind. The poem was intended for society in general. Cf. 'Lady Vi'.

Childhood Among the Ferns

Autobiographical; cf. *Life*, 15–16, JO.1.ii (where the experience is adapted to the context), and 'He Never Expected Much'.

A Countenance (1884)

In 'A Watering-Place Lady Inventoried' Hardy describes an attractive personage who is 'Flawlessly oval of face'. In this poem, he finds attractiveness in a little irregularity. It seemed to him an important principle in art (*Life*, 105). Cf. Tennyson, *Maud*, 1. ii (of a face): 'Faultily faultless, icily regular, splendidly null'.[30]

A Poet's Thought

On the misunderstanding an original writer suffers; cf. 'Not Known', 'Lausanne. In Gibbon's Old Garden' (the words of John Milton), and 'He Resolves to Say No More'.

Silences

Hermann Lea lived at the Hardy cottage, Higher Bockhampton, from the early part of 1913 (after Henry Hardy and his two sisters had left for Talbothays, West Stafford) until 1921. The 'rapt silence' which is the main subject of the poem may have been experienced when Hardy revisited his old home after Lea's departure; see the note to 'Concerning His Old Home' (p. 242).

'I Watched a Blackbird'

Based on an observation of 15 April 1900, which, although included in the typescript, was omitted from Hardy's *Life*: 'Easter Sunday.

Watched a blackbird on a budding sycamore near enough to see his tongue and even his coloured bill parting and closing as he sang. He flew down, picked up a stem of hay, and flew up to where he was building.' The penultimate line of the poem is much inferior to the prose. [31]

A Nightmare, and the Next Thing

Compare 'Christmastide'. Unlike the poet, the girls on their way (up the High Street, Dorchester) to a dance see nothing nightmarish in their foggy surroundings. For Hardy, to whom death was 'the Next Thing', the phantasmal scene suggested 'the Nether Glooms' of the dead (cf. 'To my Father's Violin').

To a Tree in London (192–)

This must be the tree 'in the midst' of 'Bede's Inn' (*PBE*.xiii), where Knight had his chambers. They were drawn from the offices of the architect Raphael Brandon, for whom Hardy worked in 1870, in an 'old-world out-of-the-way corner of Clement's Inn' (*Life*, 77).

The Felled Elm and She

A cross-section of a tree-trunk shows a series of rings from the centre outwards, each representing a year's growth.

He Did Not Know Me

The poem is an allegory. Cf. *TD*.xxi, xxix ('What was comedy to them was tragedy to her') and the dictum of Horace Walpole in the note to 'The Coquette, and After' (p. 49).

So Various

The contrasting aspects which Hardy gives of himself are not complete. A strange one arises from poems which express the urgings of an evolutionary meliorist and those which indicate the wish to escape into 'nescience'. More characteristic and important is that of the Spirit of the Years and the Spirit of the Pities in *The Dynasts*; the two are inseparable if one is to view his tragedy in perspective. The title of the poem is from John Dryden's *Absalom and Achitophel*:

> A man so various that he seem'd to be
> Not one, but all mankind's epitome.

A Self-Glamourer

undoubt, confidence.

Though the past seems to indicate that his cheerful optimism has been justified, even this 'self-glamourer' has moments when he is not completely assured about the future. He wonders whether his luck will hold, whether he will continue to escape 'the Frost's decree'.

The Dead Bastard

Natural love is deeper than conventional views.

The Clasped Skeletons

colled, embraced.

Conquer Barrow has not been excavated. Writing to Paul Lemperly in September 1922, Florence Hardy said that a barrow near Max Gate had been opened the previous week, and that eight skeletons had been unearthed, one being that of a Stone Age man (about four thousand years old, Hardy said) with a complete set of teeth. The excavations took place at Bincombe Barrow on the downs about four miles south-south-west of Max Gate. The 'clasped skeletons' may have been imagined. The theme of the poem is the insignificance of life relative to the ages. Hardy thinks of famous lovers of remote eras whom the uncovered pair predeceased: Paris and Helen (the Trojan War), David and Bathsheba (II Samuel, xi), Jael and Sisera (Judges, iv), Aholah (Ezekiel, xxiii), the Greek statesman and orator Pericles and his mistress and wife Aspasia, Alexander the Great and Thais, Antony and Cleopatra, Procula pleading with her husband Pilate not to condemn Jesus (Matthew, xxvii. 19), and the twelfth-century French theologian Abelard, who was married privately to the youthful Héloise. Her uncle had him mutilated ('scarred') to debar him from ecclesiastical preferment, and he became a monk. Yet the two lovers who lived before all these belonged but to yesterday compared with the fossils among which they were buried.

In the Marquee

Hardy's rough notes for the poem indicate that he chose as the background to his story a party at Westbourne Park Villas, London (where he lodged from 1863 to 1867). The dream-dance recalls Eustacia's after her 'perfervid' imagination had made her fall in love with Clym Yeobright (*RN.*II.iii).

getting and spending. From Wordsworth's 'The world is too much with us'.

After the Burial

The scene seems to be near St Peter's, Dorchester.

The Mongrel

Which is the mongrel, man or dog?

Concerning Agnes

The death of Lady Grove in December 1926 made Hardy recall dancing with her at Rushmore, south-east of Shaftesbury. Larmer Avenue is named after the Larmer Tree by which, according to tradition, King John's hunters assembled. See *Life*, 269, 281.[32]

Kalupso, Calypso, one of the sea nymphs, daughters of Oceanus. *Amphitrite . . . Mid-sea,* the wife of Neptune . . . Mediterranean. *the Nine,* the Greek muses.[32]

Henley Regatta

The 'half-crazed tears' and her subsequent behaviour suggest that it was Nancy's frustration on Regatta Day which finally unhinged her mind.

An Evening in Galilee

The juxtaposition of this and 'Henley Regatta' shows that Hardy was as willing as ever to shock contemporary readers. From her house at Nazareth, Mary, the mother of Jesus, looks west to Mount Carmel, east to the Jordan valley and the Sea of Galilee, and reflects on her son's strange behaviour. His opposition to the priests is best illustrated towards the end of his life (Matthew, xxi. 23-27); 'Woman, what have I to do with thee?' relates to the marriage at Cana (John, ii. 1-11). Hardy assumes that Mary was too literal-minded to understand what was meant by 'Who is my mother?' (Matthew, xii. 46-50). For the question 'Who is my father?' and her vague look towards Jezreel, from which the 'one other' came to Nazareth, see 'Panthera'. The woman who follows Jesus is Mary Magdalene, 'out of whom he had cast seven devils' (Mark, xvi. 9).

The Brother

Bollard Head is Ballard Point on the coast north of Swanage.

We Field-Women

Tess Durbeyfield worked with Izz Huett and Marian at Flintcomb-Ash, 'a starve-acre place', during a bitterly cold winter, after they had been dairymaids in the lush Froom valley. One of Tess's companions may be imagined recalling this winter and contrasting it with conditions at Talbothays in the spring. Tess did not return with them; the 'love – too rash' refers to her misfortunes the previous autumn before finding work at Flintcomb-Ash.

Trimming swedes for the slicing-mill. Described at the beginning of *TD*. xlvi. *drawing reed.* See *TD*.xliii. It was harder than hacking up swedes outside in the worst of winter. The sheaves of corn were placed in a press, and the straws drawn out by hand. The reason for this process is given by Hardy (Orel, 234). The straw was required for thatching houses; drawn by hand from ricks or presses, it would be 'unbruised' and last twice as long as straw 'which had passed through a threshing machine in the modern way'.

A Practical Woman

frame, physique.

Squire Hooper

Hardy found the suggestion for this poem in Hutchins, III. 384-5. Squire Edward Hooper showed his hospitality at his house near Cranborne, but died at his principal home, Hurn Court in Hampshire. Feeling 'worn out', he politely took leave of his company and retired to his chamber to die in September 1795 at the age of ninety-four. The detail of the poem has been supplied by Hardy.

'A Gentleman's Second-Hand Suit'

The title seems to be the advertisement.

'We Say We Shall Not Meet'

On partings between the old, such as Hardy must often have experienced during the period when he wrote *Winter Words*.

Seeing the Moon Rise (August 1927)

conned, looked at, examined.

Hardy remembers walks with his wife Florence by a path past Conquer Barrow to the tumulus on the hill by the road which runs down to the Frome valley and Lower Bockhampton. Beyond, to the right, he would see the outline of Puddletown or 'Egdon' Heath; cf. 'At Moon-rise and Onwards'.

Song to Aurore

He Never Expected Much

leaze, pasture.

See 'Epitaph'. It could be said of Hardy's outlook generally that his disappointment arose because he expected too much (compare Carlyle's comment on Margaret Fuller's 'I accept the universe' – 'By Gad! she'd better!'). Few writers have been as wrung by the cruelties of the natural world as Hardy. His own life had proved his belief that human beings are the victims of chance. The stanza pattern and its repetition contribute greatly to the appeal of the poem.

Since as a child. See 'Childhood Among the Ferns'. *neutral-tinted*. Hardy had read Henry James's *Hawthorne* (London, 1879), and had probably noted the statement that Americans love the picturesque and find it in places where others would see only 'the most neutral tints' (p. 12). See the note to 'On an Invitation to the United States', p. 38.) The first chapter of *The Return of the Native* expresses the idea of Hardy's poem in much gloomier tones.

Standing by the Mantelpiece

Hardy remembered his last impression of Horace Moule in his rooms at Queens' College, Cambridge, standing by the mantelpiece and looking unconsciously at the candle-shroud as he talked. At the time Horatio Mosley Moule was a Local Government Board inspector for East Anglia. He had influenced Hardy during his formative years as a thinker and writer, encouraging him with reviews of his first novels. He had taught classics at Marlborough. Yet he was temperamentally unstable, and suffered from incurable bouts of depression. This lead to drinking and threats of suicide. His intemperance, an affair with a girl in his father's parish which he could not expect to remain concealed (Gittings, 181), and above all his powerlessness in the face of recurring temptations to suicide, led to the breakdown of his engagement to a woman whose identity has not been established. These two are the *dramatis personae* of the poem. Hardy must have had the 'affair' in mind when he described one feature of Mixen Lane, that 'mildewed leaf in the sturdy and flourishing Casterbridge plant . . . close to the open country' (*MC*.xxxvi). See 'The Place on the Map' (p. 98), *AHC*. 419–20, and *Life*, 32–4, 84, 87, 93, 96.

candle-wax . . . shroud . . . claimant. Moule is the speaker, and Hardy makes use of an old superstition. The link with Moule may also be found in Hardy's visits to King's College Chapel, Cambridge (*Life*, 93, 141). *wintertime*, an image of ill-fortune, as often in Hardy. *what has come was clearly consequent.* The breaking of the engagement. Does this suggest that the woman to whom Moule was engaged was 'full-advised' of his suicidal nature or of his intemperance? And how far does he enter into *Jude the Obscure*? See Gittings, 218. *drape*, drapery (indicative of a shroud).

Boys Then and Now

Based perhaps on one of Hardy's boyhood beliefs; cf. 'You little children think there's only one cuckoo' (*RN*.i.viii).

That Kiss in the Dark

The dramatic quality of the verse is much more convincing than the probability of the incident.

A Necessitarian's Epitaph

Though Hardy accepted Shelley's views (cf. *Queen Mab*, vi. 197ff. and Shelley's note) in his youth, and called Jude his 'poor puppet', he was not consistent, and cannot be regarded as an unqualified 'Necessitarian' (cf. *LLE*. Apology).

Burning the Holly

holm, holly.

Twelfth Night (6 January), twelve days after Christmas, was regarded as the end of the festive season. The burning holly forms a partial counterpoint to the story. The stanza pattern, with three consecutive rhymes and final lines all rhyming, is adapted from 'Helen of Kirconnell', which Hardy knew from *The Golden Treasury* (where its title is 'Fair Helen'. His copy was the gift of Horace Moule.).

Suspense

The similes 'like a clout' and 'Like the lid of a pot that will not close tight' are appropriate, but were probably not regarded by many as the stuff of poetry when the poem was first published. The weather provides a framework of indifference to a vague romantic situation.

The Second Visit

mill-tail, water flowing away from the mill-wheel.

The mill can still be seen at Sturminster Newton (by the river, half a mile or more from where the Hardys lived in 1876-8). The 'old house' has been demolished, but remnants of the orchard were visible in 1972. Hardy revisits the scene with Florence Hardy (who stands on the footbridge); he recalls a former visit with Emma during their 'happiest time' (*Life*, 118); the fond plaints were the lover's 'Do you love me?' This second visit could have taken place in 1916 or 1921 (*Life*, 373, 413).

Our Old Friend Dualism (1920)

The title suggests that the poem resulted from Hardy's reading a copy of his letter to Dr C. W. Saleeby, where the phrase occurs (*Life*, 369–

370), when he and Florence were preparing his *Life*. In philosophy Dualism asserts that mind and matter are separate, a principle which leads ultimately to the idea of a God or Creator outside the created universe. Monism, on the other hand, teaches that mind and matter are indivisible. Hence Hardy's change from the concept of the First or Prime Cause to that of the Immanent Will.

the Protean. Dualism appears in many forms. *Spinoza* (1632–77) equated God and Nature. Cf. Xenophanes (p. 209). *Bergson* (1859–1941), French philosopher. *James*, William James, American psychologist and pragmatic philosopher (1842–1910). *flamens*, priests (Roman), theologians.

Faithful Wilson

Based on an epigram in J. W. Mackail's *Select Epigrams from the Greek Anthology*. As in 'The Bad Example' (from the same source), Hardy makes the Greek epigram more real by giving it a personal and dramatic form.

Gallant's Song (November 1868)

A Philosophical Fantasy (1920, 1926)

unlisting, heedless.

The novelty of the poem lies not in the ideas but in their presentation, which was suggested by Bagehot's statement on God in Milton's *Paradise Lost*:

> He has made God *argue*. Now the procedure of the Divine mind from truth to truth must ever be incomprehensible to us. . . . A long train of reasoning in such a connection is so out of place as to be painful; and yet Milton has many. . . . Even Pope was shocked at the notion of Providence talking like 'a school-divine'. And there is the still worse error, that if you once attribute reasoning to Him, subsequent logicians may discover that he does not reason very well.

Hardy seems to have ignored the last sentence. His poem is a humorous conglomerate of some, if not all, of his ideas on the Immanent Will. The answer to the question of why its intention remains unfulfilled (after some by-play on how the Will should be addressed) is that it has no purpose, no ethical sense (which is man-made), no awareness of what is happening to mankind – though there may be improvement in this respect. In conclusion, the Will states that it is driven by a blind force or 'purposeless propension', not by attempts to carry out its first 'dreams' or plans.

life-shotten, exhausted of its vitality, blighted. *unfulfilled intention*. See 'The Mother Mourns' (pp. 38–9). *feminine I had thought you*. Particularly when associated with Nature, the 'Mother' or source of life. *my own confections*. Man's thoughts, like all events, are set in motion by the Will. His ideas about the Creator are 'freaks of my own framing'. *dream-projected*, driven on with the aim of achieving the 'dream' or 'intention'. *blind force persisting*, the 'purposeless propension' which the Will admits itself to be. The idea is Schopenhauer's, but Hardy met it often in his reading of, and on, contemporary philosophy.

A Question of Marriage

The irony is underscored when the countess wishes she had been the 'wench' of a genius rather than the wife of an undistinguished 'spouse' of rank and wealth such as hers. The remark 'We dine our artists; but marry them – no' seems to bear the guinea-stamp of authenticity rather than of invention, and may have originated the story, which has a kinship to that of Hardy's first novel *The Poor Man and the Lady* with its architect hero.

The Letter's Triumph

A subject which would probably have fared better in the hands of an Elizabethan or Cavalier lyricist.

A Forgotten Miniature

stark, completely. *Fair*, Beauty.

There seems to be little doubt that this is the miniature portrait of Emma Gifford in 1870 or earlier. See 'On a Discovered Curl of Hair' (p. 192).

Whispered at the Church-Opening

A satirical picture underlining Hardy's view that true work can be overlooked even in the Church. The essence of Christianity for Hardy was 'charity and good will'; cf. *JO*.VI.iv. For a comment on heartlessness and ambition in the Church, see *LLI*. 'The Son's Veto'.

In Weatherbury Stocks

The scene is in the square at Puddletown, not far from St Mary's, the parish church. Hardy was thinking of the occasion during his boyhood (*Life*, 21) when he dared to speak to a man who had been placed in the same stocks for being, as he guessed, 'drunk and disorderly' (Archer, 33–4).

Blooms-End. Best known from *The Return of the Native*; see *AHC*. 243, 313.

A Placid Man's Epitaph (1925)

Besides being idiomatic ('cared about it'), 'it' signifies life, or what life offers. In all lines except one it is part of the rhyme. Generally it helps to suggest that life is colourless. The speaker is indifferent to life rather than 'placid'.

The New Boots

The Musing Maiden (1866, recopied)

A sentimental poem with a metaphysical touch. Hardy's interest in coasters from Dorset to London is seen in *WB*.II.v.

hog-backed down, steep-ridged hill. *touch at will*. This seems to imply a compact between the lovers before parting.

Lorna the Second (1927)

A disappointed lover of Lorna the First (daughter of Reginald Bosworth Smith, a friend of Hardy) married her daughter, also named Lorna. Bosworth Smith lived at Bingham Melcombe in Dorset, and had been a master at Harrow (*Life*, 127, 342). Hardy and his wife attended the wedding of Lorna the First in 1906. The marriage of Lorna the Second took place in July 1927 (Bailey, 612).

A Daughter Returns (17 December 1901)

vamp, shoe-sole.

The cold sneer of dawn reflects the way in which the father thinks fate has treated him; the tempest mouthing in the flue-top makes him think of the curse which he feels in consequence.

The Third Kissing-Gate

This consists of modified verses (comparable, though very different in setting, to Browning's 'Meeting at Night') from 'The Forsaking of the Nest', published in *Nash's Magazine*, February 1912, with an illustration by Edward Blampied. An anxious father at home imagines his daughter leaving the town (Dorchester) and the lamps, hurrying along the elm-lined eastern road, and turning off along the path through the Frome meadows until she passes the garden wall (below Stinsford House) and reaches the third kissing-gate. She should soon be home, he fondly thinks. The truth is given in the last verse. In the original, another verse follows, placing the emphasis of the poem on the father's distress:

> The waiting father counts the clock
> And still no footstep nighs,
> For new delight has come to mock
> All early filial ties!

The clock in the illustration indicates 8 p.m. Romantic though the revised extract is, there can be no doubt that 'The Forsaking of the Nest' is imaginatively the richer of the two poems.

kissing-gate, a swing-gate, partially fenced in, enabling one person to pass through at a time. *waterfall*. Rather slight, near the end of the third meadow she crosses, i.e., near the third kissing-gate.

Drinking Song

rathe, soon.

The song suggests that the subject – human fallibility as seen through the ages in man's views of the universe – should not be taken too seriously. The poem is marred by one poor rhyme.

Thales, a Greek philosopher of the sixth century B.C. *Copernicus*, a

Polish astronomer (1473–1543) who disproved the Ptolemaic theory that the earth is the centre of the universe. *Hume*, a Scottish philosopher and historian (1711–76) whose 'famous principle' (for Hardy) was that 'no testimony is sufficient to establish a miracle' (Archer, 39); cf. his essay 'Of Miracles'. *Darwin* (1809–82) substantiated the theory of evolution by natural selection. *Doctor Cheyne* (pronounced *cháy nee*) was an English biblical critic (1841–1915) who did not accept the parthenogenic birth of Christ. *Einstein* (1879–1955). Hardy studied his theories of Relativity, with what effect may be seen in 'Drinking-Song' and his letter to Dr J. Ellis McTaggart (31 December 1919): 'after what [Einstein] says the universe seems to be getting too comic for words'.

The Tarrying Bridegroom

shalloon, light woollen dress.

The title alludes to Matthew, xxv. 5. The subject of the poem is the dread of a bride as she sees no sign of her bridegroom before she enters the church. 'Where the lane divides the pasture' is hardly true of the approach to Stinsford Church; the general setting suggests no particular reference.[33]

The Destined Pair

Hardy sees (in the abstract) circumstances leading up to a marriage, and asks the unanswerable question whether the pair would have been happier had they never met. For the philosophy, compare 'The Convergence of the Twain'.

A Musical Incident

June Leaves and Autumn (19 November 1898)

Does Hardy suggest here that, whether we die early or late, naturally or by accident, makes no difference, since (as is commonly said) we all come to the same in the end? Such a view is consistent with one he sometimes expressed that it is better never to be born.

quickened fall, its 'autumn' made premature, brought forward.

No Bell-Ringing

There was a traditional belief that Divine condemnation of sacrilege was expressed supernaturally. In the notebook kept for 'Facts', Hardy transcribed an account of the appearance of an apparition after a clerk and sexton had taken some of the Communion wine late on Christmas Eve, 1814. The same kind of sacrilege is transferred to 'Durnover' on New Year's Eve. Divine displeasure makes all the impious efforts of the bell-ringers abortive. How much is supernatural and how much psychological in the story is not clear. What causes the blast around the 'tall church tower' which makes the boy think of a gibbet skeleton (a detail which sets the event back in the remote past)? What is the apparition on the tombstone? And is the old man who confesses affected with cramp naturally?

the three-mile road. 'Road' means 'way'. Hardy seems to imagine the boy proceeding along the main road he knew so well from the neighbourhood of Higher Bockhampton to Dorchester, and turning off at Grey's Bridge to Fordington, as Dick Dewy did (*UGT*.iv.vii). *treble-bobbed,* rang the treble bell in peal-changes.

'I Looked Back'

Cf. 'We Say We Shall Not Meet'.

The Aged Newspaper Soliloquizes (March 1926)

The poem was written for a special number of *The Observer* on 14 March 1926, when it reached its one hundred and thirty-fifth anniversary (*MGC*. 191, letter 4498). The antitheses suggest the wide range of its news.

Beyond all mummed on any stage. Truth is stranger than fiction. It was in newspapers that Hardy found hints for exciting episodes and fine effects in his stories.

Christmas: 1924

'I said, We (the civilized world) have given Christianity a fair trial for nearly 2000 years, and it has not yet taught countries the rudimentary science of keeping peace: so why not throw it over, and try, say, Buddhism?' (*ORFW*. 92). For a more positive view, see *LLE*. Apology.

The Single Witness

The opening is reminiscent of *CM*. 'What the Shepherd Saw'. The story seems to originate from a historical source rather than from the imagination.

How She Went to Ireland

There seems to be little doubt that, as suggested (Purdy, 260), Dora was the wife of Hardy's editor friend Clement Shorter. She died in January 1918 and was buried in Dublin.

Dead 'Wessex' the Dog to the Household

See 'A Popular Personage at Home' (p. 225) and *Life*, 434–5 for more on the dog which Hardy at first did not welcome but which became his dear companion. The bold but not obtrusive double repetition of lines and the continuation of the rhyme in each verse seem to express both the insistence and the appeal of Wessex. His behaviour often made his mistress think that he would have to be 'put to sleep'; on 27 December 1926, 'in misery with swelling and paralysis', he was.

grassy path up the hill, the path to Conygar Hill (cf. 'The Walk', p. 103).

The Woman Who Went East

The MS title 'The Woman of the West' and the opening of the poem immediately suggest Emma Hardy, but the association is not borne out by the story. The 'weird old way' of the 'west land' refers to custom, and, although only relatively west, Portland was more peculiar in this respect than Cornwall. The story bears a remarkable resemblance to that of Marcia Bencomb and Jocelyn Pierston. They fall in love, but are parted; she travels. Forty years later, when she is 'the image and superscription of Age', they meet again and marry (*WB*.III.viii).

Not Known (MS, 1914, after reading criticism)

phasm, anything visionary.

Compare 'A Poet's Thought' and the more spontaneous and amusing 'I am in a Novel' (*Pansies*) by D. H. Lawrence, on Aldous Huxley's impression of him.

The Boy's Dream

The poem is animated by Hardy's love of birds and animals.

A Gap in the White

tass, cup or small goblet.

Another example of the poetry of life for Hardy. That such a misfortune would be a catastrophe to the woman is obvious, but few poets would have responded imaginatively to the subject as Hardy did.

Family Portraits

The story adumbrated in this poem belongs to the remote past, to 'far-off years' when the protagonists were 'forceful' and 'expert/In the law-lacking passions of life'. The sense of some looming disaster is enhanced by the recurrence of the first line (or its conclusion), and the frequent iteration of a single rhyme, in each verse. Were the story related to Hardy's family, he would probably have referred to it as 'a family tradition' (cf. 'In Sherborne Abbey'). No reference to such family portraits has been found. The poem seems to be an imaginative dramatization arising from the poet's interest in heredity, as it is seen in *Jude the Obscure* and 'The Pedigree'. The conclusion has no significance for Hardy in his later years; it hints at the fear of some hot-blooded act of intemperance by the descendant who 'speaks' throughout this dramatic lyric.

white-shrouded candles. Hinting at disaster (cf. 'Standing by the Mantelpiece'). *puppet-like movements*. As if chance (hereditary characteristics and circumstances) controlled their actions. *fear . . . like frost*. Frost is associated with misfortune, or the fear of it, in Hardy; cf. *TT*.xxxviii, 'A fear sharp as a frost settled down upon her'. *balked future pain*. The poem was first printed in December 1924 and subsequently much revised. There is nothing to indicate that it was an early poem (compare the conclusion of the general note).

The Catching Ballet of the Wedding Clothes (1919)

The period is the reign of William (1830–37), a time when belief in witchcraft was widespread in remote rural areas. White witches or wizards were not harmful; they claimed magical powers, and were consulted by superstitious people. Yet the ballad tale is supernatural from first to last, and reminiscent of the Mephistophelian strain in Hardy's fiction (cf. *AHC.* 156–8).

yes, my word . . . has, Jack has my word (a risky inversion).

A Winsome Woman
drouth, drought.

The Ballad of Love's Skeleton

George III of England (of Hanoverian descent) stayed nearly every summer at Weymouth at the end of the eighteenth century and during the early years of the nineteenth (cf. *The Trumpet-Major,* the main action of which belongs to 1804–5). He and his daughters danced at the town assemblies in the Royal Hotel, 'a red cord dividing the roya dancers from the townspeople' (*Life,* 229). The lady's lover, a baron of the King's Court, is a pleasure-seeker. He suggests they should go to Culliford Hill and Wood. She is disinclined because the latter reminds her of her crime in not allowing the child of their former amours to live. His thoughts remain fixed on enjoyment, and she agrees to accompany him to the Assembly Rooms. Her love for him remains, but she wonders how it will end. The closing lines give the title a dual significance.

'Culliford Tree' ('Cuilvertestrie', A.D. 1195) was the name of a large county area or 'hundred'. It is now restricted to a tumulus on the chalk downs on the east side of Came Wood, and this is the landmark Hardy could see to the south from Max Gate (*Life,* 173).

A Private Man on Public Men

These Horatian sentiments were shared by Hardy; ll. 13–14 recall the title 'Far from the Madding Crowd'. There is a parallel between the author and Clym Yeobright, in their return to their native heath from London and Paris.

Christmas in the Elgin Room (1905, 1926)

The humour of the poem seems to be coloured by Hardy's own view of Christmas and Christianity (see the note to 'Christmas: 1924', p. 256).

We are asked to imagine that the marbles (saved from vandalism by Lord Elgin, purchased for the nation in 1816, and placed in the British Museum) speak when they hear Christmas bells for the first time.

Pheidias, the Greek sculptor who was responsible for the sculptural decoration of the Parthenon and its gold and ivory statue of Athena. *Borean*. Boreas was the Greek god of the north wind. *Aurore*, dawn (Aurora, its Greek goddess). *Athenai's Hill*, the Acropolis, overlooking ancient Athens. *Helios*, god of the sun. *Ilissus*, a river near ancient Athens. *Demeter*, goddess of harvests. *Poseidon*, god of the sea. *Persephone*, goddess-queen of the underworld.

'We Are Getting to the End'

Hardy had moved a long way from 'A Plaint to Man'. His 'meliorism' had dwindled almost to despair of the human race. Though he speaks of 'some demonic force' at work, his impatience seems to be with the human race; cf. 'Thoughts at Midnight'. The poem makes it clear that Hardy could see the Second World War in the making.

as larks in cages sing. Cf. Thomas Carlyle (in an essay which Hardy alludes to in *MC*.xvii): 'The Soul of Man still fights with the dark influences of Ignorance, Misery and Sin; still lacerates itself, like a captive bird, against the iron limits which Necessity has drawn round it' ('Goethe's *Helena*').

He Resolves to Say No More

The same gloomy thoughts are continued. In a letter to Sir George Douglas, 7 May 1919, Hardy wrote with reference to the First World War: 'if it has ended, as I hope; but how it is to be prevented beginning again at some future year I do not pretend to understand'.

Pale Horse, Death (Revelation, vi. 8). It is followed by Hell, 'And power was given unto them . . . to kill with the sword and with hunger'. *Let Time roll backward . . . Magians*, let the future be brought forward and disclosed, as magicians claim it can be; cf. the 'belief in witches of Endor' (*LLE*. Apology). *souls in bond*. Cf. 'Unthoughtful of deliverance' in the previous poem. *By truth made free*. John, viii. 32. The Apology (*LLE*) voices Hardy's dismay at finding men's minds appear 'to be moving backwards rather than on' despite 'the Darwinian theory and "the truth that shall make you free" '.

9

Additional Poems

WITH minor exceptions, all these poems, including the first six lyrics from *The Dynasts*, are to be found in *The Complete Poems of Thomas Hardy* (London, 1975). They are here arranged alphabetically, three poems for children being listed separately. The poem 'When wearily we shrink away' has been omitted, as its authorship is uncertain and its style does not appear characteristic of Hardy. The five asterisked poems on pp. 263-4 were first published with an introductory essay by Evelyn Hardy in *The London Magazine*, 1956, pp. 28-39.

A. H., 1855–1912

Major-General Arthur Henniker died suddenly at his London home, 13 Stratford Place, on 6 February 1912, after being kicked by a horse and sustaining a broken leg. With the assistance of Florence Dugdale, Mrs Henniker prepared a collection of tributes and reminiscences for publication in his honour. The Hennikers had been friends of Hardy since 1893, and the poem was written specially for the memorial volume (*Arthur Henniker, A Little Book for his Friends*, London, 1912). Mrs Henniker hoped it would be included in *Late Lyrics and Earlier*, but Hardy never sought to reprint it, probably because its conclusion was borrowed from an old epitaph (*Life*, 336), possibly because he had discovered that it contained two syntactical blemishes to which he had been prone in his prose. For the text, see Bailey, 632 or *ORFW*. 152.

At a Rehearsal of One of J. M. B.'s Plays

The play was *Mary Rose* (1920), and the rehearsal occurred during Hardy's last visit to London (*Life*, 404). The poem consists of two quatrains, which were printed below the frontispiece portrait of Barrie in *The Complete Plays of J. M. Barrie*, 1928. The MS shows 'mumming' for 'mummery' (Purdy, 324).

Domicilium

The introductory note on the *subject* of the poem (see *Life*, 4, where 'Domicilium' appears as a footnote) is inaccurate: 'Some Words-worthian lines – the earliest discoverable of young Hardy's attempts in verse – give with obvious and naïve fidelity the appearance of their paternal homestead at a date nearly half a century before the birth of the writer . . .' The poem, in fact, contrasts the setting of Hardy's home at the time 'Domicilium' was written (between 1857 and 1860) with impressions of it which he had formed in 1851 from his grandmother's description of what it was like fifty years previously, when she and her husband began their married life in the lonely house on the edge of the heath.

'The Dynasts', Prologue and Epilogue

Both were written at the request of Harley Granville-Barker for his London production of scenes from *The Dynasts*, which ran from November 1914 to January 1915. The war which had broken out with Germany gave this production a contemporary significance which Hardy had in mind when he wrote these verses.

Epitaph

The text of this brief poem on the 'literary contortionist' G. K. Chester-ton is incomplete (see Bailey, 647). In the third line, 'Who'd' seems intended for 'Who'. The ending shows very clearly that Hardy had not forgotten what Chesterton had written in *The Victorian Age in Litera-ture*: 'Hardy became a sort of village atheist brooding and blaspheming over the village idiot.'

Epitaph

In the sixth and seventh chapters of *Conversations in Ebury Street* (1924) George Moore disparaged Hardy's writings and criticized his style with contempt. A withering reply soon came from John Middleton Murry (see 'Wrap me in my Aubusson carpet', *The Adelphi*, April 1924). According to Newman Flower (in *Just As It Happened*, 1950),

Hardy's resentment did not express itself until he lay on his deathbed, when he wrote this poem – 'his last'. It is quoted by Bailey (648).

Eunice

It seems most probable that this was written for *Desperate Remedies* in the winter of 1869–70. In the novel it appears as the work of the villain Aeneas Manston (xvi. 4).

*The Hatband

The dramatic setting and the varied rhyme scheme suggest that this 'satire of circumstance' is not one of Hardy's early poems, though it fails climactically. How much can be judged by appearances is conjectural (cf. 'The Slow Nature'), but the poem implies that the love of the friend for the girl who died is deeper than that of the lover whose mourning is shown in the traditional way. As in 'Retty's Phases' and 'Julie-Jane', Hardy's interest in old rural Wessex customs led to his recording them in narrative and dramatic contexts. The hatband which was worn by the male mourner at the funeral and the following Sunday service hung down to the waist; 'when the deceased was a young married woman', it was fastened to the hat with a white ribbon.

A Hundred Years Since

In writing this for the centenary of *The North American Review*, Hardy's basic preoccupation was the First World War and the unpredictability of progress.

A Jingle on the Times

This consists of nine eight-line stanzas, in which artists and a preacher are successively told that the world has no use for them in wartime. It was written in December 1914 in response to an appeal in aid of the Arts Fund.

Looking Back

See Purdy, 149. Although it appears in the MS of *Time's Laughingstocks*, its place in the published volume was taken by 'In the Crypted Way' (subsequently 'In the Vaulted Way').

On the Doorstep

This grimly realistic poem is the only one of the twelve 'Satires of Circumstance' in *The Fortnightly Review*, April 1911, which Hardy did not collect. A wife is sitting in her nightdress outside the door when her father appears and asks whether her brutal husband has been ill-treating her again. When the latter comes to drag her in, he is felled by her father, whom the daughter thereupon curses. If only her husband lives, he may treat her as he will.

*She Would Welcome Old Tribulations

This is a firm, rounded lyric, written 'about 1900'. Perhaps it was based on one of Emma Hardy's recollections.

'They Are Great Trees'

See *Life*, 386. Hardy recalls the Avenue, Wimborne, where he lived from 1881 to 1883 and wrote *Two on a Tower*.

*Thoughts from Sophocles

This sonnet is a paraphrase of the leading thoughts in the chorus within ll. 1200–1250 of *Oedipus Coloneus*, where the view that life offers nothing better than 'the good of knowing no birth at all' is expressed. Hardy's modification of the headland image in the sestet is more impressive than the original.

*To a Bridegroom

An abridgement of verses written in 1866, it asks whether love will withstand specific inevitabilities and accidents of Time and Chance. The main thought is memorably repeated in the first verse and the last:

> Swear to love and cherish her?
> She might moan were beauty's throne
> Beauty's sepulchre.

*The Unplanted Primrose

Hardy's footnote shows that this was written at Westbourne Park Villas some time during the 1865–7 period. His absence from home and the sight of a dead, forgotten plant could have engendered this brief emblematic narrative. A country girl, hoping to send her absent young man a primrose from the root she had reared at the 'time of love' and given him at his home the previous year, hurries there only to find that, though other flowers are blooming, it is a 'withered skeleton' on the ledge where he laid it when she left.

A Victorian Rehearsal

See Evelyn Hardy, 'An Unpublished Poem by Thomas Hardy', *The Times Literary Supplement*, 2 June 1966. The poem ultimately suggests more tragedy in the lives of the actors than in the play they are rehearsing; the scene and perhaps the crucial subject may owe something to Hardy's limited experience of 'stage realities' in London (*Life*, 54).

'The Woodlanders' (title-page epigraph)

'I have been looking for a motto for the title page . . . and not being able to find one, composed it' (*ORFW*. 44). This was in August 1895, when Hardy was revising his novels for the first uniform edition. The lines undoubtedly allude to his own matrimonial discords.

Hardy also wrote three poems for children's books ('Descriptions by Florence E. Dugdale', illustrations by E. J. Detmold) which his second wife prepared before or after her marriage:

The Calf

In *The Book of Baby Beasts*, London, 1911. See Purdy, 314.

The Lizard

In *The Book of Baby Pets*, London, 1915. See Purdy, 317.

The Yellow-Hammer

In *The Book of Baby Birds*, London, 1912. See Purdy, 316. The text of all three is found in Bailey (635, 661, 671–2).

So much depends on the context that it is often difficult to judge what units of verse in poetic drama constitute 'poems'. Hardy included the following 'lyrics' from *The Dynasts* in *Selected Poems of Thomas Hardy*, 1916:

1. 'The Night of Trafalgar' (1.v.vii), a song by sailors who knew Budmouth well.
2. 'Budmouth Dears' (3.11.i), a song on the eve of the battle of Vitoria by soldiers who recalled happy times when they were stationed at Budmouth.
3. 'My Love's gone a-fighting' (3.v.vi), a song sung by a woman on Durnover Green while an effigy of Napoleon is burning.
4. Chorus on the eve of the battle of Waterloo (3.vi.viii). The most notable feature is Hardy's altruism, and his emphasis on the distress and destruction of smaller creatures, and on damage to corn and wild flowers, in consequence of battle preparations.
5. Chorus of the Pities (3. After Scene). This is a hymn addressed to the Will. The opening is based on the Magnificat, and the Pities retain a traditional trust in Providence:

> So did we evermore sublimely sing:
> So would we now, despite thy forthshowing!

6. The final Chorus (3. After Scene). The Semichorus of the Years maintains its detached view that the Immanent Will continues

> Moulding numbly
> As in dream,

Apprehending not how fare the sentient subjects of Its scheme.

It is the Pities who express the heartfelt hope of mankind 'That the rages/ Of the ages/Shall be cancelled' as the Will becomes conscious of human suffering.

Of the other lyrics which could be detached from *The Dynasts* without serious impairment, the follow may have the greatest appeal or interest:

(*a*) 'We be the King's men, hale and hearty' (1.1.i), the song of infantry-men marching beyond Ridgeway towards the coast in March 1805, when a French invasion was expected.
(*b*) Chorus of Ironic Spirits (1.vi.iii). During the battle of Austerlitz these spirits insist that the Pities would not cry out if they knew what destruction of species had taken place in an earlier evolutionary era as a result of the blind activity of the Will.

(*c*) Chorus of Pities (2.i.iii). Here the Will may be seen at work in the Prussian nation ('no voice of reflection/Is heard').

(*d*) Chorus of Pities (2.iv.viii). The feelings of the fever-stricken army on the island of Walcheren are expressed in highly wrought verse.

(*e*) Chorus of Pities (2.vi.iv). On the final assault and carnage at Albuera. Hardy included this in *Chosen Poems* (first published in 1929).

(*f*) 'Mad Soldier's Song' (3.i.xi). A French soldier, crazed by severe wintry conditions and starvation on the long retreat from Moscow, gives expression to his feelings on hearing that Napoleon has deserted the remnants of the army. That night he and other survivors are frozen to death.

For satirical verse of the comic opera and music-hall varieties, see the Chorus of Ironic Spirits, i.vi.v and 2.v.vii.

The Famous Tragedy of the Queen of Cornwall is a competent rather than poetical work, and contains only one lyric of note. This is Tristram's song in Scene xi. Second verses were added to Iseult's song (vii) and Tristram's (xix) for the second edition of 1924 (in which the number of scenes is increased from 22 to 24 by the expansion of Scene xiii). The prologue and epilogue are plainly intended for speech.

Hardy's own Cornish romance had always made him associate Tintagel with 'an Iseult of my own', and the link with Emma Gifford may be seen in the references (xi) to St Nectan's Kieve (see 'The Runic Stone', p. 135) and Condolden, a neighbouring height crowned with a prehistoric barrow overlooking the Tintagel coast. Hints of her unhappiness in marriage are found in the Iseult of Brittany scenes; the additional verse to Tristram's song in Scene xxi (1924), for example, conveys a regretful recollection of the crisis when Hardy wrote 'Sept. 1896 – T.H./E.L.H.' against the lines in Arnold's 'Dover Beach' which begin, 'Ah, love, let us be true to one another' (see p. 60).

Supplementary Notes

12	92	The first explanation is supported by the light Elfride throws on her father's sermons (*PBE*.iv).
13	93	The music metaphor may be continued through 'note' to 'the spheres' (with an allusion to 'the music of the spheres'). The thought is Positivist, 'loving-kindness' being essential to the progress of civilization; cf. 'A Plaint to Man', p. 99.
14	95	Even if Emma showed interest in the dying of the clergyman's consumptive son (aged twenty-three) at St Clether, the ballad story is still implausible.
15	95	See *Life*, 291, which makes it clear that Hardy gave up novel-writing in order to preserve his self-respect with friends who did not read him. His wife must have felt vindicated (cf. Alfred Sutro, *Celebrities and Simple Souls*, London, 1933, p. 58). See 'In Tenebris' (p. 59).
16	97	The story was publicized by Ford Madox Ford in *Mightier than the Sword*, London, 1938, pp. 128–30. It has been questioned recently, but is so circumstantial that it seems strange it was not denied by any of the Garnetts if it is not reasonably accurate. Lack of confirmation may be due to Dr Garnett's efforts to hush up the story for the sake of the Hardys.
17	125	See also the last paragraph of Walter Bagehot's essay on Shakespeare in his *Literary Studies*.
18	129	Emma's note suggests that her visit to London was after that to Bath, in June 1873 (*Life*, 93).
19	131	For the images of the vision, compare the boy Jude's irradiation at a glorious idea, as if a supernatural lamp . . . (*JO*.i.iv).
20	136	A virtual engagement was reached in 1870 (*Life*, 83).
21	143	See *Life*, 321 ('the brother of the present Bishop of Durham').
22	144	Wind and rain are images of affliction for Eustacia (*RN*.v.vii) and Jude (*JO*.vi.viii,ix).
23	162	This suggests that the cryptic note of 1892 (*Life*, 243) may refer to Hardy's own poems (1867–92). If this inference is correct, it indicates that Hardy thought his most lyrical poems were those 'inspired by music'. John Buchan admired the 'flute' notes in *Late Lyrics and Earlier*, and thought that, particularly in this volume, Hardy had reached 'the very heart of seventeenth-century melody'.
24	163	For Hardy's positive meaning, see *Life*, 376, 415.
25	185	Emma's rapt inattention seems to be described in *PBE*. xvii (paragraph beginning, 'Elfride, in her turn'). Her revitalizing effect on Hardy (who describes himself as Clym Yeobright at the opening of *RN*.ii.vi) may be seen in *Under the Greenwood Tree*, which was written rapidly soon after his third visit to Cornwall. She is alluded to in Fancy Day's preoccupation with her attire, and especially with her blue dress (cf. *Life*, 78).
26	207	The almost parodic 'infallibly' may hint at Emma Hardy's assurance of reunion after death in her religious thoughts entitled 'Spaces', published in 1912 before her death.
27	215	As a 'young' lover (cf. x).
28	223	See Hardy's novelette, 'An Indiscretion in the Life of an Heiress'.

29 236 Hardy's spirit is more faithfully reflected in 'Candour in English Fiction': 'All really true literature directly or indirectly sounds as its refrain the words in the *Agamemnon*: "Chant Ælinon, Ælinon! but may the good prevail" ' (Orel, 131).

30 243 Hardy's reference to a poem by Hartley Coleridge (*Life*, 114) is very relevant.

31 244 The omission of the observation illustrates a principle which biographers and critics of Hardy often overlook: that the *Life* was intended to be complementary to the poems, in which so much of his private life had been disclosed.

32 246 Hardy described the occasion (when he started the country dances with the beautiful Mrs Grove in September 1895) as his 'most romantic' since he met Mrs Henniker at the Vice-regal Lodge, Dublin (*ORFW*. 45).

33 255 For a light-hearted treatment of the subject, see *UGT*.v.i.

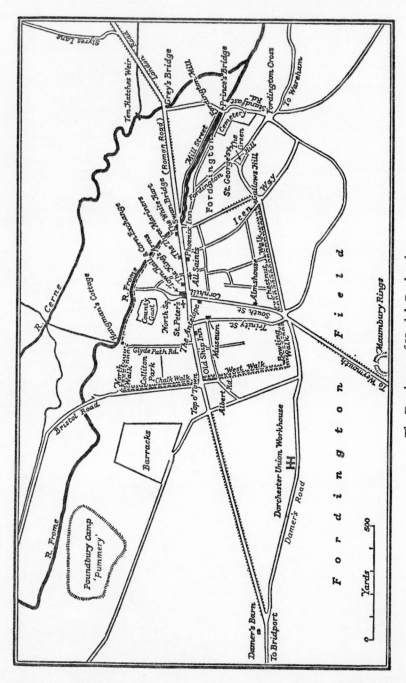

The Dorchester of Hardy's Boyhood

The Heart of Wessex

Miles

Roads ——
Railways +++++++
Footpaths ++++
Actual place-names—Druce Farm
Wessex names — Tolchurch

To Shottsford
Forum

To Longpuddle

To Wellbridge

To Wareham

To
Budmouth

Tolchurch
East Egdon
Egdon Heath
Cliffe House
Stickleford
Athelhall
Weatherbury
Elsenford
R. Froom
Woodsford Castle
Valley of the Great Dairies
Druce Farm
Kite Hill
Tsington Wood
Castle Hill
Mistover
Higher Mellstock
Rainbarrows
The Quiet Woman
Waterston House
Ridge Way
Roy Town
Yalbury Wood
Egdon Heath
Roman Road
Mellstock Cross
Blooms End
Lower Mellstock
West Stafford
Froom-Everard House
R. Piddle
Grey's Wood
Cuckoo Lane
Kingston Maurward
Park
Stinsford House
R. Froom
Slyres Lane
Mellstock Lane
Mellstock Hill
Mellstock Moor
Mellstock Ch.
Max Gate
Durnover Moor
Grey's Bridge
Durnover Hill
Durnover
Mellstock Lodge
Maumbury Rings
Conygar Hill
Charmley
Wolfeton House
R. Cerne
CASTERBRIDGE

Glossary of Wessex Place Names

ATHELHALL	Athelhampton Hall, just east of Puddletown
BLACK'ON	Black Down or Blackdon, 654 ft, 3 m. west of Maiden Castle, and site of the monument to Admiral Hardy
BUDMOUTH	Weymouth
CASTERBRIDGE	Dorchester
CASTLE BOTEREL	Boscastle, Cornwall
CERNEL	Cerne Abbas, 8 m. north of Dorchester
CHRISTMINSTER	Oxford
DURNOVER	Fordington, south-east Dorchester
EGDON HEATH	the heaths stretching eastward from Higher Bock-hampton
EGGAR	Eggardon Hill, 828 ft, site of a prehistoric camp, 5 m. east-north-east of Bridport
ESTMINSTER	Yetminster, 4½ m. south-east of Yeovil
EXON, EXONBURY	Exeter
EXON MOOR, EXON WILD	Exmoor
FROOM	the Frome river
GLASTON	Glastonbury, Somerset
HAVENPOOL	Poole
HINTOCK	Melbury Osmond, 5 m. south of Yeovil
IVEL	Yeovil
IVEL-CHESTER	Ilchester, 5 m. north-north-west of Yeovil
KING'S HINTOCK	Melbury Osmond (see HINTOCK); the park is that of Melbury House, south of Melbury Osmond
KINGSBERE	Bere Regis, 6 m. east of Puddletown
LONGPUDDLE	Piddlehinton, 3 m. north-west of Puddletown
MAIDON	Maiden Castle, a large prehistoric hill fortress 2 m. south-west of Dorchester
MARLBURY	Marlborough
MELLSTOCK	Stinsford with Higher and Lower Bockhampton, 2 m. east of Dorchester

MOREFORD	Moreton, in the Frome valley, 7 m. east of Dorchester
RIDGE-WAY, RIDGWAY	the old road crossing the downs between Dorchester and Weymouth
SHASTONBURY	Shaftesbury ('Shaston' in *Jude the Obscure*)
STOURCASTLE	Sturminster Newton
TONEBOROUGH	Taunton
WEATHERBURY	Puddletown, 5 m. north-east of Dorchester
WEYDON-PRIORS	Weyhill, 3 m. west of Andover, Hampshire
WINTON	Winchester
YALBURY	Yellowham (Wood), between Dorchester and Puddletown

General Index

Subjects clearly indicated in the Index of Titles are not included unless
there are other references to them in this index
Most of the textual references to Hardy's fiction are excluded

H. A. 6, 268
Arnold, Matthew 29, 36, 125, 162,
    163; 'Dover Beach' 53, 100, 202;
    'Isolation' 25; 'Sohrab and Rust-
    tum' 62; 'Stanzas from the
    Grande Chartreuse' 100
Ascham, Roger 89

Bacon, Francis 86
Bagehot, Walter 251, 269
Barnes, William xvi, 5, 137, 177, 194;
    his poems 23, 25, 137, 140, 241
Barrie, J. M. 261–2
Barthélémon, F. H. 165
Bath 111, 129, 216
Beeny Cliff 91, 98, 105, 106, 138, 147
Bincombe Barrow 245
Bishop, (Sir) Henry 164
Blackmore, R. D. 26
Blake, William 18, 59–60, 141
Blomfield, (Sir) Arthur xvi, 26, 74
Bockhampton Cross 139, 181–2, 238
Bodmin 124, 151
Boer War, the 30–34, 87, 199, 221
Boscastle 105, 107, 147, 166
Bossiney 105
Bournemouth 121
British Museum, the 48, 97, 113, 259–
    260
Brontë, Emily 136
Browning, Robert 9, 10, 13, 27, 35,
72, 77, 81, 93, 102, 126, 153, 155,
167, 176, 182, 183, 188, 198, 223,
254; 'By the Fire-side' 93, 123;
'Cristina' 40; 'St. Martin's Sum-
mer' 4, 195; 'The Statue and the
Bust' 49; 'Youth and Art' 178–9
Brownlow, Emma Sophia (Countess)
190
Buchan, John 269
Byron, Lord 34, 226

Campbell, Thomas 80
'Candour in English Fiction' 98, 270
Cardigan, Countess of 127
Carlyle, Thomas 248, 260
Caroline of Brunswick 212–13
'A Changed Man' 50, 70
Channing, Mary 216
Chaucer 102
Chesil Bank 108–9
Chesterton, G. K. 262
Clodd, Edward 37
Comte, Auguste *See* Positivism
Conquer Barrow (near Max Gate) 115,
    240, 245, 248
Conygar Hill 103, 257
The Cornhill Magazine 65, 66, 98, 116,
    268
Crabbe, George 7, 58
Cross-in-Hand 61, 195
Culliford Tree 103, 108, 259

Swanage xvii, 5, 142, 220, 224, 228, 241, 247

Swinburne, A. C. 4, 61-2, 94, 99, 130, 157, 165, 226; *Poems and Ballads* (1866) 4, 9, 99

Talbothays (West Stafford) xviii, 145, 154, 192

Tate and Brady (metrical psalms) 122, 178

Tennyson, Alfred (Lord) 6, 15, 24, 40, 42, 62, 64, 94, 163, 199–200, 243

Tess of the d'Urbervilles 5, 43, 44, 58, 61, 75, 77, 96, 97, 126–7, 247; quoted, 7, 24, 27, 94, 139

Thackeray, W. M. 118

Thompson, Mrs Edith 219

'The Three Strangers' 10

Tintagel Castle, 104, 135, 267

Tintinhull 67, 186

The Titanic 92

'To Please His Wife' 191

Tolbort, T. W. Hooper 143

Tomson, Rosamund 192–3

Tooting *See* Upper Tooting

Topsham 16, 22, 23

Tresparret Posts 169, 170

Treves, Sir Frederick 231

The Trumpet-Major 10, 12, 84, 152; quoted, 33, 227

Tussaud, Mme 142–3

Two on a Tower 4, 5, 6, 9, 16, 41, 144

Under the Greenwood Tree 20, 66, 73, 79, 269

Unfulfilled Intention, the 22, 26, 38–9, 45, 85, 89, 149–50, 209, 215

United States of America, the 34, 38, 158

Upper Tooting 55, 94, 133, 210

Upwey 41, 175

Valency valley 49, 102, 105, 129, 135, 158, 185, 187, 196, 230

Victoria (Queen) 30

Virgil 102, 128

'The Waiting Supper' 49, 56

Walpole, Horace 49, 87, 103, 140, 244

Weippert, John 170

The Well-Beloved 5, 25, 27–8, 47, 123, 194–5, 253, 257, 268

Wells Cathedral 116

Wessex (the Hardys' dog) 225, 257

Weymouth ('Budmouth') 13, 71, 73, 110, 118, 137, 145, 146, 169, 205, 207, 218, 221, 259, 266

'What the Shepherd Saw' 212, 257

Whymper, Edward 37

Wight, Isle of 99, 110

Willey, Basil 21

Wimborne 52, 56–7, 125, 146, 227, 264

Winchester 24

Winterborne Came 103, 137, 177

The Woodlanders 21, 22, 89, 160, 166, 265, 268; quoted, 7, 83, 161, 172, 194–5

Woodsford Castle 192

Wordsworth, William 24, 47, 49, 50, 82, 85, 150, 156, 159, 162, 163, 172, 175, 176, 246, 262

Wynyard's Gap 65, 145, 213–14

Yarborough, Marcia (Lady) 136

Yeats, W. B. 108

Yellowham ('Yalbury') 12, 55, 87, 89, 97, 193, 211, 222

Yeovil ('Ivel') 5, 11, 221, 227

Index of Titles

The principal page references are in italic type